Lance

For Shirley, who dances with such grace to the Ojibwe drums of her kinsmen at Lac Courte Oreilles.

Bill

To Mom and Dad—For everything.

Table of Contents

Table of Contents (continued)

List of Maps

Photos have been added throughout for the convenience of the reader.

Introduction

The idea of a fog-of-war book on one battle and using two authors to write from the Confederate and Union sides came from our publisher, the insightful Theodore P. Savas of Savas Beatie, during a phone call three years ago. The idea intrigued me. He assured me he could find someone to pen the Confederate side of the fence. That was enough for me.

I soon discovered I knew too much of the Iron Brigade of the West in its first battle as a unit. That made it difficult to describe the engagement using just the information on hand at the time to evaluate the fighting and the role of various officers.

Prussian military analyst Carl von Clausewitz used the word "fog" to describe the uncertainty facing military officers on a field of battle. Were they confident of their own ability and the ability of their commands? What were the capabilities of officers and commands on the other side? What were the possibilities and hindrances of the field? What about the weather conditions?

It is easy long afterwards—especially by writers of military history—in describing a battle to see the errors made at the time and make judgmental statements about the conduct of various officers.

Yet, there is much gained by putting yourself in the place of this officer or that and how he reacted with only the information he had at the time. This is especially true looking at the Union side of the fighting at Gainesville on the field now called Brawner's Farm.

There is even confusion about the name of the engagement. Iron Brigade veterans never knew they were fighting on a farm leased by John Brawner. They always called it "Gainesville" for a nearby crossroads community, and that was the name put on their battle flags. The name "Brawner's Farm" was first used by Alan Nolan in his powerful 1961 book, *The Iron Brigade.*

In writing this account I was reminded of a day in August 1981 when I was on hand for the first unrolling of battle flags of the Wisconsin regiments. They had been rolled a century before and bound in cheese cloth and were now being prepared for restoration and preservation.

The flags were unrolled on a long table. They were musty and smelled of smoke, whether campfire or tobacco I could not discern. Several of the early issue flags were in tatters, and the stars and battle names painted on them a handful of paint chips. Several of the wooden staffs were marked by bullets. In one flag was found the wood sapling cut by 7th Wisconsin men the night after the first day of Gettysburg. The original had been shattered by an artillery blast.

The early banners showed the most damage. Painted on some of them was the name of the Iron Brigade's first fight as a unit—"Gainesville."

Lance J. Herdegen
Town of Spring Prairie
Walworth County, Wisconsin

Acknowledgments

Writers spend much time alone as they work on a book, but it is never an individual achievement. Many people have an impact on the finished work. In fact, they are often woven into the very words themselves.

First I would like to acknowledge what a pleasure it was to work with Bill Backus as we completed this unusual project. How much did I enjoy reading his sections.

We are both indebted to Theodore Savas and his Savas Beatie team. It was a pleasure to work with Sarah Keeney, Veronica Kane, Ian Hughes, Sarah Closson, and David Snyder. They are dedicated professionals and made this entire experience enjoyable and worthwhile.

A special thanks to Phil Spaugy, Dan Netteshiem, Dan Joyce, and all those descendants of the Black Hats who came forward with letters, diaries, and photographs of their ancestors. Others who deserve mention include Paul Johnson, Steve Victor, Brett Wilson, Doug Dammann, Alan Gaff, William Washburn, William J. K. Beaudot, Pat and Bob Sullivan, and the late Howard Madaus and Alan T. Nolan. Many others helped, so many it is all but impossible to name them here. My thanks to all.

Introduction

When publisher Theodore Savas approached me with his idea for this book, I was immediately intrigued. The concept of a fog-of-war study returns the drama back into the story. What interested me even more was Ted's idea to use this concept on Brawner's Farm, the opening engagement of Second Manassas.

Sandwiched as it was between the drama of Gen. Robert E. Lee's Seven Days' battles and his strategic defeat in Maryland at Sharpsburg, the Second Manassas campaign has yet to generate the study it deserves. John Hennessy's magisterial 1993 *Return to Bull Run: The Campaign and Battle of Second Manassas* might have something to do with that; following in Hennessy's footsteps is rather daunting. But for a campaign that was arguably Lee's greatest victory, new studies (and lots of them) are warranted and needed.

I have the great fortune to live, work, and play in the area described in this book, so I have a good sense of the topography and have walked and driven the terrain too many times to count. For this book I had to take an entirely different approach and relearn the campaign from one side as it was happening.

Using mostly firsthand accounts, I have endeavored to present an accurate description (as far as such a thing is possible) as seen through the eyes of the generals, line officers, and rank-and-file soldiers as these events unfolded. This includes the storied flanking operation (and the famous endurance) of Thomas J. "Stonewall" Jackson's men, their actions around Manassas, and the sudden eruption of the battle of Brawner's Farm on the evening of August 28, 1862. This, of course, is in addition to the fighting itself.

Researching, walking the ground, and writing this manuscript without an omniscient viewpoint has changed my perspective of the Confederate high command. Victory mitigates many mistakes, but it never completely buries them. Despite his storied Civil War career, I find it difficult to match Jackson's performance here with the legendary plaudits many historians laud upon him. Time and time again, Stonewall's renowned tendency toward secrecy exposed his command to unnecessary risks. Such was the case during the Manassas campaign. In the end, the men themselves and Jackson's outstanding subordinates, especially Richard

Ewell, were perhaps more responsible for the Second Manassas accolades that have typically been bestowed upon Jackson. This became even more clear to me while walking with the men in real time without knowing what was coming, or why.

Trying to piece together what someone knew and when they knew it is a difficult task. Thankfully, much of the core battlefield survives because of the exhaustive research and efforts of archaeologists, archivists, preservationists, and public historians, who have returned much of the landscape to its 1862 appearance. This made my task easier. Archival sources are precious, but there is no substitute for preserved battlefields.

Bill Backus
Manassas, VA

Acknowledgments

The writing of any book requires the assistance of many people. A book with this unique premise requires more than its fair share.

Ahead of everyone else are Ted Savas and Lance Herdegen. The genesis of this book was Ted's. Writing a fog-of-war study would have been difficult had it not been Ted's shepherding in all the various stages it takes to get to publication. Writing a book about the first baptism of fire for the Iron Brigade is a lot easier when you have a co-author like Lance. The foremost expert on the Wisconsinites (and Indianans), it was a joy to work with Lance.

In no particular order are Kevin Pawlak, Tom McGinley, Brian Ross, Gary Haskins, Lionel Raymond, and Rob Orrison. All have been a sounding board, and debate team, to discuss the Second Manassas Campaign. A chat with any of them always left one thinking about the campaign in a new perspective.

A book of this type needs maps. Thankfully Edward Alexander was able to produce fantastic maps that give an idea of how the Confederates viewed the battlefields in 1862.

The staff at Manassas National Battlefield are some of the best in the business. Chief among them is Jim Burgess. In my opinion Jim is the expert on both Manassas battles and the Civil War in Prince William County. It is a pleasure to call Jim a colleague.

Family has been a constant source of encouragement. Gregg and Kathy have been amazing parents-in-laws. Mom and Dad have cheered me on every step of the way, from a history obsession in grade school to a professional historian. Finally, Paige has spent countless hours exploring Civil War battlefields and talking history, sharing a beer, and now raising a family.

Chapter 1

"Johnny Stole a Ha-a-am"

Virginia: August 28, 1862

The infantry brigade moving east along the Warrenton Turnpike at a steady route step was nearing the battlefield of Bull Run. It was a warm late summer day and the sinking sun cast dancing shadows ahead of the moving soldiers. The march had started at 4:00 a.m. and the men now looked forward to a quiet camp where they could cook the chunks of raw beef issued a few hours earlier. Six horse-drawn artillery pieces and transport wagons rumbled and clunked behind the four regiments, the whole compact column filling a half mile of the turnpike. It was second in the line of four brigades ordered to Centreville, Virginia. The first brigade was about a mile ahead and the third and fourth brigades a mile or more behind.

The division had been on the move the past week marching here and there in a frantic search for a Confederate force moving in central Virginia. It was the end of a long, tiring day marked only by occasional enemy horse artillery fire that tried to delay and disrupt the long line of the four brigades. The soldiers chatted and joked as they moved along the roadway in what seemed a leisurely fashion. At one point earlier in the day a far-off brass band could be heard playing the jolly notes of a popular soldier song, and here and there in the sprawling ranks men and boys took up the chorus:

> Johnny stole a ha-a-am,
> And didn't care a da-a-a-m.

To the north of the marching brigade was a farmhouse and outbuildings and ahead, on the turnpike, a thin wood where the road had been excavated leaving a three-foot embankment. Passing through trees, rays of sunlight flashed now and then on the bright musket barrels carried by soldiers at the head of the column.

On the wooded low ridge several hundred yards to the north, a man on a dark horse came out of the trees. He watched the marching soldiers as he moved from one spot to another. After a time, he turned and went back over the ridge line out of sight. It was near 6:00 p.m., August 28, 1862, a Thursday. It was a day long to be remembered in homes in far off Wisconsin and Indiana.

One Month Earlier

The brigade review ordered nearly a month prior on the heights above Fredericksburg, Virginia, came off in what one soldier called "a very poor style." The regiments stepped off promptly as ordered at 6:00 p.m. on August 1, 1862, but the formation soon faltered. Even though the brigade had been together almost a year and heavily drilled the past months, the lines of marching soldiers carelessly bent this way and that as the sergeants and officers tried to correct the alignment. "The boys did not care how they went," the private wrote in his journal that evening, "and the officers could not make them do any better for they were all together, and when they take a notion and hang together, the officers never could handle us as they pleased."[1]

The reason for the "very poor style" may have been that the review came at the end of a long and wearying day preparing a new camp above the city. The weather was hot and the soldiers tired. And it did not help that the whispering in ranks was that the review was ordered to show off the brigade to an elderly civilian watching with division commander Rufus King—and that the watching gent just might be the general's father.

The brigade contained four regiments from the nation's frontier—the 2nd, 6th, and 7th Wisconsin, and the 19th Indiana. The move to the new location was an attempt to escape the malaria prevalent along the Rappahannock River in late summer in central Virginia. In many ways, the summer camps near Fredericksburg and environs were rather pleasant. The city on the south bank of the river midway between Washington and the new Confederate capital at Richmond was noted for its history and location. Now, however, the quiet that once marked the community was disturbed by movement and noise as it was home for various elements of the Union army. The units arrived from the Washington camps the past May as part of George B. McClellan's much-hailed

1 William Ray, *Four Years with the Iron Brigade: The Civil War Journal of William Ray, Company F, 7th Wisconsin Volunteers*, eds. Lance Herdegen and Sherry Murphy (Cambridge, ME, 2002).

General Rufus King. *Library of Congress*

grand advance on the Confederate capital. General Irvin McDowell's force, including the Western regiments, however, was stopped at Fredericksburg to protect Washington and central Virginia as well as being poised to go overland if needed to join "Little Mac." But the order to join the Army of the Potomac outside Richmond never came.

Nowhere was the latest war news followed with more sharp and lengthy discussion than in the four regiments in King's division. The soldiers were singled out as the only all-Western infantry brigade serving in the East. They had been together since mid-summer of the previous year and—except for the 2nd Wisconsin which fought at First Bull Run—saw only limited action. "Of course, we feel eager to be something more than ornamental file-closers," a frustrated Wisconsin officer wrote home. "Our regiment has been more than a year in service, and in soldierly bearing, perfection in drill, and discipline, we do not yield the palm to the regulars in any service." The four regiments brought 4,000 men to Washington the previous year, but transfers, other duties, desertions, and disease had reduced the brigade numbers. Now, the officer noted, only some 2,800 soldiers remained in the 40 companies.[2]

The news from the great Federal army assembled outside Richmond was troubling. Little Mac was stalled outside the city gates and the bright hopes of early summer grew darker with the passing weeks. The war itself seemed to be taking on a more serious tone with dimming hopes of a quick conclusion. The Northern public was still stunned and reeling by the long casualty lists from the fighting in April at Shiloh near Pittsburg Landing in Tennessee. The Confederates were still in the field in force across the whole front, East and West, and it seemed Federal leadership did not know what to do about it.

Adding to the grim outlook was a troubling new order from the War Department combining commands, including McDowell's corps, into a new "Army of Virginia." It placed the Western volunteers another step removed from their beloved "Little Mac" and any hope of rejoining the Army of the Potomac. Around their coffee fires, the boys wondered aloud how they could ever explain their lack of real service to the folks back home. "I feel more like fighting than ever but as yet have not had a chance to show our boasted bravery but hope the [day] will soon come when we will have the orders to join Mclelen," one of the 7th Wisconsin boys wrote in his journal. An officer grumbled in a letter home that "General McClellan presses steadily on to Richmond. We are left out in the wet."[3]

2 Rufus Dawes, *Service with the 6th Wisconsin Volunteers* (Marietta, OH, 1890), 51–52.

3 Ray, *Iron Brigade*, 119; Dawes, *Service*, 44. See also Frank A. Haskell, letter to his brothers and sisters, Sept. 22, 1862, Frank Haskell Papers, Wisconsin Historical Society [hereafter "WHS"].

Despite the dark headlines over the latest war developments, the move to the new camp was welcomed and the volunteers spent the last two days of July constructing tree branch arbors for shade over their tents along the new company streets. The site included a large clover field and timber on three sides and the handy Westerners began digging two wells at each end of the camp. Their small canvas shelter halves and other improvements were soon "all so covered up that you can scarcely see a tent," one soldier wrote in his journal. "There is plenty of wood nearby and tolerable plenty of water."[4]

In their letters, the Western boys described a city "surrounded by high land and being built with strict regularity." It contained "many handsome private residences and public buildings"—one soldier observed—and was supplied with waterpower by the Rappahannock Falls. The city is "a place of great wealth and beauty," a Wisconsin officer wrote to his wife. But he added a disapproving note that the city residents "made their living by furnishing negroes for the Southern market that furnished them with large incomes. So they built themselves beautiful homes and enjoyed them. . . . I would want a more sterling life." Also discovered was the marble monument marking the grave of George Washington's mother. "It was shamefully mutilated and disfigured by reckless soldiers," one soldier wrote home.[5]

The brigade had its beginning in the Washington camps in the summer of 1861. The 2nd Wisconsin reached the war front in June 1861 and the boys always believed they were the first of the three-year regiments to reach the city with the earlier organizations enlisting for 90 days. The Wisconsin men arrived just in time for the battle of Bull Run in July and got whipped along with the rest. The next two arriving regiments—the 5th and 6th Wisconsin—reached Washington shortly after the battle. The 7th Wisconsin, the last of the Badger infantry regiments to be sent to the East, was held at home until after the fall harvest. When it did arrive, it was attached to a holding brigade under the command of Gen. Rufus King comprised of the 2nd, 5th, 6th Wisconsin, and the 19th Indiana.

The Western nature of the unit raised speculation about the creation of an all-Wisconsin brigade under King. One of the strongest encouragements for that idea came in early August 1861 from Col. John Starkweather of Milwaukee.

4 Ray, *Iron Brigade*, 123.

5 Henry F. Young, letter to wife, May 24, 1862, *Dear Delia: The Civil War Letters of Captain Henry F. Young, Seventh Wisconsin Infantry, 1861–1864*, eds. Michael J. Larson and John David Smith (Madison, WI., 2019) 68; George H. Otis, *The Second Wisconsin Infantry, with letters and recollections by other members of the regiment*, ed. Alan D. Gaff (Dayton, OH, 1984), 51–52.; E. B. Quiner, *The Military History of Wisconsin: A Record of the Civil and Military Patriotism of the State in the War for the Union* (Chicago, 1866), 992–993.

He commanded the 1st Wisconsin Infantry, just then nearing an end to 90-days of active service north of Washington. His was a big name back home where he was a prominent attorney and well known for his activity in the pre-war Wisconsin state militia. Always forceful in manner and speech, his Milwaukee Light Guard was regarded as one of the finest militia organizations of the Upper Middle West. It was a "crack company," one observer noted, and displayed a "high degree of proficiency in drill and discipline" in which Starkweather, as captain, "took much pride." As a result, it was the first company selected when Wisconsin formed the three-month 1st Wisconsin regiment of active militia and Starkweather was named colonel.

With his regiment presently in the Department of Shenandoah and scheduled to be sent home, the always ambitious Starkweather wrote to fellow Milwaukeean King, a longtime friend and militia colleague in the Light Guard. King was now—because of his graduation from the U. S. Military Academy—commanding a volunteer brigade at Washington. The letter concerned two matters. The first involved the recent promotion of Lucius Fairchild of Madison, a captain in the 1st Wisconsin, to the 2nd Wisconsin in King's brigade. Could Fairchild be allowed to return to Wisconsin with the 1st Wisconsin before coming back to Virginia to report to his new post, Starkweather asked? "I would like it much that it be so arranged."

The second matter was more far-reaching. The colonel wanted King to write an order assigning his regiment to the general's brigade. The 1st Wisconsin would return to Milwaukee as scheduled, he said, and would be maintained as "a skeleton" pending recruitment for three-years. Within three weeks' time, Starkweather could fill it with at least two-thirds of the veterans of his old regiment. "I want you to get an order to such effect for me and at the same time place the Wis. 1st in your Brigade," he wrote. "It ought to be done. The governor [Alexander Randall] wants us to go in, and the whole of Wisconsin is anxious for it."

The only thing his men would need, he explained, were new Federal uniforms to replace the state issued militia grey. "The 1st could be put in the field again in short order perfectly disciplined, sound in condition . . . Ready for hard work and would be well informed in its duty." Lawyer Starkweather knew how to shape a request in the most forceful language: "Get me the order General to muster out at once in Mil. And pay off—3 weeks' time and I am with you heart and body with as fine a body of men as ever started up. . . . You can do it for me General. . . . For my sake—for the Regt's sake for Wisconsin and our Country's sake, do this swiftly."[6]

6 Quiner, *Military History*, 993; John Starkweather to Rufus King, Aug. 8, 1861, private collection.

Fairchild was given permission to return to Wisconsin before reporting to his new assignment, but for reasons never clearly explained, Starkweather and the 1st Wisconsin did not join King's brigade. It returned to Milwaukee where it was mustered out and then reformed as a three-year regiment with orders to serve in the Western Theater of the war where Starkweather was now commanding a brigade.

The idea of an all-Wisconsin brigade was dashed for good when the arriving 7th Wisconsin was placed in King's command, as expected, but the 5th Wisconsin was surprisingly transferred to another brigade. The loss of the Badger regiment controverted King's wishes and the wishes of most of the field and line officers and men of the departing organization. The decision to move the Wisconsin regiment, instead of the Indiana regiment, might have been the careless error of an army clerk, but many believed that Army officials—Eastern army officials—objected to an all-Wisconsin brigade under the watchful eye and influence of a powerful patron like the governor of a faraway state.

Chapter 2

"Splendid Looking Fellows"

Washington: Late 1861

From the very first days at Washington, volunteers from Eastern states camped nearby did not know quite what to make of the soldiers from the far West. Sightseers and the curious from nearby Washington and other places came down to the Western camps to stand off to one side or the other to gawk and take the measure of those young fellows still wearing their home state militia gray uniforms. They were considered backwoods rustics. Nearby soldiers from larger states mocked them as "the Country Brigade."

But the soldiers from Wisconsin and Indiana, observers noted, somehow seemed taller and different than the soldiers from New York, New Jersey, and even Pennsylvania, and they moved with what was then regarded as an easy and lanky Western stride. The new volunteers, it was whispered, had lived side-by-side with the native tribes of the frontier, and it was pronounced with solemn tones and firm nods that those Badgers and Hoosiers were used to sleeping on the ground and did not need tents or other shelter. Confirmations flowed when the 2nd Wisconsin passed through Chicago on the way to the front. One of the big city newspapermen watched with awe and described the new volunteers as "all young, stalwart, vigorous, splendid looking fellows." The regiment, he reported, included "200 lumbermen, hardy, cast-iron fellows from the north, who have not properly slept in a civilized bed in a dozen years."[1]

1 Whether born in America or "bred beyond her borders, or in foreign climes," one volunteer explained, the Western men were proud of their states and with the firing on Fort Sumter in 1861 they rushed to fill the volunteer companies. "Not infrequently," one said, "every civilized nation on the face of the earth was represented in the rank and file of the same regiment. Every condition of social, religious, and political faith, all the trades, occupations and professions were represented. The same tent covered the banker, lumberman, medical student, lawyer, merchant and machinist. The millionaire's son touched elbows with the son of his father's hired man." "Wisconsin in the Civil War," *History of Wisconsin* 1, no. 2, n. p.; *Janesville* [WI] *Daily Gazette*, June 1861.

In truth, however, the men in the new Wisconsin and Indiana regiments were often not native to their states but were sons of New England and Pennsylvania and Ohio and New York—even Virginia, North Carolina, Tennessee, and Kentucky. The ranks also included young, tough fellows from Germany, Ireland, Norway, and other places across the sea. In some of the backwoods companies could also be found—against all army regulations—one or two free Blacks or runaway slaves just then living on the frontier. In the Wisconsin units were also found unauthorized representatives of the Ojibwe, Oneida, Potawatomi, and other tribes—all signed up to carry a musket with the rest.

A few of those who stepped forward in Indiana or Wisconsin said they signed the roll because they were bored or wanted to be considered brave or sought advancement. Others saw the war as a fight against the evils of slavery, and some felt they were protecting the sacred Union created by their grandfathers and great-grandfathers. No one saw it clearer than Edwin A. Brown of Fond du Lac, a young attorney and father, who was among the first to join a company in the 6th Wisconsin. He wrote home "Thousands of patriotic lives may be laid a sacrifice on the Altar of our Country's good, but this Country will be purified of this blighting breath of treason and corruption, and history will record of the Republic, that in the year 1861, her patriotic children rallied around the emblem of the early fathers, and purged the land of the great curse of secession."[2]

The volunteers in the new all-Western regiments also desperately wanted to prove their mettle. "We would have died rather than have dishonored the West," one of the Sauk County boys from Wisconsin explained. "We felt that the eyes of the East were upon us, and that we were the test of the West." A Badger officer said the soldiers felt what was at stake was "the reputation of themselves and of their brothers and the reputation of their state."[3]

Inside King's brigade, however, a rivalry to be identified as the best regiment smoldered. The "veterans" of the 2nd Wisconsin provoked much of the heat that late summer and the winter of 1861–62, boasting of their service at Bull Run. The 19th Indiana had also seen action, but only a simple inconsequential skirmish in the eyes of the Badgers. The 6th and 7th Wisconsin had not had a real baptism of fire. Each regiment, one observer said, "had, nevertheless, their individuality, their rivalry, their jealousies, if you will. The 2d had been

2 Edwin A. Brown to his wife, Sept. 8, 1861, Civil War Museum of the Upper Middle West, Kenosha, WI.; Edward Kellogg, "Letters from a Soldier," *Milwaukee Sunday Telegraph*, Sept. 28, 1879 [hereafter "*Telegraph*"]; Earl M. Rogers, "A 6th Wisconsin Company," *Telegraph*, Feb. 1, 1880; Michael H. Fitch, *Echoes of the Civil War as I Hear Them* (New York, 1905), 18–19.

3 Jerome A. Watrous, *Appleton* [WI] *Crescent*, Aug. 20, 1861; Edward Bragg to Earl Rogers, Apr. 3, 1900, Edward Bragg Papers, WHS.

through the Bull Run battle and swaggered a bit in consequence. They rather patronized the other regiments, put on veteran airs. They were superbly drilled but decidedly given to sarcastic comment on the other commands. The 6th, 7th and 19th had not had the 2d's opportunities, but were cock sure that when the time camc they could fight every bit as well, stay as long in a hot place or charge just as daringly into a hotter."[4]

It was not only loud talk that gave the 2nd Wisconsin veteran airs. A 6th Wisconsin officer writing home noted the men of the 2nd "look as though they had been 'through the wars' ragged, and saucy, and without discipline." Another officer noted the soldiers "look dirty and more callus than ours. . . . The men are of good stuff, but . . . with little confidence in the officers & that they care little what they do." A third officer said with a sniff that the men of the 2nd "did not have that exuberant, dashing, self-reliant manner that distinguishes the other Wisconsin men."[5]

Contributing to the hard appearance of the 2nd Wisconsin men was the sad condition of their old uniforms, especially the trousers. Many were still wearing the state grey issued in Madison and worn for the past many weeks of campaigning and in camp. There was nothing, a comrade said, quite like the "view of their rear ranks when they attempted a dress parade" as the "lively boys . . . were more like Highlanders minus kilts than model infantry." He added that even the gentlest of breezes were not hindered in cooling their "Adonis-like forms." Of course, in hard soldier fashion, the 2nd Wisconsin boys became the "Ragged Assed Second" and not any of the angry retorts served to comfort the maligned party. The 6th Wisconsin became "King's pet babies" (because of suspected favoritism) or the "Calico 6th," a roast of the homespun shirts worn by the farm boys in the back ranks, or even the "Bragging 6th." A 7th Wisconsin man observed that the 6th "was not well liked by the other regiments." The fellows in the 7th Wisconsin liked to call themselves the "Hungry 7th," but were always known as the "Huckleberries" because they "liked to talk about pies and things to eat." The 19th Indiana men were described as "lean, lank" and a quiet set and became known as "Old Posey County" or "Swamp Hogs No. 19" and,

4 Edward Bragg to Earl Rogers, Apr. 3, 1900; Charles King, "Gainesville, 1862," *Military Order of the Loyal Legion of the United States, Commandery of the State of Wisconsin, War Papers* III (Milwaukee, 1903), 271. King was the son of Rufus King and served for a time as his volunteer orderly.

5 Brown to his father, Aug. 28, 1861; Bragg to his wife, undated; *Green Bay Advocate*, Aug. 29, 1861.

said a brigade man in another regiment, that "every man of them did not care a goll darn how he was dressed, but was all hell for a fight."[6]

It was with "great reluctance," one volunteer said, "that we got up even a calling acquaintance with those other regiments, yet some of us had friends, cousins and even brothers in their ranks." In the regiments themselves, there was also some friction between the American-born and the immigrant.

One volunteer wrote home that the four regiments were "separate and distinct communities." A 2nd Wisconsin soldier tried to explain it by saying the men in his regiment "are probably the hardest set of boys, but good natured and easy to get along with. They wear an air of fearless carelessness wherever found. The Sixth is more stately, and distant, and march to slower music than we do. The Seventh puts on the least style and crow the least . . . and is well drilled. It is the truest friend the 2d ever found. The 19th Indiana is an indifferent, don't care regiment. They pride themselves on their fighting pluck—which is undoubtedly good—more than their drill. As a brigade we get along finely together." Private J. P. "Mickey" Sullivan of the 6th Wisconsin said it in plainer terms: "If any one wanted to get into . . . difficulty, all that was necessary for him to do was go into the 19th and say a word against the 'Wisconsin boys' and the same held good in any of our regiments about them."[7]

The brigade's commander, Rufus King, was a well-known figure from back home. Born in New York City, the general was named for his grandfather, Rufus King, a delegate from Massachusetts to the Continental Congress and Constitutional Convention. He was an 1833 graduate of the U.S. Military Academy and as a newly graduated young lieutenant, King was assigned duty in the Engineer Corps at Fortress Monroe, Virginia, where his commander was Robert E. Lee of Virginia. He resigned from the army in 1836 to work as an associate editor for two New York State newspapers, *The Albany Evening Journal*, and *The Albany Advertiser*, as well as serving for a time as militia commander of the Albany Burgess Corps. He left New York in 1845 to become part proprietor

6 "A Celebrated Case," *Telegraph*, Aug. 5, 1883; "The Old Brigade," *Telegraph*, Sept. 27, 1885; Ray, *Iron Brigade*, 16. Editor Jerome Watrous said the 2nd Wisconsin early on was the "Hungry Second" stemming from an incident before the brigade was organized. A visitor inquired when he would find the 2nd Wisconsin and was "told that if he went to the front, and out beyond where the Union army found it dangerous to move, then climbed the tallest tree in the neighborhood, he would probably see the boys he was after away off in some cornfield in front helping themselves."

7 *Telegraph*, Mar. 11, 1883; "Heroes of Undying Game," *Telegraph*, Sept. 26, 1896; *Janesville* [WI] *Daily Gazette*, July 10, 1862; Sullivan, *Telegraph*, Mar. 16, 1883.

and editor of *The Milwaukee Sentinel and Gazette*, a post he held until 1859. King was also a captain of the noted Milwaukee Light Guard.[8]

In March 1861, King was appointed minister to the Papal States. He was about to depart when the news of Fort Sumter reached Wisconsin. He immediately quit the appointment and offered his services to Wisconsin Governor Alexander Randall. King was subsequently promoted by President Abraham Lincoln to the national army and then advanced to division command in McDowell's corps in late summer 1861. The senior colonel of the unit, Lysander Cutler of the 6th Wisconsin, served as acting brigade commander until May 1862.

8 Herbert C. Damon, *History of the Milwaukee Light Guard* (Milwaukee, 1875), 20–22.

Chapter 3

"Battle Is a Dreadful Experience"

Manassas Battlefield: July 21, 1861

Edward Craighill remembered being soaked as he walked back from the battlefield to the Pringle hospital on that dark July 21, 1861, evening. With the interior of the hospital literally crawling with wounded from the fighting for Henry House Hill, the young hospital steward decided to sleep outside beside a roaring fire with two other Confederate soldiers. When he awoke a few hours later, Craighill realized his companions were dead. Fifty years later their impromptu burial remained seared in the Virginian's memory. Along with others that died during the night "they were carried out and buried in the Pringle garden . . . almost certainly 'somebody's darlings' whom I expect to this day, are wondering what became of them after the battle. A bloody battle is a dreadful experience."[1]

Less than a week prior, Craighill and his comrades in the First Brigade commanded by a former Virginia Military Institute instructor guarded the entrance to their native Shenandoah Valley. Ordered with the rest of their comrades east towards a small railroad junction called Manassas, after disembarking from the railroad they marched towards immortality at the battle of First Manassas. By the end of the day the brigade and their commander both earned one of the most famous nicknames in American military history. The 2nd, 4th, 5th, 27th, and 33rd Virginia regiments were now the Stonewall Brigade, led by "Stonewall" Jackson.[2]

1 Peter Houck, ed. *Confederate Surgeon: The Personal Recollections of E. A. Craighill* (Lynchburg, VA, 1989), 15.

2 There is still considerable debate about the origins of the nickname. While some argue it was made to buoy Confederate morale, others think it was intended to be an insult. The likely true meaning will never be known.

Raised exclusively in the Shenandoah Valley, the make-up of the five regiments was as unique as its nickname. Starting in the eighteenth century as a crucial transportation corridor linking Pennsylvania and the Carolinas, the Shenandoah Valley became one of the most diverse sections in Virginia and the South. Joining older Virginians coming from east of the Blue Ridge Mountains were Scotch-Irish and German immigrants drawn south from Philadelphia towards cheap, productive land. Three generations removed from their settler ancestors, the men of the Stonewall Brigade still contained elements of their forefather's heritage.[3]

Representative of the type of leaders throughout the brigade was William S. Baylor. Born 31 years earlier in Augusta County, Virginia, to a prominent Shenandoah Valley family, he entered Washington College at the age of seventeen. Graduating from the Lexington, Virginia, school in two years, Baylor entered the University of Virginia to study law, graduating from that prestigious university within three years. Soon after returning home to practice law in 1857, the citizens of Augusta County elected him commonwealth attorney, a position he held until the outbreak of war.

Working in Staunton, Baylor found enough spare time to join the local militia company, the West Augusta Guards. Naturally the company members soon elected Baylor captain of their unit. When the Guards responded to John Brown's abortive raid on Harper's Ferry in 1859, they did so without their captain who was then suffering from typhoid fever in New York City on his honeymoon. Baylor's absence in the Guard's only prewar mobilization did not affect his standing in the unit. Remaining captain after the West Augusta Guards joined the Confederate army as part of the 5th Virginia Infantry, Baylor was soon elected major of the new regiment. Unknown to both him and his comrades, in little over a year he would be commanding the brigade.[4]

Always remaining proud that they served in the Stonewall Brigade, each regiment in the brigade received a distinctive nickname used within the larger unit. Sporting some of the more martial sobriquets, the 5th Virginia was often referred as the "Fighting Fifth" while the 27th Virginia was nicknamed the "Bloody Twenty-Seventh." The two senior regiments on the other hand carried more pacific names such as the "Harmless Fourth" and the "Innocent Second." The distinction of having the most unique nickname rested with the 33rd Virginia. In commemoration of being the first regiment in the brigade to

3 James Robertson Jr. *The Stonewall Brigade* (Baton Rouge, 1991), 12–14.

4 John Johnson, *The University Memorial: Biographical Sketches of Alumni of the University of Virginia* (Baltimore, 1871), 222–225.

become stricken with lice, the brigade called the regiment the "Lousy Thirty-Third." Like nicknames used in a close-knit family, rarely did anyone outside of the Stonewall Brigade use these nicknames in reference to these five regiments.[5]

For the companies raised in Lexington and the surrounding area of Rockbridge County, Thomas J. Jackson was not only a Confederate hero, but a neighbor. Back in their civilian lives many were not impressed by the V.M.I. instructor. John Lyle, a student at Washington College that bordered the military academy, remembered seeing Jackson trying to stay awake during a prewar church service. After enlisting, Lyle remained unimpressed with his new commander. In a letter he described Jackson "with the vizor of his cap pulled down over his eyes, leaving no part of his face visible but that covered by a full, brown beard, and his hug feet thrust to the ankles into his stirrup, he rode alone and had a far away look in his face, as if oblivious to his surroundings."[6]

John Lyle was not alone in underestimating the quirky college professor. Born in the mountains of western Virginia, Jackson's military career was cut short after a professional falling out while serving in the antebellum pre-war army. Returning to Virginia, his West Point background made him a perfect candidate as professor at V.M.I. Unfortunately for his students, Jackson had difficulty in the classroom. His struggling academic career was cut short with the firing on Fort Sumter and Virginia's secession from the Union. Traveling north to Harper's Ferry, Jackson took command of the five regiments he initially called the First Brigade.

The name did not stick for long. Along with almost the rest of the soldiers then serving in the Shenandoah Valley Jackson found himself at the pivotal moment during the first major battle of the Civil War at the battle of First Manassas. After the earlier Confederate line fell into confusion, Jackson and his men turned the battle around and stymied multiple Federal attempts to capture the key terrain of Henry House Hill. In the weeks following the war's first Confederate victory many officers were rewarded for their service, including Jackson. Promoted to major general, Jackson was ordered to return to the Shenandoah Valley with his brigade and reassert control of that critical location as the ranking Confederate officer.

Returning to a hero's welcome, his first initial campaigns to severe the Baltimore and Ohio Railroad line in Maryland or recapture the important crossroads community of Romney fizzled out. When 1862 dawned Jackson's

5 Lowell Reidenbaugh, *33rd Virginia Infantry* (Lynchburg, VA, 1987), 31.

6 W. G. Bean, *The Liberty Hall Volunteers: Stonewall College Boys* (Charlottesville, VA, 2004), 32.

sterling reputation won on the fields of Manassas appeared to be tarnishing. A host of mediocre Federal commanders blundering southward into the Shenandoah finally gave Jackson an opportunity to arrest his stagnating reputation. Enduring an unexpected defeat in March at Kernstown, Jackson's luck soon improved. Throughout the rest of the spring Stonewall managed to prevent the enemy from defeating his growing army. While not as decisive as the victory at Manassas, Jackson still managed to fight Federal advances to a stalemate at places like McDowell. Later that spring he began to win incontestable victories at the battles of Winchester and Front Royal. With his final victories at Cross Keys and Port Republic, Jackson not only cleared the Shenandoah Valley of the most serious Federal opposition, but provided the only Southern victories in a period of unmitigated disaster throughout the rest of the Confederacy.

Jackson's time as a semi-independent commander revealed a few leadership flaws that fortunately had not brought excessive losses or an outright defeat. Stonewall took the quest for operational secrecy to a dangerous extreme. The Virginian routinely kept only one or two officers abreast of his intentions and plan, usually people outside of the command sphere. Jackson's subordinates, the men tasked with implementing his plans, rarely knew his full intentions. Often resulting in miscommunication or misunderstanding, Jackson's tendency for secrecy sometimes led to unnecessary casualties.

Jackson had already skirted the damaging effects of this policy during the first battle of Kernstown, which one historian has described as "a bloody comedy of errors." Tight lipped with his two principal brigadier generals, none of Jackson's key subordinates knew anything of his larger plan or intentions for the battle. Even worse, a new habit emerged, one that continued to plague Jackson. In the course of the fighting, Jackson jumped the chain of command to direct individual regiments to plug holes in the line. Temporarily successful, it created avoidable chaos and confusion in the Confederate high command with brigade commanders suddenly and unexpectedly losing touch with parts of their units.[7]

Like their commanders, to the men in the ranks, Jackson's peculiar command eccentricities remained unknown. To them he produced a nearly unbroken string of victories in the Shenandoah Valley that spring. Those victories first produced admiration and then genuine love in the army towards their leader. John Apperson recorded that his fellow soldiers in the 4th Virginia were in fine spirits that spring and whenever Jackson appeared "he was applauded most

7 Peter Cozzens, *Shenandoah 1862: Stonewall Jackson's Valley Campaign* (Chapel Hill, NC, 2008), 221.

General Thomas "Stonewall" Jackson. *Library of Congress*

enthusiastically."[8] Another soldier in the Stonewall Brigade remembered a common saying in the army that spring: When any cheering was heard in camp or on the march, that it was either "Jackson or a rabbit."[9]

8 John Herbert Roper, ed. *Repairing the "March of Mars": The Civil War Diaries of John Samuel Apperson* (Macon, GA, 2001), 213.

9 John Casler, *Four Years in the Stonewall Brigade* (Columbia, SC, 2005), 92–94.

After the war Captain Alfred Edgar of the 27th Virginia perfectly summed up the feeling of the junior ranks to Stonewall. Jackson was given "a certain kind of precedence over every other officer in the southern army. The Confederates have implicit confidence in his ability, and the Northern army fears him more than any other thing in the South. . . . The high esteem in which he is held by both officers and men is unbounded. The great power and influence he wields over us is something wonderful." Leading an army with almost unwavering confidence in its leader, Jackson and his men were called away to the new critical point. They were going to Richmond.[10]

10 Alfred Mallory Edgar, *My Reminiscences of the Civil War with the Stonewall Brigade and the Immortal 600* (Charleston, WV, 2011), 65.

Chapter 4

"The Southern Renegade"

Virginia: Early 1862

As part of the Federal grand advance against Richmond, Irvin McDowell, commanding the I Corps, including King's division, was ordered to move from Washington overland to central Virginia. The days of marching were wearying for the new soldiers and the men in the four Western regiments in what was wet and rainy weather. The long columns slowly tramped to Fairfax, Centreville, then Bristoe Station, Catlett's Station, and on to the Fredericksburg area. Along the way there were several halts for work details to rebuild bridges destroyed by the enemy. One weary night there was snow "wet, wood scarce and mud deep, air chilly and everything in a forlorn condition." The boys laughed it off and called it "Camp Snowy." A heavy whiskey ration issued as a preventative was a miserable failure. "A thousand drunken men in the brigade, made a pandemonium of the camp all right," reported a Wisconsin officer.[1]

On April 23, the regiments marched to the small town of Falmouth and camped above Fredericksburg in central Virginia. Enemy pickets could be seen on the hills beyond the city. The brigade was given an ineffective volley by scattered Confederates from the north road at the entrance to the town, who then fled "precipitately across the river burning three splendid bridges." The bridges were tarred and piled with wood shavings. Arriving soldiers were delighted to find the "thriving little village" had three general stores which were bought out in short order with Confederate script, "an abundance of which was in the possession of men at the time." A $5 U.S. bill "would buy a bushel basket full of goods, while it required a bushel basket full of confederate notes to purchase a pound of tea or coffee," one soldier said. "The most hardened rebel was even then anxious to own a U.S. treasury note."

1 Otis, *Second Wisconsin*, 47; Dawes, *Service*, 39–40.

The military appearance of the brigade when it reached the Fredericksburg area was still mixed and in disrepair. The previous October, with the state-issued grey uniforms badly in need of replacement, the acting brigade commander, Colonel Cutler, began requisitioning the Federal blue. It was done in stages so that one company might still have grey caps from home while wearing newly issued blue wool frock coats. The men in the needy 2nd Wisconsin—known in camp as the "Ragged Assed Second" because of much worn and stained grey trousers—were issued the dark blue trousers of the regulars while companies in other regiments began to get the light blue wool kersey currently in fashion. At first, they wore their new issue sack coats like shirts, tucking the tails into their new trousers.

Shortly after arriving at Fredericksburg, acting brigade commander Lysander Cutler ordered the first major issue of consistent headgear. With the fashionable flat-topped forage caps in short supply, the Badgers were given the Model 1858 dress hat of the regulars, a fancy, high-crowned affair with brass insignia and trim and sporting a black plume. The new hats were well received and immediately made the brigade recognizable in camp and on the march. One soldier wrote home: "We have this week all in the regiment received new regulation hats. They are tall and rather heavy but much better in the sun and rain than our caps."[2]

A more far-reaching development than the new uniforms was the May 8 announcement that Capt. John Gibbon of Battery B, 4th U.S. Artillery, was being promoted to brigadier general of volunteers and given command of the Western Brigade.[3] Gibbon was already a familiar figure to the soldiers in infantry ranks. His battery (famous in the Old Army for its service at Buena Vista in the War with Mexico) had been attached to the brigade from the earliest days and when Gibbon, who was also McDowell's chief of artillery, needed men to fill the ranks of his gunners he went to the infantry regiments to select volunteers.[4]

2 T.H.R.S., letter, May 1, 1862, WHS.

3 The battery was one of the most famous organizations of the Old Army and one of 36 artillery companies (the "companies" officially became "batteries" in 1861) created in the artillery reorganization of 1821. Battery men fought as dragoons in the Seminole War and served with distinction as artillery at Monterrey and Buena Vista during the War with Mexico. It was stationed at Camp Floyd, Utah, for the Mormon Uprising and was serving as cavalry escorts to guard the Pony Express route. In fact, it was a Pony Express rider who brought word of the firing on Fort Sumter. The battery was ordered to move overland to Fort Leavenworth in Kansas and then traveled by rail to Washington. Battery B was equipped with six Model 1857 muzzle-loaded 12-pound bronze smoothbores, often called "Napoleons" or "Light Twelves" to distinguish them from an earlier model. They were officially categorized as "gun-howitzers" and got their name in part by the weight of the ammunition—a 4.62-inch caliber, round 12-pound solid shot.

4 Born in Pennsylvania in 1827 into the family of a physician, Gibbon grew up in North Carolina. It was from that state he was appointed to the U.S. Military Academy, graduating in the class of

Private Jasper Daniels, 2nd Wisconsin
Institute for Civil War Studies

In the 6th Wisconsin he labored to convince soldiers to join his battery, partly due to the volunteers' distrust of West Pointers. Only one man stepped forward following his opening appeal. Finally, Colonel Cutler explained again what was wanted, and then a "large number stepped forward" and Cutler cautioned, "There, there, that will do—you needn't all come out—they don't want the whole regiment for the battery." Gibbon, along with two battery officers, carefully picked the men at the rate of two, three, or four from the various companies.[5]

Those selected became among the best artillerymen in the Army of the Potomac. One volunteer explained in a letter home why he made the transfer: "I pity the poor infantry when they move, for they have got to carry five days' rations in their knapsacks and three days in their haversacks, besides their

1847. He was assigned to the artillery and briefly saw occupation duty in Mexico, then against the Seminole Indians in Florida. He returned to West Point as an artillery instructor from 1854 to 1859. He won attention in 1859 for the publication of his highly regarded *Artillerist's Manual.* He left West Point when he was promoted to captain and joined Battery B at its duty post at Camp Floyd in the Utah Territory.

5 Jerome Watrous, *Telegraph*, Sep. 7, 1884; Augustus Buell, *The Cannoneer: Recollections of Service in the Army of the Potomac* (Washington, D.C. 1897,) 33–39, 24–25. Buell's memoir has been questioned, see Milton W. Hamilton, "Augustus C. Buell, Fraudulent Historian," *Pennsylvania Magazine of History and Biography* (156), 478–492. Hamilton documented that Buell, in fact, did not enlist until Aug. 21, 1863, six weeks after Gettysburg, and then joined the 20th New York Cavalry. Author Silas Felton, however, has demonstrated that details of Buell's account of Battery B included solid information and was supported by veterans who were with the battery. Felton concluded Buell's accounts were probably based on extensive oral interviews with at least three Battery B veterans. In addition, Felton noted, Buell's story was first published in the major veteran newspaper of the day, *The National Tribune*, and later reprinted in book form, a path of publication that would be avoided by an author putting together a bogus record. Obscure Wisconsin sources also confirm additional minor details of Buell's account. Silas Felton, "Pursing the Elusive Cannoneer," *Gettysburg Magazine*, no. 9 (July 1993), 33–39.

General John Gibbon. *Library of Congress*

clothing and blanket, while we have only got a canteen of water to carry. When we get tired of walking we can ride. I never have been better suited than I am at present."

Gibbon's first published order as a general, however, was not well received. His regiments, he proclaimed, should "emulate the gallant deeds of their brave Statesmen in the West, and prove to them that the heroism displayed at Fort

Donelson and Pittsburg Landing, can be rivaled by their brothers, who have come East, to fight the course of the Union." The order was a sour reminder that the brigade had not seen any real active service and immediately cast a long shadow over the new commander.[6]

If the new general of volunteers seemed pleased with his new command, in ranks there was grumbling over his appointment, and the loudest came from ambitious and politically well-connected Col. Sol Meredith of the 19th Indiana. Meredith resented the fact that the new commander was a regular army officer. Surely—Meredith mentioned aloud to anyone who would listen and explained in letters to his powerful political friends—volunteers should be commanded by volunteer officers. One soldier called the new commanding general "a most thorough disciplinarian," and said that "the manner in which he put the brigade through drill will never be forgotten by those who participated. There were early morning drills, before breakfast, forenoon drills, evening, and night drills, besides guard mounts and dress parade." He speculated that "Probably no brigade commander was ever more cordially hated by his men." Another Badger reported: "He is very strict—too much West Point and white gloves to suit the boys at first sight."[7]

That fact that Gibbon was raised in North Carolina and had brothers in the Confederate service was also noted and discussed around the coffee fires. Behind the general's back, the soldiers laughed and called him "The Southern Renegade" and the "Gigadier Beneral" and made jokes about his "comical appearance . . . when mounted because . . . his legs were abnormally long and he rode a small horse." One of his first orders required each soldier to take a bath once a week. Another instituted a daily review—at 5:00 o'clock in the morning—to be followed immediately by the drinking of a cup of hot coffee by each member of the brigade whether he liked it or not. Regimental officers who had not attended the early morning roll call were now required to do so. "The impression in relation to our new Brigadier, on first sight, is rather unfavorable," a Hoosier wrote in his diary.[8]

As he worked to train his new soldiers, the uneven appearance of his regiments troubled Gibbon. Uniforms varied from company to company with some soldiers in caps and others in the tall black hats. Trousers varied from

6 *Gibbon's Brigade, General Orders*, U.S. National Archives, Records of the U.S. Army Continental Commands; John Gibbon, *Personal Recollections of the Civil War* (New York, 1929), 12–14.

7 Gibbon's General Order No. 52 is cited in Alan D. Gaff, *On Many a Bloody Field: Four Years in the Iron Brigade* (Bloomington, IN, 1997), 124, 12–14, 27–28; T.H.R.S., letter, May 4, 1862.

8 "His Pilgrimage," *Telegraph*, July 1, 1888; William Murray diary as cited in Gaff, *Bloody Field*, 125.

Colonel Sol Meredith, 19th Indiana
Civil War Museum, Kenosha, WI

dark blue to sky blue. The transition began before he took command when it was decided to make the Model 1858 dress hat a consistent item. Gibbon took the uniform matter a step further and required that all soldiers be issued the nine-button dark blue frock coat of the regulars along with white linen leggings and cotton white gloves. A 7th Wisconsin volunteer wrote home: "We have a full blue suit, a fine black hat nicely trimmed with bugle and plate and ostrich feathers, and you can only distinguish our boys from the regulars by [our] good looks."[9]

If the additions were at first generally greeted with "the greatest merriment," there was loud grumbling when it was discovered that the cost of the gloves and leggings would come out of the soldiers' clothing allowances. The required items included extra underwear, stockings, and shoes. A soldier in the 2nd Wisconsin was so outfitted and it was determined it added 85 pounds to his marching weight. "It is impossible for men on the march, in active service, to transport on their persons anything more than they actually need. And the Yankee soldier won't," said one volunteer. To Gibbon's regular army dismay, the extra clothing was thrown away on the first practice march. Requisitioning supplies for his regiment, Meredith slyly asked for four extra mule teams to transport the Indiana regiment's extra luggage. The colonel's request was denied.

The displeasure over the issue of linen leggings lingered into the summer. In addition to the additional cost, they were cumbersome to put on and uncomfortable to wear in warm weather. The angry mood in the ranks was expressed one morning when Gibbon came out of his tent and found his "pet horse" equipped with four leggings. Upset with the break in discipline, the general never discovered the culprits.

9 For a description of the uniform, see "The uniform of the Iron Brigade at Gettysburg, July 1, 1863" in Herdegen and Beaudot, *In the Bloody Railroad Cut at Gettysburg*.

Private Charles Keeler, 6th Wisconsin
Alan T. Nolan

One bright spot was that the "sheet metal" smoothbore guns altered from flintlock to percussion and first issued to the regiments were mostly gone and all the regiments were armed with rifled weapons. This was important because the perception of the Badgers and Hoosiers was that they "were all crack shots with the rifle" as they "came from away out West and always lived in the woods." Of course, it was not true.

If the new rifles helped morale, they created an ordnance supply nightmare. The 2nd Wisconsin now carried the Model 1854 Austrian Lorenz rifles in their original .54-caliber ("a splendid gun to shoot," one said) while the shoulder arms of the other regiments were in the more standard U.S. patterns of .58-caliber. "Is there any wonder, then that we should weep for joy rather than sorrow," a 2nd Wisconsin man wrote home when the old muskets were exchanged for "true and trusty rifles that will bite as well as bark and kick. We now have the best guns in the Brigade, and I think they are in the hands of men who know how to use them." After a firing drill a week later, he reported that the new weapons proved satisfactory. "They are a splendid piece, rough as they look; and in the hands of the Second will do good execution when the opportunity for their use occurs."

The men in the 6th Wisconsin and the 19th Indiana were issued the Model 1861 Springfield pattern rifle muskets, with the length of a musket but a rifled bore. Many in the two regiments believed they were superior to the Lorenz. In the 6th Wisconsin, Pvt. J. P. "Mickey" Sullivan mounted his rifle-musket with "some silver ornaments and fixed the screw in a stock against the dog [sear] so it [trigger pull] worked almost as easy as a squirrel gun, and I felt very proud of it." During an inspection, an officer asked about the screw in the gunstock. "I told him so that I could hit a canteen at one hundred yards and he asked me no more questions."

The 7th Wisconsin had also been issued Austrian Lorenz rifles but unlike the smaller caliber guns of the 2nd Wisconsin they were re-rifled or reamed to .58-caliber—the standard being adopted by the army. The new rifles had been exchanged in the regiment for the old muskets in February before it moved to central Virginia. One private said his regiment was formed and then "they were given out as the roll was called and the guns being numbered, we took guns accordingly." The new rifles were "colored black except for the lock guard and rammer, which are bright." The rifles were four inches shorter than the old musket and a half-pound heavier, but "they carry very nice and much easier than the musket. So we are ready for the secesh now."[10]

10 Mickey of Company K, "The Charge of the Iron Brigade at Gettysburg," Feb. 13, 1883, *Mauston* [WI] *Star*; Ray, *Iron Brigade*, Feb. 16, 1862, and June 19, 1862. Ray wrote: "We got everything pertaining to the new guns, which are as follows. First a brass Stopple, a very pretty one, a good wormer and a good screwdriver and wrench. They are in one piece." The Lorenz was the second most common imported shoulder arm used by both sides in the Civil War. It was regarded as a sound weapon to be used while production of U.S. arms caught up with demand. The Union reported purchases of 226,924 and the Confederacy as many as 100,000.

Chapter 5

"The Whole Yankee Army Is Played Out"

Richmond: July 5, 1862

The warm, humid air in the swampy lowlands surrounding Richmond was a shock to men recently used to campaigning in clear, cool mountain air. After marching across the Blue Ridge Mountains and boarding trains for the capital, Jackson's command became part of a much larger Confederate concentration effort to drive away the enemy army rapidly approaching that city's outskirts. After defeating numerous Federal forces in the Shenandoah Valley, Jackson's men were confident they would save Richmond.

As his men snaked through Richmond, Jackson was returning to a command system he had not known since Manassas. Although he remained subordinated to Joseph Johnston as the main Confederate general in Virginia, once he arrived in the valley Jackson found himself as a *de facto* independent commander. Tied up leading the main element of the Confederate army in northern Virginia, Johnston's limited spare time was more often used to spar with his political superiors in Richmond rather than overseeing Jackson. Instead of receiving instructions and orders from Johnston, Stonewall instead started working with President Jefferson Davis's military advisor, a white bearded general named Robert E. Lee.

By the time Jackson reached Richmond, Johnston was absent, recovering from an earlier wound. Lee commanded the main Confederate army now called the Army of Northern Virginia with Jackson becoming a senior subordinate. His army growing, in late June Lee launched his first campaign in charge of the Army of Northern Virginia. Starting at Oak Grove, Lee attempted to destroy McClellan and his Army of the Potomac thereby saving Richmond. Unfortunately for Lee the army proved to be too large and unwieldy with some commanders not fit for service under the demanding Lee. In a series of costly battles Lee drove McClellan from the gates of Richmond but without destroying the main Federal army.

Robert E. Lee's first campaign in command of the Army of Northern Virginia buoyed Southern morale after months of Confederate defeats. Quoting a New York newspaper, Richmond's *Daily Dispatch* crowed "We are entering upon a new campaign. That which was commenced in Virginia with the rebel evacuation of Manassas was ended with General McClellan's abandonment of the line of the Chickahominy." Pushed back to nearly the gates of Richmond, the Seven Days' campaign shifted the course of the war in Virginia. The Seven Days' campaign was subsequently transformed into a turning point where both the Confederate capital was saved, and the war shifted to another section of Virginia. In July and August 1862, it was not clear yet that the battles were so decisive.[1]

The outlook for Lee following the Seven Days remained more challenging. Planning the campaign around Richmond, Lee had two overall objectives that he set out to meet in the Seven Days: 1) Drive the Federal army away from Richmond and 2) destroy as much as possible of the Army of the Potomac to eliminate it as an immediate threat to the capital. In the course of the fighting, Lee's army fulfilled the first objective, driving the Federal army 21 miles to the east into a confined space along the James River at Harrison's Landing. However, Southern success did not come cheap. While inflicting 15,000 casualties on his opponent, Lee lost nearly 20,000 men killed, wounded, or captured. The Army of the Potomac remained a viable fighting organization at the end of the affair, frustrating Lee who thought, "under ordinary circumstances the Federal army should have been destroyed." Instead of its destruction, Lee's campaign drove the Army of the Potomac into a concentrated position protected by earthworks.[2]

During the retreat, the Army of the Potomac's commander, George B. McClellan, transferred his supply route from the York River to the James River at Harrison's Landing. Soon Lee received intelligence of reinforcements reaching the Federal army. On July 5, Lee informed President Davis that seven large steamers had arrived at Harrison's Landing "crowded with soldiers." Reports also suggested McClellan was evacuating a portion of his army, but Lee thought the evacuees contained the "sick wounded & demoralized," not combat troops in the middle of a major redeployment. If the steamers were indeed reinforcing McClellan's army, Lee potentially faced an opponent as strong as it was at the

1 *The Daily Dispatch*, July 29, 1862.

2 U.S. War Department, *The War of the Rebellion: A Compilation of the Official Records of the Union and Confederate Armies*, 128 vols. (Washington D.C., 1880–1891), Series 1, vol 11, pt 2, 497. Hereafter cited as *OR*. All references are to Series 1 unless otherwise noted.

start of the Seven Days. With no reinforcements to Lee's army in the foreseeable future, for the time being the Confederates were likely to remain outnumbered.[3]

Even if the Federal steamers in the James River did not carry reinforcements, their presence changed the operational options available to McClellan, or at least so Lee thought. Lee worried that McClellan could use steamers to "transfer his troops on the other side of the river" and potentially renew the campaign against Richmond from a new direction. Intelligence reports from Confederate pickets across the river from Harrison's Landing confirmed Lee's fears. If the troops were indeed being transferred to the James River's southern bank, Lee was unable to attack his opponent in transit owing to the U.S. Navy gunboats anchored in the river. Lee's best available option, he told President Davis, was to leave a small cavalry force watching Harrison's Landing while the rest of the army returned to Richmond "where it can be better refreshed & strengthened, & be prepared for a renewal of the contest, which must take place at some quarter soon."[4]

Returning to Richmond after an active campaign, many soldiers felt they had returned to civilization. Not all was leisure, however; rest was interrupted by the tedious routine of drill and camp duty. A soldier in the 5th Texas remembered "drills in the morning and evening, roll calls three times a day, and a general inspection of dress, arms and accouterments on Sunday morning." To combat the boredom in camp and to reward good performance in the army, many regiments issued a small number of daily passes allowing select soldiers to escape to the city. The small number of passes was never enough to satisfy the numbers of men wishing to get away from camp. If caught outside of camp without a pass, a night in the guardhouse and some extra duty typically was the punishment. Getting into Richmond without a pass became a sport for the daring known as "running the blockade."[5]

On one occasion Private Morrell of the 5th Texas ran the blockade after convincing the regimental surgeon that he was ill. Unfortunately for the Texan his surgeon discovered the ruse and threatened a week in the guardhouse. Thinking quickly, Morrell found a large supply of mustard which he used to make a poultice applied to his back. Waiting an hour or so, the Texan started to groan "most piteously." Examining Morrell's back, the regimental surgeon and assistant surgeon determined that the best solution to the Texan's affliction was

3 Lynda Crist, *The Papers of Jefferson Davis*, vol. 8, *1862* (Baton Rouge, LA, 1995), 278.

4 Ibid., 279.

5 George Skoch and Mark Perkins, eds., *Lone Star Confederate: A Gallant and Good Soldier of the Fifth Texas Infantry* (College Station, TX, 2003), 51.

to remove the poultice, causing his back to be "perfectly raw." After applying a soothing ointment, Morrell was placed back on the sick list. As soon as the surgeon left, "up jumped Morrell, brushing his hair, tying on a dilapidated necktie, borrowing a 'V'—he starts out to run the Blockade, and was gone four days."[6]

Soldiers unable to obtain a pass or run the blockade whiled time away in camp. While gambling remained popular, many soldiers focused their idle time catching up on correspondence. In letters to family and friends, or to newspapers, soldiers attempted to evaluate the results of the recent fighting and speculate on future campaigns. A soldier-correspondent thought that the "crushing defeat of the Federal armies in the series of battle before Richmond" had significantly damaged the Union war effort. Confederates were interested in how the recent fighting impacted the North, and thought themselves fortunate that "information reaches here regularly from the North through various channels. It is an easy thing for a person in Richmond to keep well posted as to the condition of things in Abe's dominions." Another Confederate victory, some thought, would destroy the U.S. government and that "the Northern people will soon have to re-enact the bloody scenes of the first French revolution. Mark the prediction."[7]

A Maryland artillerist concurred with his unknown compatriot. Writing to his family back home behind Federal lines, the Marylander concluded "I don't think there can be many more days before the big fight will take place, when I sincerely believe the Yankee army will be annihilated. . . . I believe that the whole Yankee army and Government, to use a camp phrase, are about 'played out.'"[8]

6 Ibid., 51.

7 William Styple, ed., *Writing & Fighting from the Army of Northern Virginia: A Collection of Confederate Soldier Correspondence* (Kearny, NJ, 2003), 125–126.

8 Rick Richter, *Three Cheers for the Chesapeake! History of the 4th Maryland Light Artillery Battery in the Civil War* (Atglen, PA, 2017), 24.

Chapter 6

"A Pleasant Place"

Fredericksburg: Summer 1862

The move to the Fredericksburg area was a welcome change from the used-up and crowded Washington camps. The burned bridges were rebuilt, and supply trains began to arrive, day and night. One bridge was made of canal boats anchored lengthways. They were planked so teams could cross. Despite the drills, work details, and other duties during those weeks of early summer, the Westerners carefully followed the newspaper reports of the fighting in the far West where friends and relatives served in Wisconsin and Indiana regiments. More interest was given to the accounts of McClellan's main force move on Richmond. "We expect 'Little Mac' will celebrate the 'Fourth' in, or near that place," one Westerner wrote to his sister shortly after arriving in Fredericksburg. "We will not participate, but will move to there soon after it is taken."

As they settled in at Fredericksburg, there were indications the brigade might, in fact, be needed for serious work. A force of Confederates in the Shenandoah Valley under a "General Jackson" defeated and routed a Union army under Gen. Nathaniel Banks at Front Royal May 23. That sent off alarms in skittish officialdom at Washington. The setback was followed soon after by the defeat of two other Union forces in Virginia at Cross Keys on June 8 and Port Republic on June 9. The defeats seemingly made the decision to halt McDowell in central Virginia to protect the capital the prudent and correct one. In the ranks, a rumor circulated King's division might be on the move. "It is said that Banks has retreated to the Potomac River and that Jackson was following him up," a Wisconsin soldier wrote in his journal. "I have an idea that we are going to the rear of Jackson, thereby cutting off his retreat, and have him between two armies." Bank's retreat, he explained "was done on purpose to draw him on and get us in the rear so as to take Mr. Jackson and his all." In the end, however, that order never came.[1]

The news from McClellan's army outside Richmond was encouraging at first. Newspapers reported how the general extended his lines and brought up necessary armament and supplies. It was not until June 25, however, that "Little Mac" began a serious movement, winning a minor victory at Oak Grove. Troubling telegraph reports followed, however, telling of heavy fighting and setbacks at Beaver Dam Creek, Gaines' Mill, and at Savage's Station, where the rear guard of the Union army was sharply attacked. In the end, McClellan retreated toward the safety of Harrison's Landing and the cover of Union gunboats on the James River. McClellan's grand advance—started with such bright hope and loud talk—was stalled. At Harrison's Landing, he told anyone who would listen that the setback was Washington's fault for failing to release McDowell's corps and other troops that he had requested.

"There has been terrible slaughter, but we are well satisfied that McClellan is safe," a soldier in Gibbon's brigade wrote of the news. "We did not have half force enough. When we get there we will make them skedaddle, where ever we meet them we drive them back, but it must be admitted they fight like devils." A rumor also circulated that one of the Confederate generals—"Stone wall Jackson"—was killed during the fighting. "I consider when they lost him [they] lost their most dangerous man, that is their best fighter, but the papers will keep you posted," a Wisconsin officer wrote his wife. The rumor proved false, and what followed the setbacks was wild speculation that Confederates were being pulled from the defenses at Richmond to again move into central Virginia. Especially troubling was concern that Rebel forces might be under command of the very much alive "Stonewall Jackson."[2]

As the dismayed Wisconsin and Indiana men watched war developments from a distance, they spent the days in training and on work details. One such effort involved rebuilding a railroad track destroyed by the Confederates. A party of Wisconsin men was marched out to one site along a railroad line where a bridge was being constructed and issued shovels. The Badger officer in charge looked over to a nearby wood and saw troops from New York City "hacking around trees until they could push them over and then trying to make railroad ties from the trees." The Western officer in charge, one soldier said, with "his face the picture of disgust" turned to the New York colonel: "If you will give

1 Ray, *Iron Brigade*, May 29, 1862.

2 John Gibbon, *Personal Recollections of the Civil War* (New York, 1928), 34. Young to wife, July 4, 1862, *Dear Delia*, 76.

those shovels to those counter jumpers and give us the axes we will cut all the ties and bridge timber you will need on the road in a week but if you give us the shovels we could not dig a hole big enough to bury a cat in a month." The Wisconsin men got the axes. In short order the wood needed for the roads and bridge was made available. The bridge was completed in three days.

The Western boys also had the run of Fredericksburg, commandeering wagon shops, blacksmiths, and other workshops, and even the abandoned local newspaper. "Our troops are in full possession of this hot secession hole and the soldiers are running the machine shops and mills on an improved 'yankee' Plan," a Badger wrote home. The Potomac & Richmond railroad bridge burned by the "skedaddling secesh" was rebuilt, he said, and cars crossed over regularly between Acquia Creek and Fredericksburg.[3]

The former printers in the regiments quickly put together and began issuing a soldier's newspaper called the "Christian Banner" on brown store wrapping paper. The local shopkeepers had run up their prices for the intruders. Common-sized note envelopes were $1 per package and tea $7 a pound. At first, the store owners refused to accept U.S. greenbacks and wanted only Confederate money. As a result, and until officers halted the practice, enterprising printers made facsimile Confederate "notes" available at 10 cents per $1,000. "We accommodated them and bought out the town in the line of supplies they had that we thought we wanted and did not kick on the price charged, as we got our money cheap," one Badger said. "The boys felt that all was fair in war."[4]

The summer of 1862 at Fredericksburg passed quickly with few major incidents. There were several reports of Confederate cavalry in the area and some exchange of gunfire. In addition, now and then, a deserter or two would show up. One of the Rebels had on "a fine pair of boots," one Wisconsin soldier observed. The Johnny said the footwear "cost him $18.00 in Richmond." Of more importance was the explosion of powder and other munitions housed in a small brick building used as a magazine. It killed one of the guards. "He was blown on top of a building some 4 or 5 rods distant," said a Wisconsin man. "One leg blown [off] close his body & and the other just below his knee." It was a sight never forgotten: "The hair was burned off his head. He had scratches all over his body and besmeared with blood, blood and dirty. There was not a thread of clothing left on him. I saw him & it was the most horrible sight I have

3 George H. Brayton, May 23, 1862, in "Civil War Voices: Letters and Diaries of Some Columbia County Soldiers (and a few others relevant thereto)," ed. W. K. Wright, no date, unpublished, 5.

4 Loyd G. Harris to his sister, July 2, 1862, Loyd Harris Papers, WHS; Cheek and Point, *Sauk County*, 8, 24–26, 29–30.

A Fredericksburg campsite of the Jayhawkers of the Prairie du Chien Volunteers, Company C of the 6th Wisconsin, displaying some of the new 1858 dress hats. *Institute for Civil War Studies*

ever seen. It is beyond description. His brother was the first to get hold of him, he being on another post not far distant. I have not heard as there was any body else got even a scratch."[5]

One more important matter of interest was the growing use of the issued tents as hammocks. The practice began in a company of the 6th Wisconsin which included men who worked in the Mississippi River boats. The practice soon spread. At first the use of hammocks made from the half-tent issued each soldier got a mixed reception. "I didn't rest well last night, the cause of it is that I slept in a hammock and it was so soft and easy" compared with sleeping on the ground, one soldier noted. But he soon added that he now found it "more comfortable living without a tent and with a hammock." Soon the whole campground was named "Hammock Ridge."[6]

5 Gibbon, *Recollections*, 34–35; Otis, *Second Wisconsin*, 48; Ray, *Iron Brigade*, May 26, 1862, 88–89; George Eustice to Mother, Apr. 20, 1862, Carroll College Institute for Civil War Studies, Civil War Museum, Kenosha, WI.

6 Ray, *Iron Brigade*, July 12, 1862.

The weather was pleasant, the countryside lush and beautiful, and the lonesome Western boys were soon thinking of more tender matters. One Wisconsin officer wrote home: "Fredericksburg can boast of two things beautiful, Flowers of every description and pretty Women. There is certainly some of the finest looking women here I ever seen. They sit out on the stoops and verandahs every pleasant evening. That is the regular Southern fashion." The Southern ladies, however, were quick to show their scorn. The "women and girls are worst of all," a soldier in the 7th Wisconsin wrote home. "When ever they would pass a Yankee soldier they would twist their pretty faces all out of shape."

A 6th Wisconsin soldier described the city inhabitants as "mostly colored, a few old hoary headed white men, rosy cheeked damsels (all in their sweet sixteenth). They all think we are 'right smart looking fellows and wear right good clothes' but can't become reconciled to that name Yankee." Some of the more zealous of the fairer sex, another soldier said, showed their patriotism for the Confederate cause by "making mouths at the Union soldiers as they pass through the streets, in some cases even spitting at them and threw water upon them from the windows."

The boys got their own form of revenge. A Union flag hung over a sidewalk on Caroline Street where the Federals had an office. A group of ladies were nearly under the flag before seeing it, then walked out into the muddy street to escape passing beneath the banner. "The boys looked on and enjoyed the scene," said one who was watching. Soon there were seven flags strung across the whole street and the ladies "did not walk on that street at all."

No soldier had a more bittersweet incident than young Lt. Loyd Harris of Prairie du Chien, Wisconsin. He was a soldier with an outgoing and sunny manner, a love for music (he took his violin with him to war), and an eye for a pretty girl. He first encountered "the rudeness" of the local inhabitants while walking along the principal street as "two young ladies" approached. "As we neared each other, I gave away toward the outside of the walk. When the ladies crowded me into the gutter and swept by[,] I had just time to raise my hat and say Thank you my pretty 'secesh.'" He wrote of the encounter in a letter to his sister.[7]

Troubling as well were the hundreds of runaway slaves who flocked to the army seeking safety in the circle of "Massa Linkum's men." The fugitives were young and old, men and women, family groups and alone, and they "came in

7 Young to wife, May 24, 1862, *Dear Delia*, 68; George Eustice, undated; Jerome A. Watrous, *Appleton* [WI] *Crescent*, May 31, 1862; Edward P. Kellogg, "Another Regiment," *Telegraph*, Sep. 28, 1879; Philip Cheek and Mair Pointon, *History of the Sauk County Riflemen, Known as Company "A" Sixth Wisconsin Veteran Volunteer Infantry, 1861–1865* (N.P., 1909), 29–30.

Lieutenant Loyd Harris, 6th Wisconsin
Lance J. Herdegen

clouds," one Badger officer said. There were no regulations for dealing with runaways, no plan to free them or care for them. The enlisted men looking into the hard face of slavery at first backed away and then accepted them as part of army life. They called them "contrabands" from a statement to the newspapers by Union Gen. Benjamin Butler who declared such fugitives reaching his lines were "contraband of war" and refused to return them to their previous owners. By the time the Black Hat Brigade reached Fredericksburg, every company had at least one "contraband" attached to the mess and other details of the various officers.

Chapter 7

"Lee's Dilemma"

Richmond: Late July 1862

While many of his soldiers predicted that the decisive battle of the war was about to be fought, Lee focused on reorganizing his army and finding replacements for casualties. Unlike McClellan, reinforcements to Lee's army came from men returning from extra duty or the hospital. Few new regiments reached the Army of Northern Virginia after the conclusion of the Seven Days' battles. In the space of ten days, from July 10 to July 20, 13,472 men returned to the army. With Longstreet's Division numbering over 8,000 men and A. P. Hill's Division numbering over 11,000 men, these returning soldiers were the equivalent of a division reinforcing the army. As welcome as these returnees were, the number of soldiers who either remained in the hospital or on detached service continued to plague the Confederate war effort. A July 20 army return noted 94,692 officers and men present. The problem was that the number of officers and men present *and* absent numbered 139,110. Nearly 45,000 soldiers, the equivalent of about four divisions, were absent. Some of these men did return to the army, providing a slow trickle of reinforcements during the later 1862 campaigns. However, the problem remained that about a quarter of Lee's entire army was unavailable for the foreseeable future.[1]

In addition to finding replacements for his army, Lee set about the task of reorganizing his command structure. Unsatisfied with the results of the previous campaign, some commanders found themselves reassigned to distant theaters while others were promoted. A recurrent problem during the fighting was the unwieldy organization of the army. The largest authorized subordinate unit in the Army of Northern Virginia was the division. In the July 20 return, Lee had eight infantry divisions, a small division of cavalry, and a large artillery reserve.

1 *OR* 11, pt. 3, 645.

Controlling nearly a dozen divisional commanders in the midst of a rapidly changing battle proved chaotic and confusing. To alleviate the problem during the Seven Days' battles, ad-hoc larger commands were formed with a general such as Jackson or Longstreet given temporary command over additional units. While this achieved only limited success at Gaines Mill and Glendale, Lee decided to transform the scheme into a semi-permanent command structure. Unfortunately for Lee, the Confederate Congress had yet to authorize corps in the Confederate military. Lee tried to get around this bureaucratic hurdle by splitting his army into two semi-permanent wings.[2]

Lee decided to divide his army in half. In command of the Right Wing, Lee placed Maj. Gen. James Longstreet. Destined to be Lee's "Old War Horse," Longstreet proved himself in the fighting around Richmond. Like Longstreet, Maj. Gen. "Stonewall" Jackson demonstrated an aptitude for higher command and was given Lee's Left Wing. Rounding out the upper echelons of the Army of Northern Virginia, Maj. Gen. J. E. B. Stuart retained command of the cavalry while Brig. Gen. William Pendleton remained in command of the army's artillery reserve. Four divisions remained independent and reported directly to Lee.

The fighting around Richmond also demonstrated that many divisions were too large for one officer to control effectively. Longstreet's former division was broken up into two new ones, along with Benjamin Huger's Division. This shake-up in command allowed for the promotion of officers who exhibited promise, while also permitting the removal of officers deemed unsatisfactory. Brigadier General William Whiting was replaced by Brig. Gen. John B. Hood and reassigned to command Wilmington, North Carolina. Three more general officers were banished from Lee's army and sent to the Trans-Mississippi Department.

With the army readying for another campaign, the question of how to use it to the best advantage continued to plague Lee. Firmly entrenched at Harrison's Landing, an assault to drive the Army of the Potomac into the James River would likely be prohibitively costly to the Confederates. The only reasonable option left for Lee was to closely observe the Federals at Harrison's Landing and wait for future movements. While McClellan and his army remained the primary target, Lee remained abreast of other enemy commands. A large Federal presence under Maj. Gen. David Hunter continued to operate on the coast of South Carolina near Port Royal. With little campaigning in that region in May and June, the Confederate War Department transferred many regiments from South Carolina to Richmond to augment the army. The remaining troops successfully repelled a haphazard advance towards Charleston at the battle of

2 Two divisions recently transferred to Gordonsville are not reflected in this return.

Secessionville in June, although defeated Federals remained a potential threat. A new advance towards Charleston by Hunter could trigger a return of troops from Lee's army back to the Palmetto State.

In North Carolina lurked another threat to the rebel army around Richmond. A corps-sized Federal force under Maj. Gen. Ambrose Burnside had been operating on the North Carolina coast since early 1862. A series of Federal victories at Roanoke Island, New Bern, and Fort Macon all but destroyed Confederate resistance in the eastern third of the Tar Heel State. A combination of disease and lack of adequate wagon transport stalled further advances by Burnside. The unexpected reprieve allowed many North Carolina regiments to be transferred to the Army of Northern Virginia in time for the Seven Days' battles while a small Confederate presence remained back home. If Burnside received enough reinforcements and wagons to restart his campaign, the critical communication center of Goldsborough, North Carolina, could be threatened. Burnside could potentially then advance north, threatening the important railroad hub at Petersburg, Virginia.

Yet another Federal presence worried Lee. A large Federal army now appeared in central Virginia. Scrapping together the debris of Federal forces from the disastrous Shenandoah Valley campaign along with soldiers serving in northern Virginia and Fredericksburg, the new Army of Virginia conceivably could be a more dangerous threat to Lee than McClellan's army bottled up in Harrison's Landing. Similar to the Carolinas, after the multiple Federal advances in the Shenandoah Valley and central Virginia were repulsed that spring, most of the Confederate soldiers serving in those areas were reassigned to the main Confederate army around Richmond.

Lee faced a potentially cataclysmic strategic situation after saving Richmond. The victory at the Seven Days derived from many different factors, but a significant reason was the concentration of most of the Confederate forces along the East Coast to the Confederate capital. Fortunately, the Federals had yet to capitalize on that concentration by launching new thrusts into a lightly defended section of either of the Carolinas or Virginia. That such an offensive had yet to transpire did not guarantee continued peace in those regions. If either Hunter or Burnside, or worse a coordinated offensive, advanced in the Carolinas, Lee appreciated the very real possibility of losing substantial numbers of soldiers as parts of his army were sent to confront those threats while Lee dealt with McClellan in Virginia. If Lee detached part of his army to preemptively strike either Hunter or Burnside, McClellan could seize upon the weakened Confederate army for a renewed drive towards Richmond. Likewise, a move north towards the Federal Army of Virginia could create another opportunity for McClellan to swiftly drive towards Richmond. Until Federal plans became clear, Lee determined to keep his army concentrated around Richmond. Once a Federal threat materialized, then Lee would act.

On July 12 the garrison commander at Gordonsville, Virginia, forwarded a report to the secretary of war in Richmond. The eleven-word message set in motion a train of events that first transferred the war to central and northern Virginia and ultimately to Maryland: "Federal army in large force occupied Culpepper to-day at 11 o'clock." The Yankee Army of Virginia was on the move.[3]

3 *OR* 51, pt. 2, 590.

Chapter 8

"Mule Racing & 4th of July"

Fredericksburg: July 4, 1862

The Union army camps at Fredericksburg were already stirring when 36 artillery guns opened the Fourth of July 1862, with a thunderous salute that echoed off the hills along the Rappahannock River.

It was the 86th birthday of what one soldier in John Gibbon's Brigade called "this great and once happy Republic." William Ray of the 7th Wisconsin also added in his journal: "Oh, awful to think that a portion of its inhabitants have tried to & Disgraced it to their utmost."[1]

Another of Gibbon's men—James Northrup of the 2nd Wisconsin—mentioned the holiday in a letter home. "I suppose you will have a good time," he offered ruefully. "I hope so at least and hope you will not forget us Volunteers but enjoy a little fun for us." Of the current military situation, he wrote: "We are still laying on the north bank of the Rappahannock having an easy time of it. We have been expecting that we would be taken down to reinforce McClellan but at present it looks as if we were elected to stay where we are for some time to come. The fact is somebody has got to stay here in case of a reverse to McClellan the rebels could march on to Washington without opposition."[2]

The brigade had been together since mid-summer of the previous year and—except for the 2nd Wisconsin which fought at First Bull Run—saw only scattered and limited engagements with the enemy over the past months. "Of course, we feel eager to be something more than ornamental file-closers," a frustrated Wisconsin officer wrote home. "Our regiment has been more than a

1 Ray, *Iron Brigade*, 110.

2 James Northrup to brother, July 3, 1862, *Drifting to an Unknown Future, The Civil War Letters of James E. Northrup and Samuel W. Northrup*, ed. Robert C. Steensma (Sioux Falls, SD, 2000), 35, 36. Northrup enlisted April 21,1861, at Lodi. He was wounded and captured at the Wilderness in 1864 and was absent, a prisoner, in the muster out of his regiment in 1864.

year in service, and in soldierly bearing, perfection in drill, and discipline, we do not yield the palm to the regulars in any service."[3]

Planning for the brigade's patriotic celebration had been underway for more than a month. The site selected for the event was "opposite Fredericksburg on a large section of the plantation formally owned by the widow Washington, the mother of the first president and the father of the county," said Ord. Sgt. Jerome Watrous of the 6th Wisconsin. "The morning opened bright and warm and remained so all day."[4]

The holiday began on the company streets with the usual morning reveille and roll calls, but there were catcalls and shouts from the ranks as the organizations formed. Privates in the 7th Wisconsin had elected new officers from boys in the back ranks and the "officers" immediately took command of the regiment.

"There was, as a matter of course, considerable laughter in ranks but [they] behaved well and obeyed orders which Our orderly said we must obey. And he couldn't refrain from laughing himself at the novelty of the thing," said Ray. "But as soon as we had got breakfast, the old cooks called on our Orderly to have somebody carry the breakfast to those that were on duty (as that is the way it is done). Orderly called at the top of his voice, J. B. Callis (Col. John Callis) and informed that he had to carry the guards breakfast to him. This rather plagued him but go he must."[5]

Other regimental officers were assigned to the cooking and water carrying details. Non-commissioned officers made up the police details cleaning up the campgrounds under the watchful eyes of privates.

The guards came out dressed in their dirtiest and "most comical" uniforms, said Ray. "Our corporal had an old haversack for a hat, got an old knappsack which had been thrown away, and put it on with the canteen tied to the knappsack behind dangling about his legs and instead of a gun he had a verry large crooked stick, with paper stripes cut in a fantastic form on his arms."

As the unusual detail formed, the large Newfoundland dog owned by Capt. Alexander Gordon Jr. of Beloit was freed just as the guards passed. "This scattered the boys all over and the officer of guard with sword drawn tried to defend the guard and gets run over by three or four [of] the guard which caused greater confusion in the ranks of the guard."

3 Dawes, *Service*, 51.

4 Jerome A. Watrous, untitled manuscript, Jerome Watrous papers, WHS.

5 Ray, *Iron Brigade*, 110–112.

Company K, 7th Wisconsin, taken between May and July 1862 while the brigade was stationed at Fredericksburg. The officers from left to right in the center are Capt. Alexander Gordon, Jr., 1st Lt. Frank W. Oakley, and 2nd Lt. Samuel D. Morse. The town is in the background. *Beloit Historical Society*

At the guard mount, the new adjutant inspected the detail and found fault with some of the sticks used as guns "for not being clean (not having the bark and splinters off, two or three which he got in his hand). . . . But after fussing about for about an hour and as fast [as] the adjutant would get one in line another would run away." Half of the officers were excused by the doctor, the rest missing or hiding.[6]

The "large plain was used for the horse racing, foot racing, and other amusements and athletic exercises" including a "mule race, sack race and a greased pig," said Maj. Rufus Dawes of the 6th Wisconsin. The "festivities and merry-making" went on most of the day with more artillery salutes at noon and again at sundown.

"The mules without number was run, then the horses, then foot races were run," said Ray. "I guess every officer in the division was there and the whole of Gibbons Brigade and a few privates from other Brigades, but it was made for this Brigade only."

The officers had gathered money for prizes. Wagon master William Sears of the 6th Wisconsin won the mule race which littered the track with soldiers

6 Ray enlisted at Cassville Aug. 19, 1861, wounded at Gainesville, Gettysburg, and the Wilderness, and mustered out July 3, 1865. *Roster of Wisconsin Volunteers, War of the Rebellion, 1861–65*, Vol. 1 (Madison, WI, 1886), 560.

unseated along the way, said Dawes. "The prize in this case was for the mule that got through last. Each rider accordingly whipped another's mule, holding back his own." Sears, he said, "rode a bulky mule which would go backward whenever whipped."[7]

A gray mare named "Bet" belonging to Adj. John Russey of the 19th Indiana was the fastest in the horse racing and Col. Sol Meredith of the same regiment, a farmer with a good eye for horseflesh, won $140 in the wagering.

A 6th Wisconsin soldier—John Ishmael of Cassville—got the first prize of $10 dollars as the fastest runner. He was immediately challenged to a final race by Capt. Hollon Richardson of the 7th Wisconsin. The officer beat Ishmael but refused any money saying he just wanted to see if he "had lost speed any since coming to the army." Other informal races continued until evening.[8]

All was accepted as great fun by officers and men.

As the day ended, the massed drums of the four regiments called the soldiers together for a conclusion to the revelries. The soldier selected for the final oration was a regimental favorite that one officer said "can talk on any subject and entertainingly"—Pvt. Edwin C. Jones of the 6th Wisconsin.[9]

"We are assembled on sacred soil, a portion of the plantation owned by the mother of George Washington," Jones told the crowd of soldiers around him. "It was while living on this plantation, under the direction and blessed with the teaching of a noble mother, that George Washington learned those lessons . . . fitting him for leadership in war and peace, to lay the foundation of the mighty Nation that we today are fighting to preserve."

Jones went on: "Over yonder back of the City of Fredericksburg, in a little cemetery, sleeps that noble mother who gave to the Nation its richest and rarest gift. I suggest that we 3,000 Western soldiers turn our faces in the direction of Mary Washington['s] grave and bow our heads in honor and to the memory of the mother of the father of this great country of ours."

Watrous remembered that "every one of the 3,000 browned faces" looked in the direction of Mary Washington's grave and every head was reverently bowed.

"On yonder hills there is an armed force pledged to destroy the government founded by George Washington," Jones paused, then said in a loud voice. "But by the living God they shall not do it."

7 Dawes, *Service*, 51. Sears enlisted at De Soto on July 16, 1861. He died Sep. 6, 1862, of disease at Falls Church Hospital, VA. *Roster*, 531.

8 Ishmael enlisted July 12, 1861, and was discharged Jan. 17, 1863, due to disability. *Roster*, 506

9 Jones enlisted June 18, 1861, writing on his papers he was a "Cosmopolite." He rose to the rank of sergeant and was wounded May 12, 1864. He mustered out July 14, 1865. *Roster*, 514.

Up to that time the audience had listened spell-bound, said Watrous, "but in an instant hats flew in the air, cheers were given for the orator, for the American flag, for the American Nation, and such cheers as are not often heard."[10]

Back in camp, the new "officers" of the 7th Wisconsin issued a series of humorous orders, and finally, in a more sincere tone, thanked the regular commanders for their forbearance, singling out Col. William Robinson "for the levity he has allowed us &c and expressing the greatest confidence in him as a man to lead us to the battle."

In his journal, Ray admitted the brigade had made "quite a demonstration" and it was not something that could have been done at home. "But when we do get home," he concluded, "we will try to raise a Co for the next fourth after."[11]

Another soldier wrote home that the "best part of the day" was the two dollars' worth of "fire works" purchased by Gen. Rufus King.[12]

10 Watrous manuscript.

11 Ray, *Iron Brigade*, 110–115.

12 George Washington Partridge Jr. to his sisters, July 20, 1862, *Letters from the Iron Brigade*, ed. Hugh L. Whitehouse (Indianapolis, 1994), 39–40.

Chapter 9

"I Want Pope Suppressed"

Culpeper: August 9, 1862

The importance of Culpepper to the Confederacy centered on the strategic Orange and Alexandria Railroad. The main north-south railroad in Virginia, the O&A connected with the crucial Virginia Central Railroad some 30 miles to the south at Gordonsville. This small railroad crossroads was immensely important to the Confederate war effort. The Virginia Central Railroad connected the agricultural bounty of the Shenandoah Valley with Richmond and Lee's army. Federal possession of the Virginia Central would prove disastrous to the Confederacy. Writing back in March while still acting as the chief military advisor, Lee believed "the loss of the Central road & communication with the Valley at Staunton would be more injurious than the withdrawal from the Peninsula and the evacuation of Norfolk." Cut off from supplies of food and equipment, a starving army defending Richmond would be an easy target for the Army of the Potomac. Lee had to act.[1]

Since McClellan refused to budge from Harrison's Landing, the greater part of Lee's army remained around Richmond. Within 24 hours of receiving information of Federals in Culpepper, Stonewall Jackson and two divisions of approximately 15,000 soldiers under Maj. Gen. Richard Ewell and Brig. Gen. Charles Winder boarded trains north of Richmond for a slow ride to Louisa Courthouse, east of Gordonsville. Still facing an unclear situation, Jackson's remaining division received orders detaching it from Jackson's command and remaining in camp around Richmond.[2]

That summer Jackson was probably the most famous person in North America. The hero of First Manassas, Jackson's semi-independent command in

1 Clifford Dowdey and Louis Manarin, eds., *The Wartime Papers of R. E. Lee* (Boston, 1961), 139.

2 *OR* 12, pt. 3, 915.

1862 in the Shenandoah Valley stymied one Union advance after another before being called to Richmond for the Seven Days' battles. Around Richmond Jackson uncharacteristically muddled his assignments, such as the attack at Gaines Mill, but eventual Confederate victory ensured that his reputation remained unblemished. With experience leading a semi-independent command, it was natural that Lee chose Jackson to watch Pope. With a well-known aggressive drive, Jackson's orders were not only to oppose the Federal threat coming from Culpepper but if the opportunity presented itself, to "strik[e] a blow at him."[3]

Jackson's transfer to Louisa helped but did not completely solve Lee's predicament on how to confront the several Federal forces operating in Virginia. Confederate soldiers, especially cavalry, picketing and scouting in central Virginia continuously gathered new intelligence. With the Army of the Potomac unmoved from Harrison's Landing, Lee needed all the information that he could get before he could formulate a plan to attack the enemy.

A challenge with any intelligence report is the weeding of fact from rumor. In a dispatch to President Davis on July 18 Lee provided a summary of the intelligence reaching his headquarters. Jackson reported that from reports he received the Federals had abandoned Fredericksburg and were then concentrating to the west around Orange Court House. J. E. B. Stuart relayed information indicating that a large enemy force was assembling near Winchester for a possible resumption of the Valley campaign. Worse yet, Lee still believed that McClellan continued to receive reinforcements. Although Lee remained skeptical that a new threat in the Valley was emerging, he highlighted the problems of accurately interpreting reports that "are so conflicting and sometimes opposing, and our people take up so readily all alarming accounts, which swell in their progress, that it is difficult to learn the truth till too late to profit by it."[4]

Lee soon began to doubt the immediate threat posed by Pope. In a letter to Jackson, Lee admitted that he "can get no clew as to his intentions." Lee believed that Pope's position was actually further north around Manassas Junction and that his mission remained the protection of Washington D.C. The reports of Yankee excursions towards Culpepper and other stops along the Orange and Alexandria Railroad were likely detachments of scouts and skirmishers sent out for "plunder, provisions, and devastation." The main threat in Virginia remained McClellan's army outside of Richmond. Facing a secondary force that posed

3 Dowdey and Manarin, *Wartime Papers of R. E. Lee*, 232.

4 Ibid., 232–233.

no immediate threat, Lee decided against reinforcing Jackson in his effort to deal with Pope.[5]

Lee's views soon changed. On July 23 Pope issued Orders No. 11 to his army declaring that any male civilian deemed disloyal to the Union was to be arrested and given two choices: Swear allegiance to the United States or be sent south towards Confederate lines. Any man who broke his oath of allegiance could expect a summary military execution as a spy and the forfeiture of his property.[6]

Pope's orders enraged Confederate authorities. Lee told Jackson "I want Pope to be suppressed" and to inform Pope that implementation of his orders "cannot be permitted and will lead to retaliation on our part." The Confederate War Department went farther, declaring that Pope and his key subordinates enforcing the order "hereby, specially declared to be not entitled to be considered as soldiers." If Pope's army fulfilled its threat of executing civilians behind its lines, the Confederate War Department announced that a similar number of captured Federal officers would be immediately hanged.[7]

Although incensed by Pope's attempt to transform the character of the war in Virginia, Lee refused to be distracted from the greater threat posed by McClellan. Fortunately for Lee, the strategic situation appeared to offer a fleeting opportunity to deal with a portion of the Federal forces in Virginia. In a letter to Jackson, Lee admitted that a rapidly evolving intelligence picture included the possibility of sending another division to Jackson. News reached Lee that a division of Federal infantry had recently arrived at Harrison's Landing from South Carolina. More ominous reports indicated that Burnside's entire force had been withdrawn from North Carolina for an unknown destination, but more than likely Virginia. Facing an increasing number of new Federal forces, Lee hoped that if Jackson could strike and either destroy or drive back Pope's forces, Stonewall and his divisions could quickly return to Richmond to face the new threat along the James River. Jackson remained outnumbered by Pope, but Lee hoped that an additional division from Richmond could give Stonewall enough strength to deal with Pope once and for all.

Lee mulled over which division to send and narrowed to either A. P. Hill's Division or D. H. Hill's Division. However, both divisions had problems that prevented their immediate release. A falling out between Longstreet and A. P. Hill during the Peninsula campaign resulted in the latter's arrest. Likewise, D. H. Hill's

5 *OR* 12, pt. 3, 916.

6 *OR* Series 2, vol. 4, 836.

7 *OR* 12, pt. 3, 919; *OR* Series 2, vol. 4, 837.

General Ambrose Powell "A. P." Hill
Library of Congress

Division was temporarily leaderless "in consequence of confusion among the major generals."[8]

Lee released A. P. Hill from arrest and sent the young Virginian and his division to Jackson. Writing to Jackson, Lee wrote "A. P. Hill you will find I think a good officer with whom you can consult and by advising with your division commanders as to your movements much trouble will be saved you in arranging details as they can act more intelligently." As President Davis's military advisor, Lee had corresponded regularly with Jackson during his Valley campaign. After assuming command of the Army of Northern Virginia Lee gained valuable insights about how one of his chief subordinates operated. Lee understood Jackson's limitations as a commander, especially his tendency to keep brigade and division commanders in the dark. It remained unclear if Jackson would heed Lee's sound advice to work with his subordinates in a more productive manner.[9]

Lee seemed to not be completely satisfied with Jackson's conduct in central Virginia. In the same message that Lee announced he wanted Pope suppressed, he also delivered a mild rebuke to Jackson's command style. "Do not let your troops run down if it can possibly be avoided by attention to their wants, comforts, &c., by their respective commanders. This will require your personal attention; also consideration and preparation in your movements." Jackson should have already taken heed of Lee's concerns from his time in the Valley. The transformation of his army into "Foot Cavalry" sometimes produced impressive victories but could also generate specular misfires. The forced marches that allowed victories such as Port Republic also reduced the number of effective soldiers in the army to sometimes dangerously low numbers. If Jackson decided

8 *OR* 12, pt. 3, 917.

9 James Robertson Jr., *General A. P. Hill: The Story of a Confederate Warrior* (New York, 1987), 98.

to subject his soldiers to a harsh physical march, he should be certain that the odds of Confederate success were high.[10]

The transfer of A. P. Hill and his division to Jackson signaled a slow but ultimately decisive shift of the Virginia war from the eastern tidewater to the central piedmont. Piecemeal transfers away from Richmond set the stage to ultimately confront Pope's army but Lee continued to fret about the Army of the Potomac along the James. Until McClellan's army was removed from its post east of Richmond, the Confederate capital could never truly be safe, and hence it would always require a large garrison. Frustrated with his strategic impasse, in late July Lee endeavored to either drive McClellan away from Harrison's Landing or return to a campaign of movement.

An attempt in late July to establish Confederate batteries on the south bank of the James River directly opposite Harrison's Landing initially produced great confusion in McClellan's army. Abandoning their position before the Federals could attack in force, Lee later learned that McClellan sent a detachment of his army to defend this position, preventing future Confederate attacks on Harrison's Landing. However, the Federal response demonstrated that the Army of the Potomac's camp along the James River was likely temporary and that the threat to Richmond was fading. McClellan still posed enough of a threat to retain troops around Richmond, but Lee started to focus on the war in central Virginia.

Just as the threat along the James began to subside, a new potential threat emerged from Fredericksburg. On August 5, Lee received a dispatch from J. E. B. Stuart, serving with Jackson in central Virginia. On a scouting mission towards Fredericksburg, Stuart's cavalrymen encountered two brigades of Federal infantry and accompanying artillery. Stuart believed the enemy totaled around 6,000 men and twelve cannon. The most alarming piece of information in Stuart's dispatch relayed that after interrogating some prisoners, Burnside and 16,000 soldiers had disembarked at Fredericksburg after a journey from North Carolina.[11]

Stuart's intelligence could derail any concerted action against Pope, if verified. Rumors became a kind of currency for soldiers on both sides, mainly as a way to combat boredom. Army rumors often blurred the accuracy of intelligence reports gathered from cavalry raids, picket line fights, and prisoners. Until Lee could verify that Burnside was indeed in Fredericksburg, the focus remained on Pope.

10 *OR* 12, pt. 3, 919.

11 *OR* 12, pt. 3, 924.

During the first week in August Jackson learned that a portion of Pope's army had advanced to Culpepper Court House. Dangling in front of him, Jackson hoped "through the blessing of Providence, to defeat it before reinforcements should arrive." Couriers galloped about and soon Jackson's entire force began to rumble towards the Federals. The orders Jackson issued were simple: the movement would commence at dawn with Ewell's Division leading, followed by A. P. Hill and Jackson's old division bringing up the rear. [12]

The simple orders produced confusion. By dawn Hill had his command up and ready for the day's march, with his leading brigade near the road on which Ewell was expected to march. Regrettably for the future command relationship between Hill and Jackson, Ewell was absent. After issuing marching orders, Jackson realized that Ewell was farther to the west than originally thought. Instead of adding needless miles to his march, Ewell's orders changed, allowing him a more direct march to his destination. Jackson failed to send a staff officer or courier informing Hill of the change. Understandably Hill remained in position, waiting for Ewell's Division.

After dawn, Hill saw soldiers he assumed to be the vanguard of Ewell's Division. After "one or two brigades having passed" Hill learned he was not watching Ewell's Division, but Jackson's old division, the one ordered to bring up the rear of the Confederate column. Only then did Hill learn "that Ewell had taken another route. . . . Of this no intimation had been given me." With elements of another division in front of him, Hill declined to get his division marching. Instead he decided to let the other division pass him in its entirety and then begin his march, bringing up the rear of the Confederate line.[13]

After the tail of the division passed, Hill was surprised to see the army's wagon train. Hill's Light Division now found itself in the midst of a giant traffic jam. Marching in fits and starts and facing the prospect of marching longer than expected, after approximately an hour a frustrated Hill rode forward to find the cause of the delays. After marching on a separate route, near a crossing of the Rapidan River, Ewell's command returned to the main Confederate line of march. Like Jackson's old division, Ewell was also marching with his wagon train in his rear. Riding up to the river Hill discovered "a portion of Jackson's division had not crossed, and all were delayed by the passing of Ewell's troops and trains." The main culprit, at least in Hill's eyes, stemmed from the fact that "nothing had been said about the trains in the order of march." Instead of a

12 *OR* 12, pt. 2, 182.

13 Ibid., 215.

combined wagon train bringing up the rear of the column, Jackson's other two division commanders decided to have their wagons follow immediately behind their individual commands, slowing the progress of all units in their rear. Informing Jackson about the delay, by afternoon Hill received orders to turn his command around. Instead, Hill ordered his troops to camp where they were. The Light Division marched an incredible one mile that day.[14]

Jackson was not amused by the performance of his newest commander. Regarding the problem with the trains blocking the road, Jackson focused the blame not on his vague orders, but on what Jackson viewed as Hill's lack of initiative. Jackson believed "Had General Hill moved at dawn I could, had I deemed it necessary, have halted Ewell's train before it reached the road upon which General Hill was to move, and thus have brought the division of General Hill immediately in rear of that General Ewell." Jackson further railed: "If [Hill] believed that the division for which he was waiting to pass was Ewell's, he could easily have sent some one and ascertained the fact. But though the better part of two hours had elapsed since the time fixed for marching, yet it does not appear that he had taken any steps to ascertain, but appears to have taken it for granted that the division which should have been in advance of him was in rear."[15]

The confusion on the march did not endanger Jackson's forces. However, it introduced unnecessary friction and distrust into the Confederate high command. The ultimate goal of this march, an attack on a portion of Pope's army below Culpepper, was postponed for another day. On August 9, that fight arrived. Jackson planned to attack a portion of the Federal army near Culpepper in the shadow of Cedar Mountain. From scouts, Jackson learned that one of Pope's three corps was in the vicinity. If he quickly attacked, he would outnumber the Yankees on the battlefield.

The ensuing battle of Cedar Mountain ended in stalemate. Retaining control of the battlefield that evening, the Confederates viewed the battle as a Southern victory. That victory proved costly for Jackson with nearly 1,300 of his men killed, wounded, or missing. Ultimately Jackson abandoned the battlefield after intelligence reports indicated the rest of Pope's army concentrating around Culpepper. On August 11 Jackson left the Cedar Mountain battlefield and returned south of the Rapidan River. The battle of Cedar Mountain was the start of a larger campaign that in a few weeks would climax at the old Manassas battlefield in northern Virginia.

14 Ibid., 215.

15 Ibid., 217.

Chapter 10

"End of Summer"

Fredericksburg: Late Summer 1862

The current situation, stuck at Fredericksburg observing war movements elsewhere, was especially hard for Capt. Edwin Brown of the 6th Wisconsin, who was homesick and in despair as the days went on without resolution. An attorney, he had left his practice and gone to war leaving behind his wife, Ruth, and small children at Fond du Lac. The war news, often conflicting, and the realization that McDowell's corps was missing the advance on the rebel capital at Richmond, left him angry and bitter.

To add to the frustration of the men of the brigade, the new commander of the Army of Virginia, John Pope, was off to a troubling start. A native of Kentucky and later Illinois, Pope graduated from the U.S. Military Academy in 1842 and served in the Mexican War. Subsequently, after the firing on Fort Sumter, he was named to command the Army of the Mississippi and won newspaper attention, much of it through his own efforts, for capture of New Madrid and Island 10 on the Mississippi River. The successes caught Lincoln's eye and Pope was brought East. His new assignment was to protect Washington, threaten Confederate rail lines in central Virginia, and open a second front to threaten Richmond.[1]

"I come to you of the West, where we have always seen the backs of our enemies," the general proclaimed in an order under the title "Headquarters in the Saddle" which was read to the soldiers of his new Army of Virginia. "I am sorry to find so much in vogue amongst you . . . certain phrases [such as] 'lines of retreat,' and 'bases of supplies' . . . Let us study the probable lines of retreat

1 Pope was a captain in the regular army when the war started and, upon Lincoln's election, used his political connections (his father was a judge in Illinois) so he could travel on part of the president-elect's journey to Washington. Pope was rebuffed, however, in his attempt to be named the president's military secretary and instead accepted a commission as brigadier general of volunteers. *Green Bay Advocate*, July 10, 1862.

of our opponents and leave our own to take care of themselves. Let us look before us and not behind. Success and glory are in the advance, disaster and shame luck in the rear." Of course, it was a swipe at Little Mac, and it did not go down well with soldiers recently associated with the Army of the Potomac. "General Pope's bombastic proclamation has not tended to increase confidence indeed the effect is exactly the contrary," one Wisconsin officer wrote home. The "Headquarters in the Saddle" heading was ridiculed in the ranks of his new army as an indication that his headquarters were where his hindquarters should be.[2]

Despite the frustration of being left behind, endless drills, work details, and the pull and push among the regiments, the time at Fredericksburg slowly passed. There was some excitement May 23 when President Lincoln and Secretary of War Edwin Stanton arrived to review the troops and confer on the situation. Shield's division also arrived at Fredericksburg about the same time, the soldiers dirty and much used up with their commander's arm in a sling from a wound he had received in the Valley of Virginia. A Wisconsin officer wrote in his journal that Shield's men "are the dirtiest ragamuffins we have yet seen in the service." His brigade was in full uniform of dress black hats and dress coats and made a striking appearance during the review in comparison with the recently arrived regiments. But the hard veterans of Shield's regiments laughed and hooted, and labeled the Westerners and their new uniforms as bandbox soldiers. "I saw our president, the rail splitter, yesterday," a Wisconsin boy wrote home. "He was up here and we passed in review before him in heavy marching order. It was a very warm day and you better believe we sweat some." One of the Wisconsin boys observed Lincoln "looks pale, no wonder. He travels so much."[3]

The president received the general officers at the Lacy House, then being used as McDowell's headquarters. When Gibbon was introduced, Lincoln shook his hand, asking in his sly way if the general had written *The Decline and*

2 Dawes, *Service*, 51. "A good deal of cheap wit has been expended upon a fanciful story that I published an order or wrote a letter or made a remark that my 'headquarters would be in the saddle,'" Pope said. "It is an expression harmless and innocent enough, but it is even stated that it furnished General Lee with the basis for the only joke of his life. I think it is due to army tradition, and to be the comfort of those who have so often repeated the ancient joke in the days long before the civil war, that those later wits should not be allowed with impunity to poach on this well-tilled manor. This venerable joke I first head when a cadet at West Point . . . and I presume it could be easily traced back to the Crusades and beyond. Certainly I never used this expression or wrote or dictated it, not does any such expression occur in any order of mine; and as it has perhaps served its time and effected its purpose, it ought to be retired." John Pope, "The Second Battle of Bull Run," *Battles and Leaders of the Civil War*, Vol. 2, eds. Robert U. Johnson and Clarence C. Buell, 493–494.

3 Dawes, journal, May 24, 1862; Dawes, *Service*, 45; Wesley Richardson, Co. B, 7th Wisconsin to mother and father, May 24, 1862, Wright, *Civil War Voices*, 19; Zebulon Russell, Co. B, 7th Wisconsin.

Fall of the Roman Empire. Puzzled, Gibbon blurted that the only thing he had written was an artillery manual. Lincoln smiled: "Never mind, General, if you will write the decline and fall of this rebellion, I will let you off." The president also approved McDowell's call for an immediate march to join McClellan at Richmond and agreed that King's division should lead the advance.

In the Western ranks, the arrival of the president was viewed—one soldier said—as "the forerunner of something to happen. Speculations of all sorts are in order, and the boys come to believe that it was for fear of something dreadful as likely to happen that they were kept from participating in McClellan's on to Richmond via the Peninsula." The brigade received marching orders the next day and the joyful soldiers readied to leave. "As soon as old Abe saw our brigade, he knew it could take Richmond, and he has sent us to do it," one said, while another soldier reported in a letter home that the "hearts of the men in Gen. King's Division, were made glad with the cheering prospects of soon being at Richmond." The column left at noon in good spirits and camped at sundown eight miles from Fredericksburg. The next morning "all hands were ready and anxious to move," but a rider brought orders that General McDowell had ordered a halt.[4]

The stop, one Badger reported, caused "quite a sensation among high officers as well as the men." The speculation around the coffee fires was that the advance was halted because of the fears that Washington would be unprotected. But then news came of the disastrous retreat of Gen. Nathaniel Banks in the Shenandoah Valley and the swift advance of Confederate forces. On Thursday, orders arrived to march to Catlett's Station about 35 miles and 12 miles west of Manassas. "You can as well imagine the feelings of the boys, as I can," a Wisconsin correspondent reported to his hometown newspaper. "The idea of retreating and so great a distance, too, seemed almost incredible, but all were convinced in a few moments when faced toward our destination and put in motion."[5]

Part of the mission of McDowell's corps was to locate the Confederates. The Western Brigade reached Catlett's Station on Saturday. One brigade and two regiments under Gen. Marsena Patrick were put on cars and started for Front Royal, via Manassas Junction. Gibbon's brigade, and the rest of Patrick's, were expected to go sometime during the night, but Sunday morning came and no

4 Otis, *Second Wisconsin*, 48; Ray, *Iron Brigade*, May 26, 1862, 88–89; George Eustice, letter, no date; *Appleton* [WI] *Crescent*, June 28, 1862.

5 Gibbon, *Recollections*, 34–35; Otis, *Second Wisconsin*, 48; Ray, *Iron Brigade*, May 26, 1862, 88–89; George Eustice, letter, no date; *Appleton*[WI] *Crescent*, June 28, 1862.

cars. All the wagons carrying ammunition, forage, and provisions, in fact all means of transpiration, were started to meet the troops at Front Royal.

Over the next few days troops were shifted hither and yon by what Gibbon called "wild orders" by higher authorities: "One brigade was at once shipped by water whilst the balance of the command, our troops, apparently under the command of nobody, was in a few days strung from Fredericksburg to Front Royal, some marching and some on the cars rushing, helter-skelter, as was supposed to 'cut off' Jackson," Gibbon said. What was done by the other portions of the command was only learned from time to time by rumors.[6]

The marching was especially hard with a great deal of rain and sun so hot "that it fairly wilted some of the men." The issue of extra clothing added to the burden carried by the soldiers. One tramp of 20 miles saw 150 men in the 6th Wisconsin fall out exhausted. "Our young boys were broken down by the needless overtaxing of their strength," said one officer. "I can not say who was responsible for such management. I know, however, that General McDowell, whether justly or unjustly, was thoroughly cursed for it." Even General King ("a splendid officer and well liked")—another officer noted in a letter—"wants to get his Division out of McDowels Corps awful bad. The fact is McDowel has no friends in the army, and I don't know what in hell the administration keeps him for." One of the men in the marching columns wrote home that the two weeks of marching in rain and heat made it "a dear march for Uncle Sam." Soldiers threw away knapsacks, blankets, extra pants, and shoes. "We returned to Fredericksburg tougher if not better soldiers."[7]

Some of the stronger soldiers in the 6th regiment—such as Abe Fletcher of Lemonweir—carried two or three knapsacks to help "the little fellows," often "young, slight, round cheek boys, who endured their hardship with a cheerful patience that won us all." In good form was Pvt. J. P. "Mickey" Sullivan, who displayed his sharp Irish wit to ease the long hours on the road. Even Maj. Rufus Dawes shouldered a knapsack to help.[8]

In the 7th Wisconsin, William Ray of Cassville was ill. "The catarrh in my head troubles me very much of late when I get my blood heated. I was completely given out and should have had to [have] stopped for the night if they had went much further," he noted in his journal. The next day he reported on rumors that two men in the 6th Wisconsin died from the heat along with one soldier in the

6 Dawes, *Service*, 47–48; Gibbon, *Recollections* 34–35.

7 Young to wife, June 22, 1862, *Dear Delia*, 76; *Appleton* [WI] *Crescent*, June 28, 1862.

8 Dawes, *Service*, 47–48.

2nd Wisconsin killed by sunstroke and another left helpless. Two of the men in his own Lancaster Union Guards were put on the backs of the officer's horses to keep them with the column.[9]

Along the way, the soldiers continued to throw away the newly issued extra clothing and overcoats as well as discarding the overburdened knapsacks they called "Saratoga trunks." The "sides of the road were literally blue for miles," one wrote in his diary. The Western boys explained to each other with a smile that they were "issuing overcoats to the rebel cavalry." One said the first to go was the extra coat, "then the pants, then the socks, and last of all the shoes, accompanied by the shoe brush and the box of blacking." Gibbon was dismayed at the "quantities of perfectly new clothing drawn just before we left Fredericksburg" being left along the roadway but was unsure what to do about it. Confederate deserters were also flushed by the soldiers and brought in as prisoners. One ragged and dirty specimen came to the side of the road to watch the marching columns. He looked over the Black Hats with professional interest, taking in their knapsacks, coats, and many accoutrements. "We uns durst leave our mammy," he said with a sly grin. "You uns is tied to granny Lincoln's apron string."[10]

9 Dawes, *Service*, 46–47; Ray, *Iron Brigade*, 91.

10 Dawes, *Service*, 47–48; Gibbon, *Recollections*, 35; *Telegraph*, July 1, 1888; George Fairfield Diary, George Fairfield Papers, WHS.

Chapter 11

"Who Could Not Conquer with Such Troops as These"

Jeffersonton, Virginia: August 24, 1862

On August 13, Irby Goodwin Scott finally found enough time to write a letter home. A lieutenant serving in the 12th Georgia, Scott attempted to piece together the confusion of the battle of Cedar Mountain to his distant family. Scott openly wondered to his father why Jackson's soldiers retreated towards Gordonsville after scoring what many Confederates believed was a victory. "I cannot tell why we fell back, but I supose they were either to strong in position or numbers for us or the object may be to draw them out and fight them on our ground," Scott conjectured.[1]

The perceptive lieutenant had nearly as clear a picture of the strategic problem facing Jackson as his commanding officer. The unification of Pope's army presented Jackson with but one realistic option. Outnumbered by his opponent for the foreseeable future, Jackson retreated towards Gordonsville, putting the Rapidan River between his command and the larger Union force. With a river separating him from Pope, Jackson waited for reinforcements from Lee's main army. Scouting reports determined that Burnside's Union soldiers from North Carolina were being offloaded downriver at Fredericksburg. Burnside could either advance towards Richmond between Pope and McClellan or reinforce Pope's command. Burnside's appearance increased pressure on Lee and Jackson. If Lee remained on the defensive, both his army and Richmond would likely be caught in a powerful Yankee vice. Something had to be done, and soon.

As the fighting around Cedar Mountain raged, in Richmond Lee decided to act. Since the Army of the Potomac continued to be lethargic in its operations along the James River, the possibility existed to return the war in Virginia back

1 Johnnie Pearson, ed., *Lee and Jackson's Bloody Twelfth: The Letters of Irby Goodwin Scott* (Knoxville, TN, 2010), 94.

to a war of maneuver. No longer pinned against Richmond, an offensive could return Virginia territory abandoned by the Confederacy earlier in 1862 and potentially damage or destroy one of the Federal armies in the commonwealth. Lee needed to move as much of his army as quickly as possible to outnumber and overwhelm either Pope or Burnside before either command could be reinforced. To do so, the Confederates needed to take advantage of their interior lines of communication provided by the railroads.

Railroads connected Richmond to much of the state and the new nation. The Central Virginia Railroad, connecting the capital city with the important Orange and Alexandria Railroad and eventually the Shenandoah Valley, was especially important. Jackson's main source of supply and communication remained centered on the Central Virginia, and many of his soldiers rode its rails during their initial transfer to face Pope. If enough trains could be collected, more of Lee's soldiers could quickly augment Jackson's command. Reinforced, Jackson could try another offensive against Pope's army and with luck destroy it or at least drive it back towards northern Virginia. With Pope temporarily neutralized, Jackson and his enlarged command could then board the trains and return to Richmond. The reunited Confederate army could then deal with McClellan.

On August 9, Longstreet's staff penned instructions to his brigade commanders to prepare their commands to be "ready at once to march at any moment that you are called on." The destination for all six brigades was the same: Gordonsville. In total, Longstreet's command numbered nearly 20,000 soldiers. Once they arrived at Gordonsville, the Confederate army in central Virginia would double to over 40,000 men, nearly on par with Pope's command.[2] Close to half of Lee's army now either encamped in or was on its way towards Gordonsville.

The move from the James River to Gordonsville foreshadowed Longstreet's assumption of command over Jackson. Lee considered Longstreet to have seniority over Jackson in a unified command. In two dispatches from August 14, Lee referred to Longstreet as "Commanding &c. Gordonsville, Va." and referred to the soldiers in central Virginia as "that portion of the Army of Northern Virginia now under General Longstreet." Lee's decision to travel to central Virginia and take an active role in the emerging Second Manassas campaign soon made the issue of Longstreet commanding Jackson moot. However, it seems that Jackson's independent service around Gordonsville did not impress

2 *OR* 51, pt. 2, 604; Joseph Harsh, *Confederate Tide Rising: Robert E. Lee and the Making of Southern Strategy* (Kent, OH, 1998), 120.

Lee. According to Jackson's mapmaker, Jedediah Hotchkiss, "Gen. Lee came to us at Gordonsville with a rather low estimate of Jackson's ability."[3]

The delicate command situation in central Virginia soon cleared with Lee's arrival. While he wrote of Longstreet being in nominal command of the Rapidan line, Lee received new information that finally broke the impasse around Richmond. A Federal deserter revealed that McClellan's army was embarking on transports at Harrison's Landing. Stunned by the news that McClellan might be finally moving, Lee ordered D. H. Hill to immediately send scouts along the James and verify the deserter's account.[4]

The same day that he learned about the potential abandonment of Harrison's Landing, Lee also received word that Burnside's soldiers had left Fredericksburg and were marching west to reinforce Pope. This news freed up yet another Confederate division for central Virginia. Lee ordered Hood to immediately set off west "to Gordonsville and report to General Longstreet." Like D. H. Hill along the James, J. E. B. Stuart received orders to scout along the Rappahannock River and verify that Burnside was indeed heading towards Pope.[5]

Although the threat to Richmond remained, the strategic problem that had vexed Lee for most of July seemed to be solving itself. If the Army of the Potomac was finally leaving, the diminishing threat to the capital allowed for more of the army to be transferred to central Virginia. It remained to be determined by Stuart if Burnside was in fact moving west towards Pope, but the strategic picture facing Lee quickly simplified. Instead of hamstrung between three powerful Union forces around Richmond (McClellan), Fredericksburg (Burnside), and Culpepper (Pope), one army was moving off the map while another one apparently absorbed the third. If Lee could move fast enough while McClellan was in transit, he might concentrate his army near the Rapidan River and defeat Pope before the Army of the Potomac could be of any assistance. On August 15 Lee boarded a train to take field command of the Rapidan line. In a letter to President Davis, Lee declared "the war will for a season at least be removed from Richmond."[6]

Accompanied by yet another Confederate division, Lee soon reached Gordonsville. The enlarged Confederate force and united high command presented Lee with the opportunity to wrestle the initiative away from the Federals. The focus of the Confederate commander remained Pope and his army

3 *OR* 11, pt. 3, 676–677; Archie P. McDonald, ed., *Make Me a Map of the Valley: The Civil War Journal of Stonewall Jackson's Topographer* (Dallas, 1989), 118.

4 *OR* 11, pt. 3, 674.

5 Ibid., 674.

6 Dowdey and Manarin, *Wartime Papers of R. E. Lee*, 257.

at Culpepper. The longer the Confederates waited, the larger Pope's command likely grew. A strategy of dealing with Pope before McClellan could reinforce him became Lee's summer priority.

The main problem that consumed Lee and his subordinates remained the best route to attack Pope before McClellan arrived. Since the Army of the Potomac's destination remained unknown, Lee mulled over the idea of attacking Pope's left flank. If Lee could cross the Rapidan River somewhere downstream of his current position, the Army of Northern Virginia could place itself between Pope and any possible reinforcements arriving from Fredericksburg. Lee instructed Longstreet to proceed downstream towards Raccoon Ford while Jackson marched upstream towards Somerville Ford.[7]

A bold plan, Longstreet's movement required both secrecy and speed. If he was delayed crossing Raccoon Ford, Longstreet's Right Wing would be dangerously exposed between Pope and arriving Federals coming from Fredericksburg. Attacked from two sides, Longstreet risked being destroyed, wiping out a large portion of Lee's army. Before the operation could begin, one of Stuart's staff officers carrying dispatches which outlined both Lee's army and its intentions mistakenly rode into a Federal patrol and was promptly captured.

Aware he now faced a large enemy force that harbored offensive designs, Pope elected to retreat north, positioning his army north of the Rappahannock River. On August 18 Lee rode to Clark's Mountain, later joined by Longstreet. Towering over 1,000 feet, Clark's Mountain offered a panoramic view of the country between the Rapidan and Rappahannock rivers. Peering at the Federals through field glasses, the generals saw "the white tops of army wagons. . . . Half an hour's close watch revealed that the move was for the Rappahannock River." Both generals continued to watch in silence as Pope's army continued moving north. Watching his adversary slip away "General Lee finally put away his glasses, and with a deeply-drawn breath, expressive at once of disappointment and resignation, said 'General, we little thought that the enemy would turn his back upon us this early in the campaign.'"[8]

Although Lee's army took possession of Culpepper County, which remained an important transportation and agricultural center in Virginia, the main operation problem Lee faced remained: a large Union army with a river separating it and the Confederates. For Lee to go on the offensive, he first had to cross the river, potentially under enemy fire.

7 Longstreet, *From Manassas to Appomattox*, 159.

8 Ibid., 162.

Although many were frustrated by Pope's retreat, morale in the Army of Northern Virginia continued to soar. A Virginia artillerist wrote home that Lee "has an army in numbers and spirit, I believe he will wield it greatly." After the successful Seven Days' battles, soldiers viewed Lee "like a God," an attitude that spilled onto his subordinates: "even Jackson & the best among them are but strong men." Another soldier thought that the number of exchanged men returning to his company helped create high morale though he noted that the exchange was "not exactly completed and they cannot take up their arms yet."[9]

On August 20 the Army of Northern Virginia was on the move again, this time to the Rappahannock River. Marching in the middle of summer in Virginia proved uncomfortable as the army now had to march instead of ride the trains. A newspaper correspondent wrote of seeing a "good many stragglers by the wayside" but assured readers that they were "generally broken down soldiers." The large number of stragglers notwithstanding, the reporter was mesmerized by the sight of Lee's army advancing north: "Three columns—long, black winding lines of men, their muskets gleaming in the sunshine like silver spears, are in sight, moving." Not everyone was as enthralled with the march. A Virginian in the column later remembered the campaign, "marching over the hot and dusty roads blistered the back of our necks so that it was painful to raise the head, and our warm clothing chafed our limbs to a pitiful condition, while our feet were tortured by the heat and dust to such an extent that [we] were forced to walk in bare feet with shoes tied together, thrown over our rifles."[10]

An Alabamian remembered the tedium of the march broken by "the good people of Culpeper and vicinity" hailing the passing army with "enthusiasm." The mood soured when those same civilians "related many incidents of cruelty and depredations inflicted on them by the camp-followers of Pope's army."[11]

Lee initially believed that Pope was retiring further north. In a telegraph to President Davis on the 21st Lee thought that half of the Federal army appeared to be retreating east towards Fredericksburg while the rest retired further north to the town of Warrenton. Lee soon realized that reports of those movements proved false. The same day that Lee wrote Davis, Jackson encountered most of Pope's force on the bluffs overlooking the north bank of the Rappahannock

9 C. G. Chamberlayne, ed., *Ham Chamberlayne, Virginian: Letters and Papers of An Artillery Officer in the War for Southern Independence 1861–1865* (Wilmington, NC, 1992), 93; Pearson, *Lee and Jackson's Bloody Twelfth*, 97.

10 *Charleston Daily Courier*, Aug. 30, 1862; Philip F. Brown, *Reminiscences of the War of 1861–1865* (Richmond, 1917), 24.

11 Jeffrey Stocker, ed., *From Huntsville to Appomattox: R. T. Cole's History of 4th Regiment, Alabama Volunteer Infantry, C.S.A., Army of Northern Virginia* (Knoxville, TN, 1996), 51.

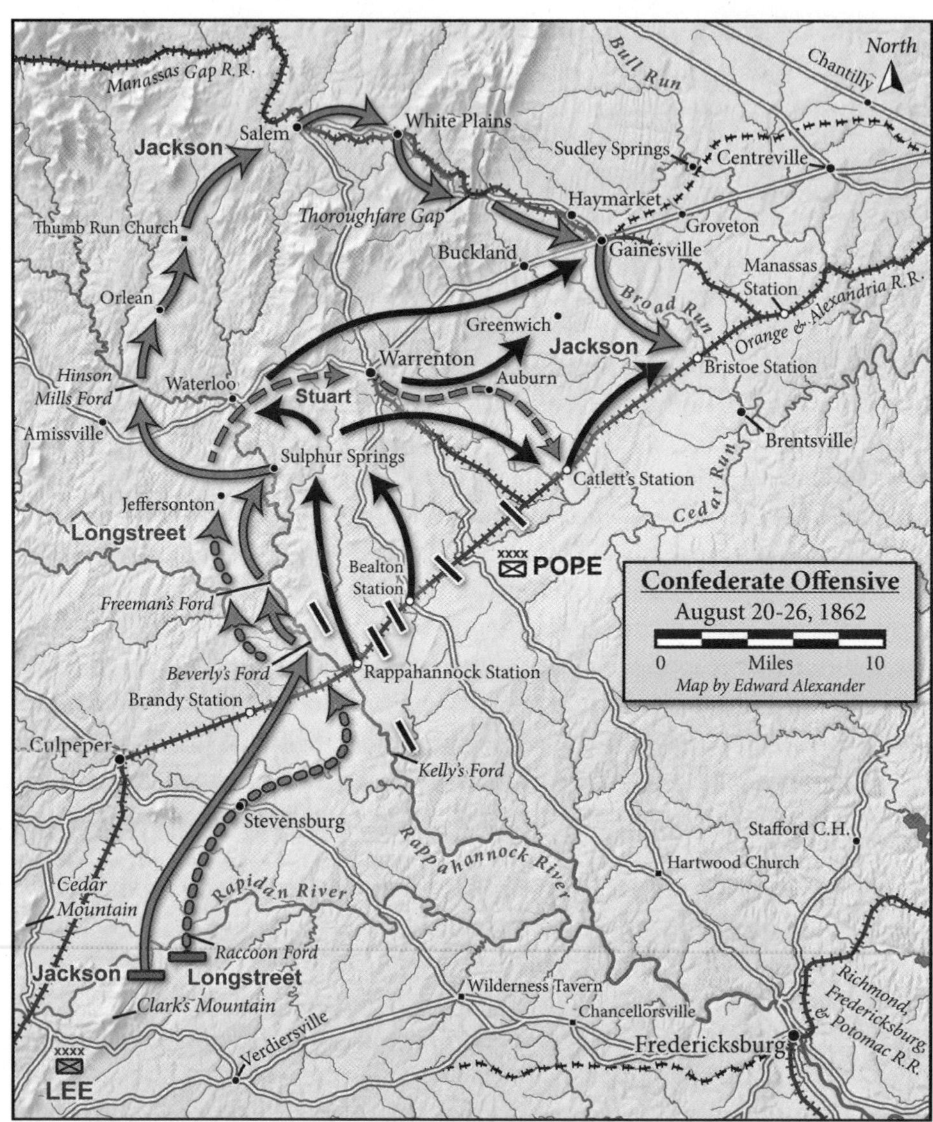

River. Jackson's cartographer, Jedediah Hotchkiss, noted the strong Federal position overlooking the river, including entrenched batteries near the Orange and Alexandria Railroad bridge by Rappahannock Station. To help mask the army's intentions, after reaching the river soldiers fanned out to find and cover as many fords as possible "so they cannot divine where we attempt to cross."[12]

12 Dowdey and Manarin, *Wartime Papers of R. E. Lee*, 261; McDonald, *Make Me a Map*, 70.

Recognizing that Pope's new position dominated the Rappahannock Valley, Lee altered plans. Facing Pope across the Rapidan River, Longstreet was the army wing commander tasked with flanking the Federals' left, placing a large portion of Lee's army between Pope and the reinforcements coming up the east. With Pope firmly in control of the river near Rappahannock Station, coupled with the Federals near Fredericksburg, Longstreet's proposed turning movement ran out of real estate. Instead of turning the Federal left, Lee decided to outflank Pope's right.

Pursuing Pope towards the Rappahannock, Jackson's Wing of the Army of Northern Virginia faced Pope near Rappahannock Station while Longstreet was downstream near Kelly's Ford. To give the army the ability to get around Pope's right, Lee instructed Longstreet to leave Kelly's Ford and replace Jackson opposite Rappahannock Station. Replaced by Longstreet's soldiers, Jackson was then to take his men further upstream in search of an undefended ford to cross.

To find Jackson's crossing site, Lee instructed Stuart to reconnoiter upstream. Supplemented by Ewell's Division, Stuart's command marched upstream to Freeman's Ford. Discovering Federal infantry and artillery on the northern bank, Stuart ordered John Pelham's horse artillery to drive the enemy away. Finding his objective blocked, Pelham continued to bombard any visible Yankees while Ewell continued upstream hopeful of discovering another ford. In the midst of the skirmish, Stuart received a message from Lee. Earlier in the campaign Stuart's command team was surprised by a Federal cavalry patrol and quickly scattered. Embarrassed, Stuart requested permission to lead a raid behind the Federal lines. Uncertain of Pope's plans and possible reinforcements from Fredericksburg, Lee wisely kept Stuart with the army. Now temporarily stymied at the Rappahannock, Lee gave Stuart permission for his raid. Lee hoped a raid against the rear of Pope's army could create alarm in the Federal high command. With luck, Pope would be focused on his rear instead of the fords over the Rappahannock.

A jubilant Stuart quickly organized his raiding party. Accompanied by nearly 1,500 troopers, Stuart forded the river at Waterloo Bridge and headed straight towards Warrenton. Finding no enemy, Stuart decided to march towards Catlett's Station and burn a small bridge of the Orange and Alexandria Railroad. A terrific summer thunderstorm overtook Stuart that evening before he reached the railroad.[13]

Fortune smiled on the young Virginian when one of Stuart's troopers captured an enslaved man known to Stuart. The enslaved man knew "the

13 *OR* 12, pt. 2, 731.

location of General Pope's staff, baggage, horses, &c." and offered Stuart a "guide to the spot." Capitalizing on this intelligence and the freshening storm, Stuart remounted his troopers and had them on a march towards the railroad. Reaching the station around 9:00 p.m., Stuart quickly settled on a plan. Colonel Rooney Lee would lead his 9th Virginia Cavalry on a direct attack against Pope's headquarters train while the 1st and 5th Virginia assaulted a nearby camp.[14]

Troopers of the 5th Virginia encountered Union pickets attempting to stay dry in a church, enjoying what one Confederate thought a "bountiful meal." With their attention fixed on their dinner plates instead of the picket line, "it was the work of a minute to disarm these men and send them to the rear." Federal pickets neutralized, Stuart's troopers trotted to the enemy camps unnoticed and unopposed. About 100 yards from the camps, Stuart gave the signal for the 1st Virginia's bugler to sound the charge.[15]

The unexpected charge combined with the nighttime storm threw everything into chaos. A trooper in the 1st Virginia thought the darkness "so intense that the whitest house could not be seen immediately in front of you, except by the lightning which was incessant." Driving the enemy away, the Virginians plundered camps while a few tried to burn the wagons, which proved too wet to ignite. Fearing a counterattack, Stuart pulled his troopers back, heading towards the Rappahannock and the main army, finally returning on August 23.[16]

Stuart's raid not only embarrassed the Federals, but during the charge one of Pope's wagons containing his personal papers and clothing was captured. For Lee and the future conduct of the Manassas campaign, the most important result of Stuart's raid was the captured papers. Before the raid, Lee sifted through incomplete, and oftentimes false intelligence reports from cavalry scouts, spies, newspapers, and deserters. Forming an accurate picture of the strength and position of the Federal Army of Virginia proved difficult, let alone trying to divine Pope's plans. The captured papers momentarily cleared away the fog of war for Lee.

Critically for Lee, the size of the Army of Virginia finally became clear. Before Lee and Longstreet joined him, Jackson estimated that Pope's forces numbered between 50,000 and 70,000. Captured dispatches put the number of men ready for combat in Pope's army at 45,000 officers and men, though Burnside's men streaming in from Fredericksburg likely increased Pope's numbers. The papers

14 Ibid., 731.

15 Robert Driver Jr., *5th Virginia Cavalry* (Lynchburg, VA, 1997), 36.

16 Ibid., 44.

also disclosed the destination of the Army of the Potomac: McClellan's men were on their way to join Pope. Worryingly, the van of McClellan's army had already arrived, with Fitz Porter's corps marching from Falmouth and deploying on the right of Lee's line. Pope intended to wait behind the Rappahannock until McClellan arrived when the combined armies, nearly 150,000 soldiers, could drive Lee south again towards Richmond.[17]

Lee drew two important assessments for future operations after analyzing Pope's papers. First, the threat against Richmond appeared to be fading. The withdrawal of McClellan from the James River allowed for the reunification of the Army of Northern Virginia along the Rappahannock. Every soldier remaining near the capital should be immediately sent north to join the main army, Lee argued to Davis. Without consulting with the president, Lee ordered his divisions around the capital to join him. If Davis disagreed with Lee, he could "countermand the order, and let me know." Any work left on the Richmond fortifications should be finished by civilian contractors. Once finished the city could be protected by a handful of field artillery batteries. Lee thought that Pope intended to remain stationary in his new defensive works until McClellan's men arrived. Since Pope opted to remain on the defensive for the time being, the Confederates could seize the initiative. Lee hoped to outmaneuver Pope from his current lines for the campaign's ultimate fight somewhere else.[18]

Possessing a clearer picture of the war along the Rappahannock, Lee believed he had a small window of opportunity for his army to take the offensive. In addition to being outnumbered by its opponent, the Army of Northern Virginia experienced supply difficulties in central Virginia. Passing armies ravaged local crops and mills, limiting the supplies available for impressment or purchase. The army's ability to live off the land curtailed, most of its supplies arrived along the single tracked Orange and Alexandria Railroad. A year into the conflict, destruction from the armies, coupled with the railroad's limited ability to repair damage, reduced the number of cars on the line as well as the speed of the trains. If Lee remained along the Rappahannock indefinitely, he courted the likely scenario of slowly starving his army.

Lee continued to search for a suitable place to outflank Pope upstream from his position. Initially Lee sought to cross somewhere between Warrenton and the Bull Run Mountains. As Jackson's Wing slowly crept northward trying to find a suitable ford, Pope responded by stretching his line north to the mountains.

17 *OR* 12, pt. 3, 942.

18 Ibid., 942.

Any flanking movement now required the Confederates to march to the west of the mountains and recross at a suitable gap.

On August 24 Lee summoned his top subordinates to a council of war to flesh out the army's coming campaign. Henry Kyd Douglas, a staff officer to Jackson, accompanied his commander to the meeting. Circled around a lone table in the middle of a field, a map of the area was laid out. Sitting at the head of the table examining the map, Lee was flanked by Longstreet, Jackson, and Stuart. Staff officers of the four generals were "lounging on the grass of an adjacent knoll."[19]

After discussing the army's situation, the council adjourned with a plan of action that allowed considerable flexibility for the men responsible for executing it. Lee likely was the main architect for the large flanking movement around and behind Pope's army. While half of the army remained along the Rappahannock pinning Pope in place, the other half would march towards the northwest with the goal of placing it "between Washington City and the army of General Pope and to break up his railroad communications with the Federal city." The flanking force retained the flexibility of choosing the best route around the Federals and the location of cutting the railroad. After severing the railroad, the Confederates were to evaluate the situation and act accordingly. Deciding to remain with the portion of the army along the Rappahannock, Lee gave the flanking force commander great latitude.[20]

Lee decided that Jackson and his wing of the army would lead the flanking movement. Jackson's considerable experience with independent command and reputation for hard marching in the Shenandoah Valley likely eased Lee's decision to send Stonewall. However, the position of Lee's army also played an important role in determining which wing of the army started the campaign. Thanks to earlier movements as the armies jockeyed for position along the river, Jackson's men found themselves positioned upstream of Longstreet. Before the column could begin the great turning movement, Jackson's Wing had to withdraw from the river and consolidate in the rear, forcing Longstreet to spread west to cover Jackson's old line. With Jackson's men already positioned to the west, their withdrawal portended to be easier than removing Longstreet from the line and shuttling him westward. Lee had expressed some unease with Jackson's command earlier in July and August while in semi-independent command around Orange and had imagined Longstreet taking command in his

19 Henry Kyd Douglas, *I Rode with Stonewall* (Chapel Hill, NC, 1940), 133.

20 *OR* 12, pt. 2, 643.

absence; Jackson's position rather than Lee's unflinching confidence in Jackson's command abilities likely contributed to Jackson's selection.

Many observers considered the soldiers readying themselves for march to be the cream of Lee's army. Jackson's "Left Wing" of the Army of Northern Virginia contained nearly 24,000 soldiers organized into three divisions. The heart and soul of Jackson's Wing was Taliaferro's Division, also known as the Stonewall or Jackson's Division. Jackson's old command from the Shenandoah Valley campaign, this division of four brigades saw extensive combat in both the Shenandoah and Seven Days' campaigns. The battle of Cedar Mountain further thinned its ranks, including a divisional commander mortally wounded in the fighting. Leaving his brigade in the hands of a nephew, Brig. Gen. William Taliaferro took over command of the division. The native Virginian had studied at both the College of William and Mary and Harvard and received a direct commission to the rank of captain during the Mexican-American War. Returning to the Old Dominion to enter politics, Taliaferro retained an ardor for the military, serving as the commander of the Virginia militia after John Brown's raid on Harper's Ferry. With the outbreak of war, Taliaferro accepted the colonelcy of the 23rd Virginia. Serving under Jackson for most of his active Civil War career, Taliaferro led a brigade in the spring and summer fighting.[21]

If Taliaferro's Division was the heart of Jackson's command, Ewell's Division was its backbone. The four infantry brigades and one artillery battalion forged a superb combat record under one of the best divisional commanders in the entire Confederate army. After serving in Jackson's Valley campaign, Ewell led his command in the bloody fighting around Richmond before traveling up to central Virginia.

Born in Washington D.C. to a Virginia family, Richard Ewell grew up on his family farm in Prince William County, Stoney Lonesome. After graduating from West Point, Ewell forged a solid if unspectacular career in the antebellum army. Sectional strife quickly proved Ewell's innate talent to large field command from First Manassas to Richmond. Known as "Dirty Dick" by his men, Ewell grew into a confident combat leader despite serving under Jackson. Unlike Lee's style of outlining broad objectives and allowing his commanders to figure out how to implement them, Jackson's command style of extreme secrecy and little command initiative inhibited his subordinates from exercising independent command. A Louisianan complained that Ewell "seems half the time not to

21 Ezra Warner, *Generals in Gray: Lives of the Confederate Generals* (Baton Rouge, LA, 2006), 297–298.

know what he is doing." Unbeknownst to this Louisiana Tiger, the problem stemmed more from Jackson's failing command style than with Ewell.[22]

The final addition to Jackson's Wing happened to be the largest division in the Army of Northern Virginia. Named for its commander, A. P. Hill's Division was sometimes referred to in grand Napoleonic fashion as the Light Division. Ambrose Powell Hill, a native Virginian and West Point graduate, rapidly advanced in rank after joining the Confederate army. Initially serving as a colonel of a Virginia regiment, within a year he jumped from brigade commander to division leader. Serving ably at both Seven Days and Cedar Mountain, the main source of concern was his tendency to feud with his immediate superiors.

A competent commander on the field of battle, in camp Hill often was a difficult and quarrelsome subordinate. After serving in Longstreet's Wing around Richmond, the two had such a falling out that Lee was forced to transfer Hill and his command to Jackson in the hopes that the two Virginians could get along better. Lee's hopes of a harmonious relationship proved short-lived. After the fiasco of the march towards Cedar Mountain, Jackson thought Hill an overrated officer who did not know how to effectively operate his command. In Jackson's mind part of Hill's failure was the unusual size of his division. Stonewall thought Hill's command "too large" and proposed to "reduce it by at least the Louisiana Brigade." The threat of downsizing did not endear Hill to his new commander.[23]

After meeting with Lee, Longstreet, and Stuart, Stonewall summoned his chief engineer. Described by his close friend Jedediah Hotchkiss as "an excellent, good-natured, honest Presbyterian," Capt. James Boswell established an exceptional relationship with his commander. On the afternoon of August 24 Jackson tasked Boswell to find the "most direct and covered route to Manassas." Growing up in the immediate vicinity, the Fauquier County native proved an excellent resource for planning a march. Boswell suggested marching to the northwest of Jeffersonton, past the community of Amissville to the road leading to Hinson's Mill Ford on the Rappahannock. By skirting further to the northwest, few Federals would likely be encountered as Jackson crossed the Rappahannock River. The column could then proceed north through Orlean until reaching Salem and the east-west road that ran towards Manassas Junction. Heading east, the troops would march through Marshall, pass through the Bull Run Mountains at Thoroughfare Gap, and proceed to Gainesville where two roads

22 James Gannon, *Irish Rebels, Confederate Tigers: A History of the 6th Louisiana Volunteers, 1861-1865* (Campbell, CA, 1998), 21.

23 *OR* 12, pt. 2, 181.

branched out to the O&A Railroad. Boswell's route achieved the objectives that Lee gave Jackson, but at nearly 56 miles was by no means the most direct route. Nonetheless Jackson approved Boswell's route and prepared his command to march early on August 25.[24]

While the generals planned for the march, the enlisted men tried to make themselves comfortable living outdoors in the midst of a Virginia summer. In a letter home to his father, Hugh White observed that the Stonewall Brigade was "as merry in camp as if the enemy was a thousand miles away." Soon the men were alerted to a pending movement after the quartermaster began issuing three days rations with orders to cook them immediately. A soldier in the 21st Virginia recalled that rumors of a march appeared in his unit while they were in the midst of cooking. With no time to finish, many men had but a "half-baked biscuit and raw dough" to subsist on during the march.[25]

A habit that never fully went away, Jackson preferred to take operational secrecy to an extreme. Lee, Longstreet, and Stuart all knew the destination of Jackson's march. Within Stonewall's command, however—the part of the army that soon would be implementing the march—only Jackson and his engineer, Captain Boswell, knew its destination. Reducing the number of men that knew the plan reduced the possibility of the enemy discovering it, but in his zeal for secrecy, Jackson increased the possibility of a Confederate miscommunication ballooning into disaster. Jackson failed to brief his three divisional commanders on the goal of the operation and what was expected of them. As long as the column remained united, the risk remained low. If subordinate units of Jackson's Wing became separated from each other, however, and a divisional commander experienced difficulty communicating with Jackson's headquarters, the lack of knowledge of the overall plan could prove catastrophic. Summarizing Jackson's reputation for secrecy, a Georgian soldier joked that if Stonewall's "coat tale knew his plans he would cut it off."[26]

In preparation for the march, elements of Jackson's Wing received orders to leave knapsacks behind and load their muskets. Many veterans viewed this as a sign of a "forced march and a flank movement." Maximizing the speed of his column, Stonewall reduced his wagon train to a minimum, leaving most of his

24 James Robertson Jr., *Stonewall Jackson: The Man, The Soldier, The Legend* (New York, 1997), 328; *OR* 12, pt. 2, 650.

25 W. G. Bean, *The Liberty Hall Rifles: Stonewall's College Boys* (Charlottesville, VA, 2004), 130; John Worsham, *One of Jackson's Foot Cavalry: His experience and what he saw during the war 1861–1865* (New York, 1912), 118.

26 Gregory White, *This Most Bloody and Cruel Drama: A History of the 31st Georgia Volunteer Infantry* (Baltimore, 1997), 40.

wagons with Lee. Proceeded by cavalry screening the roads, Jackson selected Ewell's Division to lead, followed by A. P. Hill, while Taliaferro's men brought up the rear. Jackson's selection of Ewell placed his most experienced (and trusted) commander in the vanguard. Sandwiching Hill between Ewell and Taliaferro was likely a decision to keep Hill under watch and prevent a repeat of the earlier marching fiasco.[27]

In the early morning hours of Monday, August 25, nearly 25,000 soldiers began one of the most famous Civil War marches. Leaving Jeffersonton and marching to the west, some soldiers in the ranks predicted they were returning to their old stomping grounds in the Shenandoah Valley. This scuttlebutt may have been passed along to civilians the soldiers encountered. Henry Kyd Douglas remembered on the march between Jeffersonton and Amissville that "citizens complained that we were again leaving them to the enemy." Crossing the Rappahannock River at Hinson's Mill Ford, the change in the column's direction to the north dashed anyone's hopes of returning to the Valley.[28]

To reduce the likelihood of a bottleneck slowing the column, soldiers in both Ewell's and Taliaferro's Divisions took alternative routes paralleling the main column. One of Ewell's staff officers complained that after crossing the river they instead took "a series of by-roads & no-roads a general direction towards Salem." At the tail of the column a soldier in Taliaferro's Division later complained that the column left the road and snaked "several miles right through the country, through fields, over ditches and fences, through woods until we [came] to a public road."[29]

After marching 26 hot miles, that evening Jackson approached the small community of Salem. Nearing the halfway point to Manassas Junction, Stonewall elected to bivouac overnight near Salem and finish the march the next day. Not until nearly midnight did the last of Jackson's column arrive at their camp. Nicknamed "Foot Cavalry," Jackson's men were renowned for their marching abilities. Such experience did not make the grueling march any easier, however. Marion Fitzpatrick of the 45th Georgia wrote to his wife of the "hardest marching that was ever known almost." Fitzpatrick was among many soldiers who developed blisters on their feet from the march. Fitzpatrick's feet

27 Alfred Edgar, *My Reminiscences of the Civil War with the Stonewall Brigade and the Immortal 600* (Charleston, WV, 2011), 81; John Casler, *Four Years in the Stonewall Brigade* (Columbia, SC, 2005), 106.

28 Douglas, *I Rode with Stonewall*, 134.

29 Terry Jones, ed., *Campbell Brown's Civil War with Ewell and the Army of Northern Virginia* (Baton Rouge, LA, 2001), 146; Worsham, *One of Jackson's Foot Cavalry*, 118.

were so painful that "when I start, I would have to lean over on my gun and the tears would involuntarily gush from my eyes."[30]

So fatiguing was the march, when ordered to halt for the night, "many of the men lay down right where they stopped in the road, being so completely used up from the march and heat as not to have energy to move to one side." To compound the misery, rations began to run out. Theoretically issued enough food to last until around the 27th or 28th, lack of time to adequately prepare the food combined with smaller than intended portions and large appetites generated on the road left many soldiers in caloric arrears. Many found their haversacks empty by the time they arrived at Salem. Forced to choose between sleep or procuring food from local citizens, many soldiers roamed the vicinity in search of food.[31]

In marching to their camps, the men of the Stonewall Brigade passed their original commander who stood on the side of the road, cap in hand. As a captain in the 27th Virginia remembered, "forgetting how tired we are, we begin to cheer. He instantly checks us with a wave of his hand. This we understand is a signal to be quiet, and we pass quietly along. But as we pass we catch inspiration from the noble men of our commander. Jackson, turning to his staff, was heard to say, 'Who could not conquer with such troops as these?'"[32]

30 Jeffrey Lowe and Sam Hodges, eds., *Letters to Amanda: The Civil War letters of Marion Hill Fitzpatrick, Army of Northern Virginia* (Macon, GA, 1999), 24.

31 Worsham, *One of Jackson's Foot Cavalry*, 119.

32 Edgar, *My Reminiscences of the Civil War*, 81.

Chapter 12

"One of the Meanest Generals"

Fredericksburg: Late Summer 1862

Despite the hard marching and the panic over the Confederate threat, Gibbon's brigade found itself back in camp opposite Fredericksburg without having "seen an enemy nor heard a gun fired during the time." To their dismay, the men in McCall's division of McDowell's corps were transferred to McClellan's army, but the Westerners were once again left behind.

Gibbon reviewed his brigade June 12 and in a general order soon after praised the "military bearing and appearance of the Regiments on review," but singled out the "marked contrast" between the Wisconsin units and the 19th Indiana. "Three weeks ago, when reviewed by the President, every one remarked [upon] the neat and cleanly appearance of this Regiment, and the General noticed with the regret, the contrast presented in review yesterday." Gibbon made a sour reference to the clothing discarded on the recent marches and added: "Such foolish waste of Stores provided by the Government can not be tolerated, and would never occur in a properly disciplined body of men. . . . At the approaching muster, every man of this regiment, who has not now in his possession, the clothing issued to him during the past month will be charged on the muster rolls the cost of such clothing, and have the amount deducted from his pay."[1]

Of course, the order set off a firestorm in the 19th Indiana. Upset with the insult to his command, Meredith secured a leave to meet with his Indiana political friends in Washington to see about replacing Gibbon or having his regiment transferred to another brigade. In the Hoosier ranks, there were hot words and threats against "one of the meanest Brigadier genarls that ever lived. Gibens is his name. He is a regular and if we ever get in a fight he will be the first to fall. every Body hates his very name."

1 Gibbon, *Recollections*, 33–35; General Orders No. 58, cited in Gaff, *Bloody Field*, 132.

Color party of the 2nd Wisconsin posing for a photograph opposite Fredericksburg in 1862.
Howard Michael Madaus

Opposition to the clothing orders was also felt in the three Wisconsin regiments. "The officers are coming right down on us as if we were so many slaves now," Private Ray of the 7th wrote in his journal June 18. "And they are forcing leggings and [blouse or frock] coats on us and forcing us to wear them. It's a dime for this and a quarter for that and so it goes. And whatever the General says we must have, we must take it or be arrested." Ray complained vividly and at length:

> It is said that the Col of the Indiana Regiment has gone to Washington to see if he cannot get his Regt out of his Brigade and our Colonel [William Robinson] has gone some place and been gone two or three days and the talk is that he has gone for the same purpose as the Ind. Col and if this be true, I hope he will succeed and we will be from under the old tyrant Gen. Gibbons. It is him that causes the truble. He comes down on the regimental officers and they come down on the Co officers and as a matter of course, they must come down on us and that is the way it goes. I don't blame any of them for reminding us of keeping clean but I hate this putting on so much style. The boys call it putting on French airs.

Ray added that most of the Indiana men and the soldiers of the 6th Wisconsin threw their extra clothing away and would have to draw more. "The

Private William Ray, 7th Wisconsin
Lance J. Herdegen

Gen is bound to make us carry the extra clothing, thereby causing a great many to give out on the march and then they will have to haul them & their knappsacks too. And if they oblige me to carry so much, I will sit down when tired and they have got to haul me."[2]

Despite the efforts of Meredith and his political friends, the Indiana regiment was not transferred, nor was Gibbon removed. The colonel returned to his regiment where in an unspoken manner he supported his Hoosiers in resisting a re-issue of the infamous white leggings. "This fretted the General, who, with numerous dress-parades and orders and lecturers to the officers on parade," one soldier said, "sought to carry his point. The officers exhorted, pleaded, threatened, swore, but the boys would not take the leggings." Exasperated over the refusal, Gibbon finally issued an order that if the Hoosiers did not appear in their leggings the next morning, he would order his artillery battery to open fire on their camp.

The Hoosiers came out to their company streets the next morning without leggings in defiance of the general and his order. Just as they formed sullen lines, a roar of cannon fire sent the startled soldiers to their knees or face down in the dirt. "Lay down boys, lay down!" some shouted and others called out "We'll take the leggings! We'll take the leggings!" After a few seconds, the Hoosiers found the cannon blast had not caused any injury. They discovered the watching Wisconsin boys laughing and pointing to a nearby battery drilling with blank rounds. In the end, the leggings were not reissued and those worn out were not replaced. The Indiana men viewed it a victory and told one another Gibbon in not forcing the issue "acknowledged that his brigade made a volunteer of him."[3]

2 Ray, *Iron Brigade*, 99–100. The rumor Robinson was seeking to have his regiment transferred to another brigade was not true.

3 For a detailed account of the leggings' incident see Gaff, *Bloody Field*, 130–138.

Chapter 13

"A Rapid March"

Bristoe Station: August 26, 1861

Roused at dawn on the 26th, Jackson's men marched from Salem eastward through Thoroughfare Gap and towards Gainesville. The distance of this day's march was longer than the previous, 30 miles compared to 26 miles, and the temperature rose from 78 degrees to a sultry 88. Most had only a few hours' sleep and little food.[1]

While planning the march back near the Rappahannock, Jackson instructed Boswell to chart a route to Gainesville. The small hamlet to the east of the Bull Run Mountains lay six miles from Jackson's objective: the Orange and Alexandria. Once his force arrived at Gainesville, Jackson planned to then choose which route to take to the railroad. Marching to the northeast about nine miles would bring his column to Manassas Junction where the Orange and Alexandria intersected with the Manassas Gap Railroad. The junction of the two lines transformed Manassas into a vital supply base. In preparation for an enemy advance, in 1861 the Confederate army constructed a series of forts to protect the junction from a Federal army marching from Washington. Although Jackson would be advancing from the west, he lacked intelligence reports about whether the Federals had altered the old Confederate earthworks or built additional forts to protect Manassas.

Manassas Junction was not the only place to sever the railroad. A few miles south of the junction, and only 6 miles from Gainesville, stood Bristoe Station. Like Manassas, earlier in 1861 Confederate regiments had encamped in the fields surrounding the station but, located safely in the rear of the Southern line, had built no defensive earthworks. A Federal garrison likely would be

1 Robert Krick, *Civil War Weather in Virginia* (Tuscaloosa, AL, 2007), 68.

encountered at Bristoe but the prospect of Jackson combating Yankees behind earthworks remained nearly non-existent.

In addition to the lack of earthworks and garrisons, another feature distinguished Manassas Junction from Bristoe Station. As important as possessing Manassas Junction was, to truly deprive the Federal army of Manassas, Jackson had to hold onto the railroad junction long enough to physically hurt Pope's logistical system. Burning the warehouses and destroying the track would be an embarrassment to the Federal commander, but repairs could be finished quickly, negating any long-term effect Confederates could achieve at Manassas. Separated from the main army and in the rear of the Federal army, if Jackson stayed in one place for an extended period of time, he risked fighting Pope's army alone as Lee attempted to reunite with him.

For lasting success, Jackson needed a place that he could temporarily hold but create long-term damage. The small station at Bristoe itself wouldn't produce the requisite damage. A few yards north of the station, however, the railroad crossed Broad Run on a bridge. Burning that bridge would require more time for Federal engineers to rebuild than damaged track. More bridges further afield of Bristoe could also compound the damage to the railroad provided that Jackson's men could quickly and easily capture those places.

Soldiers rubbing the few hours sleep from their eyes knew nothing of the ultimate destination of the march, but rumors continued to spread through the column. The turn eastwards at Salem dashed any lingering hopes of a return to the Shenandoah Valley. Marching towards the rising sun, some soldiers thought they were part of a great turning movement designed to attack from the rear while others thought they were marching to Washington, D.C. Spirits remained high on the resumption of the campaign after the column failed to meet any Yankee soldiers on the previous day's march.

Initially the Confederate column remained closed-up but stragglers soon appeared. Physical exhaustion began to take its toll on the men. James Harris marching in the 7th North Carolina remembered that "every man was pressed to the utmost of his walking capacity." Compounding the misery of the march, the pace set by the officers, many of whom rode on horseback, was described by another Tarheel as "a rapid march, long quick steps." Even the weather seemed uncooperative. The high temperatures, lack of rain, and thousands of men and animals pounding away on the dirt roads produced "a perfect cloud of dust, which seemed to be almost shoe mouth deep in the road." Physically taxing as the march was, morale within the ranks remained high. A captain in the 13th

Virginia infantry remembered his men "were all cheerful, full of fun as well as fight, had the fullest confidence in our generals."[2]

The first half of the march proved uneventful. Turning from Salem, the column tramped towards the Bull Run Mountains. A series of low peaks starting near Warrenton and running northeast for 15 miles, the Bull Run Mountains separated the Loudoun Valley to the west and the plains of Manassas to the east. Roads cut through the rocky and ragged peaks via the four natural gaps. A small defending force in any would ultimately be steamrolled by the large Confederate column, but the element of surprise would be lost. If that happened, Jackson faced the grim scenario that his command would receive the focus of all Federal forces operating in northern Virginia. Luckily, scouts reported that the gap containing the direct route to the railroad, Thoroughfare Gap, maintained no Federal garrison.

Southern horsemen ensured Thoroughfare Gap remained for Stonewall. Before the main infantry column moved out of Salem, the 2nd Virginia Cavalry rode ahead to both screen the force and capture the important gap. Leading the 2nd Virginia on its critical mission was 31-year-old Col. Thomas Munford. A graduate of the Virginia Military Institute, prior to the war Munford had turned to farming. The outbreak of hostilities brought Munford back into the army as a lieutenant colonel of mounted infantry. Promoted to colonel, Jackson assigned the young Virginian an ad-hoc cavalry brigade of two regiments during the Valley campaign. Stellar service in both the Valley and Peninsula campaigns burnished his reputation with both Jackson and Stuart. No cavalry officer, save perhaps Stuart himself, was as experienced and talented as Munford was in the summer of 1862.[3]

Leaving part of his regiment to hold Thoroughfare Gap until the infantry arrived, Munford continued to the small crossroads hamlet of Haymarket. There he finally encountered Federals. Few shots were fired in the encounter as Confederate cavalrymen captured "a full band with splendid instruments" in the town. Unbeknownst to anyone, these musicians and their instruments were the start of a colossal haul of prisoners and supplies the Confederates would capture over the next 24 hours.[4]

2 Michael Hardy, *General Lee's Immortals: The Battles and Campaigns of the Branch-Lane Brigade in the Army of Northern Virginia, 1861–1865* (El Dorado Hills, CA, 2018), 83; Lee Sherrill Jr., *The 21st North Carolina Infantry* (Jefferson, NC, 2015), 142; David Johnston, *Four Years a Soldier* (Princeton, WV, 1887), 176; Samuel Buck, *With the Old Confeds: Actual Experiences of a Captain in the Line* (Gaithersburg, MD, 1983), 51–52.

3 Warner, *More Generals in Gray*, 171.

4 Munford-Ellis Family Papers, Duke University.

By the time Munford passed through Haymarket and the smaller community of Gainesville to the east, Jackson decided on his destination. While the exact time Jackson made his decision is unknown, it is likely that Jackson ordered Munford to continue on to Bristoe Station after capturing Thoroughfare Gap. Arriving at any crossroads, Munford detached men from his regiment to retain possession until the infantry columns arrived. By the time Munford approached Bristoe Station that evening, he was left with about 100 troopers. Reconnoitering the station and remaining undetected was a difficult task, but some of Munford's men got close enough to the station to determine that the garrison contained one company of infantry and a company of cavalry.[5]

As Munford inched closer to the station, the head of Jackson's infantry slowly appeared. On a hilltop approximately a mile away from the station, a halt was ordered to allow the column to close up. Reverend James Sheeran of the 14th Louisiana recorded in his diary that the order to halt "was obeyed by the advanced Brigades without reluctance, but not so with those bringing up the rear; for all were anxious to see 'the fun.'" Confident that he had enough men nearby to capture the garrison and sever the railroad, near sunset Jackson ordered Munford to attack.[6]

The setting sun to their backs, Munford's troopers got to within 100 yards of the station before the Federals became alarmed. Within the first moments of the assault Yankee cavalry "scampered away with their horses" leaving a single company of infantry to defend the station. Realizing they were outnumbered, elements of the garrison retreated into buildings around the station. In the ensuing firefight the Southerners lost one lieutenant and two enlisted men badly wounded. The soldiers inside the buildings got the worst end of the fight, losing two killed and seven wounded. Recognizing they were surrounded and with casualties mounting, nearly 50 Federal soldiers surrendered to Munford's men. An unusually high number of the captives were officers including "the lieutenant colonel of the Fourth New York, a major, 3 captains, and four lieutenants."[7]

While Munford and the garrison battled, Jackson ordered the nearest infantry brigade to add its weight to Munford's attack. By the time Col. Henry Forno's five Louisiana regiments arrived at the station, Munford was mopping up the last of the garrison. A few moments after reaching the station, "the whistle of a locomotive in the direction of Warrenton, was heard in the distance; after a

5 *OR* 12, pt. 2, 747.

6 Joseph Durkin, ed., *Confederate Chaplain: A War Journal of Rev. James B. Sheeran, c.ss.r. 14th Louisiana, C.S.A.* (Milwaukee, 1960), 9.

7 *OR* 12, pt. 2, 747.

few moments' silence, the whistle was more distinctly heard to our right in the woods; and scarcely had the sound died away, when the engine with a long train . . . came puffing slowly up to the station." The Louisiana Tigers rushed to the railroad embankment trying to uproot a portion of the track before the train arrived, while Munford's troopers threw whatever obstructions they could find onto the track in hopes of a derailment.[8]

Hoping to speed up the track's destruction, Jackson ordered the two 21sts of Isaac Trimble's brigade, the 21st North Carolina and 21st Georgia, to assist the Tigers. The two sister regiments reached the railroad but "had just loosened a rail when a freight train hove in sight." Suspecting an enemy force ahead, the engineer rode full steam towards Bristoe. To staff officer W. W. Blackford, the engine seemed to come "thundering on past the depot at the rate of about fifty miles an hour." The roaring engine easily pushed the few obstructions off the track and continued north towards Manassas. Disappointed that the train remained on the tracks, the Tigers fired a volley towards the train. A few musket balls hit the engine, but the majority sailed through the train's empty boxcars. Some rounds fell around the ranks of Munford's troopers on the other side of the track but fortunately no one was injured in this instance of potential friendly fire.[9]

After the first train roared past, the Tigers and the two 21sts went back to tearing up the tracks. Soon one track was ripped off and thrown to the side. Moments later a second train was heard approaching from the south. As it neared the station, the Tigers fired another volley "into her boiler causing the steam to go in every direction." Seconds later the train hit the damaged section of track, derailing it into a nearby ravine. Soldiers exploring the engine were delighted to discover the train they just destroyed was named *President* with a picture of Abe Lincoln hung on the locomotive.[10]

The derailment of the *President* was partial. The engine and most of its boxcars were now in the ravine, but a few of the rear cars remained on the track. Anticipating a third train, a few quick-thinking soldiers attempted a ruse. Now well past sunset, the tracks were nearly completely dark. One of the main sources of light in the area consisted of two red lanterns hung on the rear of the last boxcar as a visual marker for any following trains. A soldier, likely a member of the 21st Georgia, climbed aboard the boxcar and extinguished the

8 Durkin, *Confederate Chaplain*, 9.

9 Sherrill Jr., *21st North Carolina*, 142; W. W. Blackford, *War Years with Jeb Stuart* (Baton Rouge, LA, 1993), 113.

10 Durkin, *Confederate Chaplain*, 10.

Derailed train near Bristoe Station, August 1862. *Library of Congress*

two lanterns. When the headlight of a third train was seen in the distance, a Louisianan crawled into the locomotive in the ravine and blew "'all right'—i.e. 'off brakes.'"[11]

Similar to the first two trains, Louisianans, Georgians, North Carolinians, and Virginians waited along the railroad. This train also proved too tempting a target, for the Tigers who once again loosened a volley into the mainly empty boxcars. Surprised by the unexpected gunshots, the engineer sped to escape the ambush and "into the rear of the wrecked train he went." The few remaining cars of the *President* that survived the initial derailment were destroyed and the boxcars of the third train telescoped into each other or were thrown from the track. Like the *President*, a few remaining cars remained on the track despite the force of the collision.[12]

11 Jones, *Campbell Brown's Civil War*, 147.

12 Blackford, *War Years with Jeb Stuart*, 114.

In the space of moments two trains were destroyed. Soon reports of yet another train approaching from Warrenton aroused hopes that the Southerners could destroy another one. Staff officer W. W. Blackford extinguished the red light from the rear lanterns with his saber while a soldier again blew the all-clear signal from an engine. The previous collision, though, had sparked a few fires. The light may have prevented the Confederates from successfully reenacting their recent ruse. A soldier in the 21st North Carolina remembered seeing the train "away down that straight part of the track" where it "stopped and whistled." The engineer seemed reluctant to believe the all-clear signal coming from Bristoe but to the tired soldiers along the railroad track it appeared in the distance that the train was slowly approaching their position. Any hopes of a repeat derailment were soon dashed when the train was seen "approaching but suddenly it reversed and went off at a lively rate."[13]

Campbell Brown, staff officer to "Dirty Dick" Ewell, was one reason for the quick withdrawal of the fourth train. The 22-year-old Brown heard that his commander had ridden to a house about 600 yards south of Bristoe Station. Growing up a few miles away at Stoney Lonesome, Ewell knew the local area well and was likely on a reconnaissance ride. Brown was joined in his futile ride to find Ewell by 25-year-old Lt. Henry Richardson, a recently assigned engineer to Ewell's staff. Failing to find Ewell, the two young staff officers instead found the fourth train.

While the Louisianans closer to Bristoe set a plan to lure the unsuspecting train by the all-clear ruse, Brown and Richardson also developed a plan, one more blunt than their comrades. After a quick discussion, the two staff officers decided to ride up and shoot the engineer and if any troops were aboard to "disappear rapidly." In their youthful confidence both men overlooked the fact that Richardson lacked a side arm and Brown's had been "loaded a year." Galloping in the dark against a train, Brown was fortunate that a low branch only took off his hat instead of dismounting him. Setting the train in reverse took time, and soon Brown closed on the locomotive. Riding next to the engineer, Brown ordered him to halt, which only prompted the engineer to hasten the reversal of the train. Raising his pistol, Brown cocked the hammer and pulled the trigger. The hammer struck the percussion cap and produced a spark, but the old powder refused to ignite. Brown tried a second and then a third shot from his revolver, but the dirty gun only snapped caps. The only

13 Sherrill Jr., *21st North Carolina*, 143.

shots he fired during the entire war, Brown had "the mortification to see [the engineer] get off unhurt."[14]

With Brown and Richardson unaccounted for, a rumor soon spread within Ewell's Division that the two staff officers had been killed. If true they would be the only Confederate casualties that night. Riding back towards the station in the darkness, both officers were able to locate the Tigers and the rest of Ewell's command. Failing to find his hat from his charge, Brown expected to be bareheaded for at least the near future. Fortunately for Brown, in going through the wreckage of the two trains a soldier in the 7th Louisiana took the hat from one of the dead engineers as a souvenir. Noticing Brown, the man gave the hat to him, Brown's only spoils from the raid.[15]

Within the space of 48 hours, Jackson had moved nearly 25,000 men over 56 miles into the rear of the main Federal army in northern Virginia. Severing the Orange and Alexandria railroad with minimal casualties, Jackson also destroyed two Union trains. Jackson later wrote "I regard that day's [August 26] achievement as the most brilliant that has come under my observation during the present war."[16]

Jackson's achievements between August 25 and 26 were brilliant but not perfect. After meeting with Lee, Longstreet, and Stuart about the future of the campaign and the role Jackson's command would play, Stonewall kept nearly everyone in his command in the dark. Jackson's sole reliance on Boswell is curious since his command contained units raised in both Fauquier and Prince William counties. Most curious of all, Jackson did not include Ewell in his decision-making though Ewell grew up in western Prince William County and was knowledgeable about the terrain of Jackson's destination.

Fulfilling his orders from Lee, Jackson had severed Pope's supply line. The failure to capture the first and fourth trains encountered at Bristoe Station, however, potentially alerted the Federals both north and south of Bristoe to Jackson's presence. It remained to be seen if Jackson would be squeezed on both fronts the next day. But before the sun rose on the 27th Jackson was again on the move. Stonewall was moving towards Manassas.

14 Jones, *Campbell Brown's Civil War*, 147.

15 Ibid., 148.

16 T. J. Jackson to Gen. Samuel Cooper, Sep. 22, 1862, Robert Lee Traylor Papers, VHS.

Chapter 14

"His Entire Command"

Fredericksburg: August 1862

The volunteers from Wisconsin and Indiana fretted the long weeks of summer under a heavy schedule of drills, reviews, work details, and camp policing as well as several forays into the countryside in search of Confederates. Accompanying the unending tasks, the volunteers were also plagued by a lingering and troubling doubt. They were untested as a brigade, they realized, and if the Western units were singled out for their frontier origins and new black hats, the four organizations were quite different in temperament and personality. It remained unknown how they would conduct themselves in an actual battle.

The troubling uncertainty of how the brigade would perform started at the very top where army commander John Pope proclaimed that his headquarters was located where his hindquarters should be. His boastful "Hindquarters in the Saddle" order also contained troubling implications about Little Mac and the Army of the Potomac. Around the Western Brigade's coffee fires, the volunteers raised troubling questions about why a general from the West was brought to command a new army in the East.

Corps commander Irvin McDowell, a failure as the overall Union commander at Bull Run, was also under a cloud. When in the field during the summer movements, he took to wearing an unusual large straw hat. It was whispered in the ranks that he might harbor Southern sympathies and wore the hat so Confederates across the way might be careful not to hit him. One Wisconsin soldier described the ornate headgear as a "basket cockade" and that the men in ranks believed at the time it only appeared "when there was any probability of fighting."[1]

1 Sheldon Leonard, letter, Oct. 21, 1877.

In a letter to his father, a young Wisconsin officer blamed McDowell for not being sent to join McClellan. The general, he wrote, "by preventing any men of whatever [officer] grade from visiting Washington on any pretence and by his continued presence there, he bids fair to thwart the wishes of his entire command. Thus, the Country if they do not suffer from his treachery or the betrayal of that command to the enemy, will at least have to pay the expenses of 30 or 50,000 troops in the field who will not be permitted to strike one blow at treason or rebellion." He added a few other bitter lines: "If McDowell had given McClellan his hearty cooperation Richmond would be ours today. As it is if McClellan should be defeated in the approaching great battle which will doubtless determine the fate of the Southern Confederacy, the loyal American people have no one to blame, no one to *curse* but McDowell and the Blindness of the War Department."[2]

Rufus King was also blamed. The general, the Wisconsin officer wrote colorfully,

> is a sluggard, a man of no force of will. King will play up the "gentleman General," have luxurious headquarters, dispense hospitality to notable individuals, get up parades shows for their edification, have fine band playing evenings around "these Head Quarters," pass the wine cup around to his satellites and friends, ride splendid horses when he goes out to see, be seen attended by his parasites and staff. Ah! it is a great thing for men Bankrupt politically & financially to hold high place in the Army . . . without rending if any aid in its death struggle with rebellion.

He concluded: "Too many men who are entirely satisfied with the place they hold have been appointed as Generals. When the war is ended they will go back to the obscurity from which they came."[3]

In ranks, John Gibbon was regarded as simply an artillery officer who never commanded infantry. With brothers in the Confederate service, his loyalty was also questioned, and his Old Army discipline and manner made him the most hated man in the brigade along with Adjutant Frank Haskell of the 6th Wisconsin, who for all his frosty military manner, was known as just an attorney from back home in Madison. "For God's sake, kill us off in battle, and don't do us to death as pack mules," a 7th Wisconsin man grumbled about the brigade

2 Brown to father, June 14, 1862.

3 Ibid.

commander while a member of the 19th Indiana described the general as "a little too strict to suit us."[4]

Of the four regiments, the 2nd Wisconsin was the most senior and the only regiment to have seen any real combat, even if the soldiers fresh from Badgerdom were swept off Henry House Hill at Bull Run by heavy rebel volleys and the unfortunate circumstance of having been fired on by a New York regiment behind them. The New Yorkers, in the noise and confusion, saw the gray Wisconsin militia uniforms in the smoke and decided they were the enemy. It was only after the Wisconsin national flag was brought into view that the friendly fire was halted, but not before several Badgers were wounded.

But the 2nd Wisconsin was also troubled. The colonel, lieutenant colonel, and major resigned as failures in the aftermath of Bull Run and replacements were appointed. The new colonel was Edgar O'Connor of Beloit, a lawyer and judge, and more importantly, an 1854 graduate of the U.S. Military Academy with a record of active service. Back home, however, his appointment came under a cloud because of O'Connor's earlier political views as a Democrat and the troubling fact that his wife came from the South and her father previously owned slaves. In truth, however, his father-in-law was a Union man who had moved his family to the North. The new colonel was forced to respond in an open letter to the Wisconsin newspapers to refute the rumors. He had "relations, friends and property in the rebel States," he wrote, and regretted the course the South had taken. "The separation has been painful, but when traitors take up arms, all personal relations, the ties of consanguinity and property, are to be merged in our higher duty to the Constitution."[5]

The lieutenant colonel was Lucius Fairchild of Madison, just promoted from captain in the 90-day 1st Wisconsin. He was a man of reputation in the pre-war Wisconsin militia, an adventurer who had gone to California in the gold rush, and a somewhat dashing young fellow openly regarded by his comrades as a ladies' man. The final regimental promotion lifted the well-regarded Bull Run veteran Thomas Allen, a former newspaper man, from his Mineral Point Company in the 2nd Wisconsin to be the major.

Given it had more time to organize, the 6th Wisconsin seemed of more steady temperament, but the regiment did not escape turmoil. "For some reason not known by the department," the state adjutant general reported, "there has been more change in the Sixth Regiment than the commissioned officers by

4 *Wisconsin Daily Patriot*, Aug. 18, 1862: Hank Gaylord to *Steuben* [Angola, IN] *Republican*, Sep. 13, 1862.

5 *Wisconsin Newspaper Volumes*, Vol. I, 135–136, 129.

Lieutenant Colonel Lucius Fairchild, 2nd Wisconsin. *Howard M. Madaus*

resignation and otherwise than all of the other regiments combined." Part of the problem was that the unit was caught in McClellan's 1861 purge of those he deemed unfit officers, especially those of Irish or other ethnic background.

The colonel, who was with them from the beginning, was 53-year-old Lysander Cutler of Milwaukee. After Fort Sumter, he immediately went to Madison and assisted in organizing and equipping the state's first regiments. He had some experience leading a regiment of militiamen in the brief but unbloody 1839 border dispute between the U.S. and Canada known as the "Aroostook War." One of his privates said Cutler had a "stern, rugged, determined, yet kindly face," and one of his captains said the old colonel would tolerate no nonsense and was "rugged as a wolf" and the regiment had great confidence in him.[6]

The initial lieutenant colonel was Julius P. Atwood, a Madison attorney, who soon resigned and was replaced by Benjamin Sweet, who then also resigned to take a promotion in another regiment. He was replaced by Edward Bragg, a Fond du Lac attorney and outspoken War Democrat who raised a company with volunteers from his city and nearby Appleton. Named to replace him as major was Capt. Rufus Dawes, a native of Ohio, who raised a company in Juneau

6 Dawes, *Service*, 18, 25, 32–33; *History of Milwaukee, Wisconsin* (Chicago, 1881), 789–791. Born in Royalton, MA, in 1808, Cutler was a farmer, surveyor and schoolmaster before moving to Dexter, ME. He and a partner built what was then the largest woolen mill east of Massachusetts—employing 2,000 workers at one point—but the Panic of 1856 destroyed the business. Cutler then moved to Wisconsin to make a fresh start and worked for a time in the rough Lake Superior mining country. For two winters, he worked organizing a mining town that was 30 miles from the nearest supply post. The Indians and mixed blood Métis who worked for him called him "Gray Devil" because of the color of his long hair and trimmed whiskers.

Colonel Lysander Cutler, 6th Wisconsin
Library of Congress

County, Wisconsin, where his father ran a general store and engaged in land speculation.

The 7th Wisconsin command situation was also somewhat in disarray. The first colonel was Joseph Vandor, an old Hungarian campaigner just then living in Milwaukee. A local newspaper touted the new colonel as educated at the "Imperial Military Academy of Vienna" and an "officer in the army of the celebrated Field Marshal Radetsky" who enjoyed a distinguished role in the Hungarian Revolution of 1848–1849. One difficulty not mentioned in the newspaper columns, however, was the fact that Vandor was just barely able to make himself understood in English. He resigned after trouble with the inexperienced young volunteer officers of his regiment who balked at his old-world discipline.[7]

Replacing Vandor as colonel was William W. Robinson of Sparta, a 42-year-old native of Vermont whose kinsmen included Mayflower Pilgrims. Robinson was a veteran of the Mexican War. As an officer, he was described by an observer as "a substantial looking man and seems perfectly at home in the discharge of his duties."[8]

The lieutenant colonel was 35-year-old Charles A. Hamilton of Milwaukee, a grandson of Alexander Hamilton, a major figure in the nation's founding. His father was a New York attorney of wealth and reputation. After attending schools in England and Germany and reading law in New York, Hamilton came to Milwaukee in 1851 and developed an extensive practice. The major was the

7 Sometimes spelled Van Dor. *Wisconsin Newspaper Volumes*; Julius Murray, letter, undated, Julius Murray Papers, State Historical Society of Wisconsin.

8 Robinson was a teacher in Vermont and New Jersey and then Ohio and volunteered for the War with Mexico, serving in the 3rd Ohio Rifles. He returned to Ohio and in 1851 moved to Sparta, WI. He left Wisconsin for the adventure of the gold fields of California. He returned in 1855 and moved to Minnesota where he helped organize the town of Wilton, served in the state assembly and militia before moving back to Wisconsin in 1859.

generally well-regarded George Bill, who came into the army as captain of the Lodi Guards.

Probably because of his imposing height and political standing, the most well-known colonel of the brigade was 6-foot-7-inch Sol Meredith of the 19th Indiana. He was a great favorite with the men who enjoyed telling stories of his rustic mannerisms. They called him "Long Sol" behind his back. Meredith was raised a Quaker in his native North Carolina and as a young man walked to Indiana to start a new life. He prospered as a farmer and was Wayne County clerk at the time of Fort Sumter. He was well known as a political crony of powerful Republican Indiana Governor Oliver P. Morton.

The lieutenant colonel was recently promoted Alois O. Bachman. Born in Madison into a family of Swiss settlers, he was active in the Madison City Greys militia organization which he took as a company into the 90-day 6th Indiana. Upon the expiration of the three months of service, he was given a commission in the three-year 19th Regiment. The regimental major was the well-regarded Isaac M. May, who by unlikely circumstance was a native of Shenandoah County, Virginia. He had come to Indiana as a boy and prospered.

In the final consideration, the volunteers from the far West felt they and their officers were untested. The nagging question in the quiet of night in their camps was how would the brigade perform if called to battle?

Chapter 15

"Ran Like Turkeys"

Manassas Junction: August 27, 1862

The burning trains at Bristoe Station signaled the partial triumph of Lee's objective to sever the Orange and Alexandria Railroad. Soldiers at Bristoe prevented supplies, reinforcements, and information traveling between Washington D.C. and Pope's army near Warrenton. To achieve a longer lasting impact on Pope's ability to remain near the Rappahannock River posed a difficult challenge to Stonewall Jackson. The most effective, but least realistic, option was for Jackson to remain at Bristoe with his entire wing. With nearly half of Lee's army in his rear sitting directly on his main supply line, Pope would be forced to abandon his Rappahannock line almost immediately, fulfilling Lee's strategy of moving the Federals away from the natural defensive positions on the north bank of the river.

Remaining at Bristoe with his entire command was risky. Jackson could expect Pope to move against him from the south to clear the railroad. Possessing intelligence reports showing that elements of the Army of the Potomac had already arrived at Alexandria, Jackson could reasonably assume that some Federal soldiers might advance from the north. If both forces could coordinate their movements, Jackson faced the possibility of being attacked from both front and rear. Remaining at Bristoe for an extended period was foolish.

Jackson needed a way to focus Federal attention on the railroad while he maneuvered to a more advantageous position. Tearing the line would prevent the immediate use of the railroad to Pope but most destruction to rail lines during the Civil War was repairable within a matter of days. Tearing up track would likely only be a temporary hindrance to the Federal supply line.

At Bristoe the Confederates had not one, but two targets that could realistically put the railroad out of commission for at least a few weeks. South of Bristoe the railroad crossed Kettle Run. A modest stream, its steep banks required the railroad to cross on a wooden bridge. Similarly, just north of the station the railroad bridged another stream, Broad Run. Provided enough time and labor, engineers could be expected to replace any damaged or destroyed bridges, though not fast enough for Pope to remain near Warrenton. Burning the bridges would almost guarantee Pope abandoning the Rappahannock, allowing Lee and Longstreet to pursue him to a more favorable battlefield.

Jackson, however, had another idea. Three and a half miles to the north sat the warehouses of Manassas Junction. The subsequent Confederate advance towards Manassas Junction later devolved into partisan quarreling that frustrates a clear understanding of the thought process of Jackson and his generals on the evening of August 26. At some point during the day, Jackson decided to harass the Federals at Manassas. Part of the confusion lay in the after-action reports about the events of August 26–27. Officers that submitted reports waited months to file them with most being submitted between January and April 1863.[1]

The sequence of events culminating in the capture of Manassas Junction will likely never be determined with certainty. Two contrasting versions of the Manassas Junction operations give conflicting evidence. The generally accepted version holds Brig. Gen. Isaac Trimble as the main individual associated with the capture of Manassas. After graduating from West Point the native Virginian moved to Maryland, resigned his commission, and worked for a railroad company. Considering himself a native Marylander, Trimble left his state and traveled back to the Old Dominion to offer his services to the new nation. Directly commissioned as a brigadier general in the Confederate Provisional Army, the hard charging Marylander soon found a home in Jackson's command leading a mixed brigade of Alabamians, Georgians, and North Carolinians.[2]

Leading his brigade in the Shenandoah Valley and around Richmond, Trimble believed his record in both campaigns warranted a promotion to major general. Frustrated at seeing other generals promoted over him, Dr. Hunter McGuire remembered Trimble boasting to Jackson "By G---, General Jackson, I will be a major general or a corpse before this war is over." Campbell Brown also heard of Trimble's boast on the evening of August 26 after the Marylander expressed frustration over not participating in the fight around Bristoe Station.[3]

1 The invasion of Maryland in the fall and the winter campaign around Fredericksburg prevented any earlier submissions.

2 Warner, *Generals in Gray*, 310.

3 Hunter McGuire, "General Thomas J. Jackson," *Southern Historical Society Papers* 19 (1891): 314; Jones, *Campbell Brown's Civil War*, 148.

General Isaac Trimble
Library of Congress

Holding a burning desire for promotion, Trimble was not above enlarging his role in the march towards Manassas. The historian of the 21st Georgia later claimed that Trimble first broached the idea of attacking Manassas on the afternoon of August 26. Trimble supposedly had intelligence that warehouses along the junction contained "millions of supplies" and if given permission could take the location with but two of his regiments. How a commander of an infantry brigade in the middle of a column would have access to this intelligence was never elaborated.[4]

Instead of first proposing an attack on Manassas that afternoon, it appears that Jackson began to give serious consideration to an advance towards Manassas after successfully capturing Bristoe. According to Jackson, only after the fall of Bristoe did he learn of the "stores of great value" and he "deemed it important that no time should be lost in securing them." But whom did Jackson order to Manassas?[5]

Jackson later remembered that Trimble was ordered first towards Manassas and subsequently Stuart was instructed to follow the Marylander with his cavalrymen. If this in fact is the correct sequence of events it is a surprising example of overconfidence in Jackson's opinion of his men. After a march of nearly 30 miles, Stonewall decided to break the chain of command by directly ordering Trimble, instead of going through his division commander Dick Ewell, to march to Manassas with two regiments of his five regiment brigade. Even against a small Federal garrison, two exhausted regiments were unlikely to capture such a mountain of supplies. Desirous of promotion, Trimble welcomed a narrative in which he and his command took the prominent role.

4 Henry W. Thomas, *History of the Doles-Cook Brigade Army of Northern Virginia 1861–1865* (Atlanta, 1903), 352.

5 *OR* 12, pt. 2, 643.

A more likely scenario, one supported by more evidence, has Stuart in command of the advance towards Manassas. Campbell Brown remembered that Trimble "came to Gen'ls Jackson & Ewell to volunteer a trip to Manassas, with his brigade along with Stuart's Cavalry." Stuart remembered that Jackson ordered him to take his troopers towards Manassas followed by Trimble's Brigade "notifying me to take charge of the whole." Even Trimble reported that his men approached Manassas *behind* Stuart's troopers. An officer on Jackson's staff remembered "General Stuart took General Trimble's brigade of infantry and part of his cavalry and went from Bristoe Station towards Manassas Depot."[6]

The probable scenario is that Jackson decided a cavalry raid on the supplies stored at Manassas would deny them to the enemy. Worried that Stuart's men needed a stronger force in case the Federal garrison put up stiff resistance, a portion of Trimble's Brigade tagged along to reinforce the raid. In classic Jacksonian fashion, Trimble's taciturn orders produced enough confusion about the proper chain of command that he thought he deserved the credit for the capture of Manassas.

In charge of the combined cavalry-infantry column approaching the junction, Stuart took the most direct route from Bristoe. Nearing Manassas, Stuart sent Col. William Wickham and his 4th Virginia Cavalry on a flanking march around the important railroad junction. Wickham's instructions placed his command across the probable escape route for the Federal garrison. Meanwhile Stuart approached Manassas directly from Bristoe with the majority of Brig. Gen. Beverly Robertson's brigade of Virginia cavalry.

Approximately one and a half miles from the junction Stuart's troopers ran into Federal pickets. The advance quickly halted when an unseen Federal cannon fired a round of canister. With Trimble's infantry expected on the field at any moment, Stuart decided to wait for the foot soldiers since "it was too dark to venture cavalry over uncertain ground against artillery." Trimble soon appeared with his two "21s" behind him: the 21st North Carolina commanded by Lt. Col. Saunders Fulton and the 21st Georgia commanded by Maj. Thomas Glover. Replacing the cavalry, the two regiments formed line of battle with the Georgians to the left of the railroad and the North Carolinians to the right.[7]

Marching in the dark, the Georgian and Tarheel approach was eerily quiet. One North Carolinian remembered marching towards Manassas "as silently and stealthily as we could" while another Tarheel remembered that "the only thing

6 Jones, *Campbell Brown's Civil War*, 148; *OR* 12, pt. 2, 720–739.

7 *OR* 12, pt. 2, 734.

we heard in the stillness of the night was a canteen or sabre clatter now and then." Finding no sign of the Federals that had fired onto Robertson's troopers, Trimble's men continued toward the Junction, screened by a line of skirmishers. Within 100 yards of earthworks, Trimble ordered a halt and issued "watchwords and responses, that our men may recognize each other in case of a mingled encounter with the enemy."[8]

Waiting for the order to continue, the men of the two regiments could barely see the enemy in the darkness. Trimble soon ordered the infantryman to charge in the general direction of the enemy earthworks. The noise emanating from Trimble's command alerted the Federal artillerists and a salvo of canister and solid shot belched from the earthworks. Owing to the darkness, the Federals overshot their targets, but firing revealed the location of the artillery. The Confederates followed with "a quick dash" that overpowered the Federals before the cannons could be reloaded. During the brief fight a Georgian heard one Federal officer encourage his men by yelling "Give 'em another round boys, it's only some of Mosby's d—n guerillas." A Confederate lieutenant soon approached the Federal officer in the dark and tapping him on the shoulder said "I reckon, colonel, you have got in the wrong crowd."[9]

Capturing the earthworks, some Tarheels had trouble locating the Georgians. In frustration a Carolinian yelled out "Halloo, Georgia, where are you?" Soon a response came back in the darkness "Here; all right. We have taken a battery." "So have we," responded the Tar Heel and the air was soon filled with the sound of cheering Confederates. For the loss of 15 wounded men, Trimble claimed to have captured over 300 Federal soldiers, 4 cannon, 200 horses, as well as 200 recently escaped African American slaves. Manassas Junction had fallen.[10]

An excited Trimble jumped the chain of command in his report on the fall of Manassas. Instead of going through the officer in charge of the operation (Stuart) or his immediate commander (Ewell), Trimble directly messaged Jackson of the success and the peculiar situation in which it placed him. Soon several soldiers began ransacking the captured supplies, forcing Trimble to detach a guard in the junction. Talking to prisoners and rifling through captured correspondence, Trimble learned of a large Federal presence across the Bull Run in Fairfax County and became concerned of an imminent counterattack to recapture Manassas.

8 Sherrill Jr., *21st North Carolina*, 145; *OR* 12, pt. 2, 720.

9 Walter Clark, ed., *Histories of the Several Regiments and Battalions from North Carolina in the Great War 1861-65* (Goldsboro, NC, 1901), 153; James Nisbet, *Four Years on the Firing Line* (Chattanooga, 1914), 137.

10 *OR* 12, pt. 2, 720–721.

Trimble worried that the 500 men of the two 21s were inadequate for both guard duty and defense of the junction. He needed reinforcements.[11]

Trimble need not have worried. The Marylander's report thrilled Jackson when it arrived just before dawn. The normally reserved Jackson sent a message: "Permit me to congratulate you upon the brilliant success with which God has blessed you." More importantly in Trimble's mind, Jackson followed his congratulations with an announcement that Trimble "deserve[s] promotion" to the coveted rank of major general, which surely delighted the man who vowed to make that rank or die trying. More importantly Jackson sent the rest of Trimble's Brigade up to Manassas. Jackson finished his note with the hope that if Trimble thought the captured stores amounted to rations for 5,000 men, to send down food if he could find the transportation.[12]

The warehouses in Manassas groaned with food. A quick tabulation by Trimble found 50,000 pounds of bacon, 2,000 barrels of salt pork, 2,000 barrels of flour, 1,000 barrels of canned beef, "large stores" of oats, corn, and whisky, and 4 sutler stores filled with more luxuries. Trimble had also captured 52 wagons and ambulances pulled by 175 draft horses. While adding to the limited number of wagons in his command, most of Jackson's wagon train remained near Bristoe Station. Using the most direct route, Jackson's wagons rumbling from Bristoe to Manassas and back would travel 8 miles. Marching his men from Bristoe to the junction, though, would both halve the distance and time it would take for Jackson's command to issue the food.[13]

Shortly after sending the remainder of Trimble's Brigade to Manassas, Jackson decided the easiest option to issue the captured rations required the troops going to the food. To hinder Pope's ability to stay south of Manassas, Jackson instructed his Chief Engineer Boswell to destroy the railroad bridge over Broad Run. To protect Boswell from any Federal incursions under Pope, Jackson left behind his best division under Ewell while taking Taliaferro's and Hill's Divisions north to Manassas.

The Stonewall Brigade lead the column away from Bristoe, followed by Hill and then Taliaferro. While the success at Bristoe Station and Manassas Junction over the previous hours resulted in a large haul of prisoners, the Confederates dispersed more enemy soldiers than they captured. In the confusion, some Federal soldiers were seen milling around the area. Between Bristoe and

11 Ibid., 721.

12 Jackson to Trimble, Aug. 27, 1862, Trimble Papers, Maryland Historical Society.

13 Report, Apr. 11, 1863, Trimble Papers, Maryland Historical Society.

Manassas the 2nd Virginia unexpectedly bumped into "a large body of enemy cavalry." Lieutenant Colonel Lawson Botts halted the march and called for artillery support, and a section of the Alleghany Artillery thundered up and deployed. With the rest of the regiment held in reserve to protect the guns, two companies of the 2nd Virginia advanced against the Yankee troopers. A few cannon rounds and the advancing infantrymen sent the horse soldiers scurrying away, reopening the road to Manassas. An insignificant fight, it highlighted that Jackson's men roamed in enemy territory and encountered the Federals unexpectedly.[14]

Continuing the march, the Stonewall Brigade reached the junction around 7:00 a.m. At the head of the column, the Virginians were pushed north of Manassas to reinforce elements of Trimble's two 21s and Fitzhugh Lee's cavalry brigade on picket duty. About a mile north of the junction Confederate soldiers had erected a series of earthworks in 1861 to protect the railroad intersection from a Union advance from Washington. Vacant during the first battle of Manassas, the Southerners did not destroy the fortifications when they evacuated northern Virginia in 1862. These surviving forts thus were one major reason Jackson decided to attack Bristoe Station. Ironically their original creators would soon use them again for their intended purpose of defending the junction from Federal soldiers.

The Stonewall Brigade, along with the accompanying Alleghany Artillery, filed into a large earthen fort the Confederates christened Fort Beauregard. Built in June 1861 Fort Beauregard was one of the first major earthworks built in Virginia during the Civil War. It's cannon embrasures to the north and east commanded the Centreville Road, the main north-south road towards Manassas. Communication trenches and rifle pits allowed ample room for the Stonewall Brigade to deploy.

Around 6:00 a.m. Stuart's pickets along the old Centreville Road reported a large Federal infantry regiment accompanied by a cannon approaching from Bull Run. Officers examining this unknown force caught red insignia on some of the enemy's uniforms indicating they were fighting an artillery force acting as infantry. Skirmishing with this unusual foe, Fitzhugh Lee's troopers slowly fell back towards Manassas, hurried by an occasional shell from the single Federal cannon.

Back in Manassas, the cannon report alerted Jackson to the news of an unknown Federal force developing to the north. Jackson ordered Hill to continue north with his division to strengthen the Confederate defensive line.

14 *OR* 12, pt. 2, 721.

Confederate fort, likely Fort Beauregard, that was used in the battle of Bull Run Bridge. *Library of Congress*

After pausing briefly, Hill's Division marched through Manassas and began filing into position. Brig. Gen. Lawrence Branch's North Carolina brigade extended the line to the west, deploying on the left of the Stonewall Brigade and Fort Beauregard. The rest of Hill's Division, four brigades of infantry, lengthened the line to the east. The right flank of the new position was anchored on Fort Mayfield, another fortification the Confederates built in 1861.

Falling back towards Fort Beauregard, Fitzhugh Lee's withdrawal ended as he approached Branch's line. The infantry now took over the fight. Examining the Federal battle line, some officers in Branch's Brigade thought the force opposing them wasn't artillerymen but instead dismounted Federal cavalry. Peppering the still unknown force with deliberate volleys, after a few moments of skirmishing the Federal line about-faced and disappeared on the road back to Centreville. The first Federal counterattack towards Manassas had failed.[15]

Before the Confederates could congratulate themselves, yet another Federal force was discovered advancing from Bull Run. Clearly infantry in brigade strength, this new force was advancing towards the Confederate center rather than its left. The defensive line resembled a half-moon, with the two ends jutting north. The Federals appeared to be blindly marching into a potential Confederate

15 *OR* 12, pt. 2, 670.

trap. If the Southerners could withhold their fire long enough, the enemy infantrymen would soon be subjected to fire from their front and both flanks.

Riding from Manassas, Jackson wanted to personally supervise the defense of such a massive haul of supplies. Sitting atop his horse Little Sorrel near the Rockbridge Artillery, Jackson and his staff observed the sun reflecting from the musket barrels and bayonets of the approaching Federals. Marching in a narrow, dense column, the enemy presented a target of which artillerists dreamed. An artillery officer in the antebellum U.S. Army, Jackson wanted the nearby artillerists to wait until the Federals were nearly on top of the Confederate line before the artillery fired canister into their unsuspecting ranks. Approaching to 100 yards of the hidden line, Jackson ordered the Rockbridge Artillery to fire. Pouring fire from front, right, and left, the Confederate artillery blew huge gaps into the struggling enemy line. Within 10 minutes, and before most of the supporting infantry could fire more than a handful of minie balls, the Federal column began falling back in confusion.[16]

The scene of retreating Federals proved too tempting for some Southerners. Seeing the enemy "run, every man for himself" an Alabamian and a few friends "ran right after them, shooting as we ran." Artillerists also proved unable to resist the temptation to charge. Over near the center of the line, Capt. William Crenshaw bellowed to his battery "Cannoneers mount! Forward; unlimber! Fire by prolong!" Usually a command given during the retreat, the cannon remained attached to the horse-drawn artillery caisson by a heavy rope. The gun was reloaded and then pulled by the horses to the desired spot before the gun was manhandled into the firing position. A member of Crenshaw's battery remembered that the fighting on August 27 "was the only occasion in which this character of firing was ever practiced by our battery."[17]

Excited infantrymen and artillerists weren't the only soldiers swept up by the scene of retreating Federals. Jedediah Hotchkiss reported that Jackson advanced towards the retreating Yankees "cap in hand, hallooing 'Surrender; throw down your arms and surrender.'" William Poague of the Rockbridge Artillery likewise saw Jackson "repeatedly wave his handkerchief calling them to surrender." Edward Moore serving with Poague looked in horror as one of the retreating Federals "raised his gun and fired deliberately" at Jackson.

16 Edward Moore, *The Story of a Cannoneer under Stonewall Jackson* (Lynchburg, VA, 1910), 106.

17 William Fulton, *War Reminiscences of William Frierson Fulton II* (Gaithersburg, MD, 1986), 45; Peter Carmichael, *The Purcell, Crenshaw, and Letcher Artillery* (Lynchburg, VA, 1990), 89.

Fortunately the shot missed but was close enough that Moore "heard the Minie as it whistled by him."[18]

Protected by the earthworks during most of the fighting, most of the casualties sustained by Jackson's Wing during this fight occurred during the pursuit as men passed through open fields. A few inches saved Jackson from death or a wound that would likely have taken him out of command for the rest of the campaign. Jackson and Stuart were the only officers around Manassas that were present for Lee's pre-march conference. A dead or incapacitated Jackson would likely have forced either Stuart or Ewell into command. Stuart knew of Lee's overall strategy but was not well acquainted with Jackson's command; friction between Stuart and his divisional commanders likely would have surfaced early with infantrymen chaffing under the command of a horse soldier.

After Jackson's calls for surrender were ignored, Branch's and Archer's Brigades joined Fitzhugh Lee's troopers in pursuing the fleeing enemy. While the infantrymen kept up the pressure preventing the Federals from reforming, Lee's cavalry tried to get between Bull Run and the Yankees. If Lee succeeded, the Confederates held a good chance of capturing most of this force. Routed infantry was a cavalryman's delight, and the fields approaching Bull Run Bridge appeared almost textbook conditions for a cavalry charge. Branch and Archer prevented organized resistance, but small groups of Federals still formed mobile squares when they saw Lee's troopers. The prospect of trying to crack infantry squares, regardless of their size, proved too daunting for most of the cavalrymen. Before the supporting infantry could put enough pressure to eliminate these ad-hoc squares more Federal troops north of Bull Run arrived. Remaining on the north bank of the stream, these new Federals fired covering volleys, allowing the refugees on the south bank to cross in relative safety. Seeing this new enemy line, the Confederates pulled back to their original defensive line.[19]

The battle of Bull Run Bridge, as the fight was later called, was one of the most lopsided victories in the Army of Northern Virginia's history. Sustaining minimal casualties, the field in front of Forts Beauregard and Mayfield were covered with dead and wounded Northerners. While the identity of the first regiment alternatively identified as either artillery or cavalry was not soon established (it was the 2nd New York Heavy Artillery), prisoners from the larger brigade identified themselves as belonging to the New Jersey Brigade of the Army of the Potomac. Further conversation with the prisoners revealed that

18 Hotchkiss, *Make Me a Map*, 130; Monroe Cockrell, ed., *Gunner with Stonewall* (Lincoln, NE, 1998), 35; Moore, *Story of a Cannoneer under Jackson*, 104.

19 *OR* 12, pt. 2, 699.

the New Jerseyans had just recently arrived from the peninsula, disembarking at Alexandria. Hearing reports of Confederate cavalry raiding Manassas, the Federals were roused early and entrained towards Bull Run. Disembarking and crossing the stream, almost everyone was confident that Manassas would soon be in Federal hands again.[20]

Intelligence gathered from this new batch of prisoners revealed important information for Jackson. Most importantly, Jackson now knew sizable portions of McClellan's army were arriving in the Northern Virginia theater and could be sent to reinforce Pope in an attack against Jackson. Until Lee and the rest of the army arrived from the Rappahannock line, Jackson now knew he would be seriously outnumbered. To prevent an overwhelming enemy force destroying him, Jackson needed to keep the Federals off balance by confusing them of both the Confederate position and intentions. Jackson needed to keep moving and try to find a strong defensive position to beat back any Federal attacks before Lee arrived.

Jackson also gathered that the Federals were still unaware of what Confederate forces they were dealing with around Manassas. Concern that the two escaping trains from Bristoe Station on the 26th alerted the Federals to his presence seemed to be unfounded. The Federal high command appeared confused about what force was actually around Manassas. The repulse of the New Jersey Brigade at Bull Run Bridge would surely alert the Federals that a large portion of Lee's army operated near Manassas. However, Jackson could risk that it would take a bit of time for the Federals to process this information (the fight ended around 11:00 a.m.) so Jackson could reasonably expect a strong Federal response from Alexandria the next day at the earliest. Stonewall planned to have the remaining daylight hours of August 27 to himself.

Lacking adequate numbers of wagons to quickly move the rations from Manassas to the forts north of the junction in a reasonable time, Jackson decided to return most of Hill's Division to Manassas. The Stonewall Brigade had the unenviable duty of remaining at Fort Beauregard in case the Federals attempted another attack, while Stuart sent Fitz Lee's cavalry on a raid across Bull Run through Fairfax County looking for easy targets. By lunchtime both Hill and Taliaferro's Divisions started going through the Manassas warehouses, a scene that soon became legendary in the army.

A strict disciplinarian, Jackson attempted to establish order in distributing the captured supplies to his hungry men. Almost immediately after securing the junction, Trimble attempted to place guards over both the warehouses

20 Ibid., 670.

and captured trains. Struggling to both safeguard the supplies from arriving Confederates and also picket the area to the north stretched Trimble's Brigade to the limit. Fortunately for Trimble, as Hill's Division passed through the area, a couple regiments peeled off the column and were sent to reinforce the guards. Returning to the junction after the battle of Bull Run Bridge, first Hill's Division and then the rest of Taliaferro's men initially found slim pickings.

At Manassas, quartermasters issued food to regiments and companies as fast as possible, creating an unnecessary urgency on the part of some officers and sergeants. A private in the 21st Virginia recalled attempts by overburdened quartermasters to quickly assess needs and issue food. Rations "were issued to the men, but not by weight and measure to each man. A package or two of each article was given to each company." In the rush, John Worsham's sergeant didn't attempt to look at what he was issuing to his men, let alone try to divide it up. A ravenous Worsham remembered that the "first thing brought us was a barrel of cakes, next, a bag of hams." Later sugar, coffee, and syrup by the barrel and potatoes by the bag were given.[21]

As food was issued by both the barrel and bagful, it seems Jackson and his staff took the more optimistic view of their current strategic picture. Fulfilling his objective severing the Orange and Alexandria Railroad at Bristoe, the fall of Manassas was helpful but not critical to Jackson's mission. Throwing back a quick counterattack coming from Bull Run, pickets remained vigilant north of the junction while two of Jackson's three divisions took advantage of the recently captured stores. Jackson's best division guarded his rear at Bristoe; to the west remained numerous gaps in the Bull Run Mountains if Jackson was pressed hard enough to retreat towards the rest of Lee's army.

A pessimist would have seen a more worrying strategic picture. The repulse of the New Jersey Brigade in the morning probably took the fight out of any Federals in the immediate vicinity of Bull Run. Unlikely though it might be, there still existed the possibility of renewed action north of town. A brigade of infantry deployed in earthworks could slow down an enemy force, but depending on the size of an enemy assault, Jackson needed to have his divisions at Manassas on hand to rapidly march the two miles from the warehouses to the earthworks. The morning fight revealed the Army of the Potomac arriving in the northern Virginia theater in strength and could be expected to add its weight to the unfolding campaign.

The Army of the Potomac north of Bull Run wasn't the only Federal force Jackson need worry about. John Pope's Army of Virginia remained south of

21 Worsham, *One of Jackson's Foot Cavalry*, 120–121.

Bristoe Station. The escaping train during the previous night's raid likely warned Pope of Confederates on the railroad. Ewell had orders to protect Jackson's rear but not bring on a general engagement. If Pope reacted decisively and concentrated strength towards Bristoe, Ewell would be hard pressed. Hill and Taliaferro needed to be ready to also march back down to Bristoe Station if the need arose.

The gaps through the Bull Run Mountains had been vacant of Federal troops when Jackson passed through Thoroughfare Gap the previous day. While most of the cavalry assigned to Jackson rode through Fairfax, a single regiment remained posted at Gainesville near Thoroughfare Gap picketing the roads towards Warrenton. There were no Confederates in any force at the gaps either holding them open for Lee and Longstreet approaching with the rest of the army or holding them open if Jackson needed to retreat.

Jackson's command should have been prepared for a worst-case scenario: converging Federal attacks from both north and south. Keeping his command prepared for an attack that might never materialize while needed supplies stood just feet away from his soldiers would hardly be popular with the rank and file. However, the men in Manassas needed to be kept in relative order if exigencies arose and they were required to rush to a threatened area.

Inexcusably Jackson and his subordinates allowed discipline to break down in Manassas, potentially threatening the security of a significant portion of the South's premier army. The guards protecting the stores found themselves overwhelmed with a mass of armed, hungry, young men. A free-for-all developed, with soldiers competing for luxuries. Soon word of the abundance of such delicacies as cakes, oysters, and wine spread beyond Manassas to the unfortunate soldiers at Forts Beauregard and Mayfield. The stories of what was found at the junction proved too much for Pvt. John Casler of the 33rd Virginia. Slinking out of line, Casler soon made his way into the carnival that was then Manassas. The Virginian recalled encountering a sutler store surrounded by a "solid mass" of soldiers. Reaching critical mass, the guard "who was not very particular" about his duty gave way, allowing the soldiers free rein to the goods. An officer and a few guards arrived a few moments later, dispersing the mob that then quickly descended onto another area, repeating the process.[22]

John Worsham remembered how rations for the 21st Virginia were "issued" to his regiment in Manassas. Officers told the men to "take four days' rations with us. It was hard to decide what to take, some filled their haversacks with cakes, some with candy, others oranges, lemons, canned goods, etc. I know one who took nothing but French mustard, filled his haversack and was so greedy that

22 Casler, *Four Years in the Stonewall Brigade*, 107.

he put one more bottle in his pocket. This was his four days' rations." Mustard proved a surprisingly good choice; trading mustard for other food, Worsham's friend stretched the usefulness of the mustard for a couple of weeks. Probably most of the cakes, oranges, and lemons were consumed within 48 hours.[23]

Complicating the duty of some officers trying to bring order out of the chaos, other officers took part in the looting. One officer remembered seeing Brig. Gen. Charles Field and his staff participating. Entering "we found spread upon the table, untouched, a breakfast of cold chicken, lamb, and biscuit, and coffee that by this time, had also grown cold." After devouring the food one major retired to "a bed with feather pillows and bolster, upon which I at once threw myself, begging to be allowed to rest, if but for ten minutes." With officers taking part rather than taking command of their men, the pillaging soon spiraled out of control.[24]

Mayhem increased when alcohol was discovered. Jackson ordered the heads of the barrels containing whiskey, wine, and brandy knocked out so that "streams of spirits ran like water through the sands of Manassas." The liquor in the streets didn't prevent some men from falling on their hands and knees trying to lap it up as it flowed by them.[25]

Either the barrels were too numerous, or like Field and his staff officers, some of Jackson's subordinates hoped to keep some alcohol for their use. In the end spirits enough remained available to the troops. During the march, many of the men's rations had given out prior to Bristoe with green corn being widely eaten. Now at Manassas many soldiers were quaffing large amounts of alcohol on empty stomachs. Drunkenness quickly spread.

Experiencing dwindling results raiding sutler stores, a few Virginians decided to try their luck on some of the railroad cars sitting on a siding. Squeezing through an opening in the car, after prying a few boxes open the men realized they were in a car full of medicinal equipment. Opening crates, the soldiers continued to rummage for medical whiskey and brandy, destroying valuable supplies, especially bottles of chloroform and morphine. Passing surgeons tried to stop the destruction, pleas quickly ignored as the men found their prizes.

Reports of the loss of critical medicines brought a reaction from the Confederate high command. A guard was sent to the train to disperse or arrest the small mob surrounding the medical car. "Arrested" soldiers were taken

23 Worsham, *One of Jackson's Foot Cavalry*, 121.

24 W. Roy Mason, "Marching on Manassas," *Battles and Leaders of the Civil War*, Vol. 2 (New York, 1956), 529.

25 Ibid., 529.

outside and their loot returned to the car if it was medicine or the pockets of the guards if it was alcohol.[26]

Some inebriated soldiers attempted to swap out their worn gray uniforms with new clothing found in storage, most of which proved to be sets of unissued Federal uniforms intended for Pope's army. "We were very willing to don the blue uniforms," thought an artillerist. Foreseeing incidents of friendly fire if large numbers of his men wore Federal clothing, Jackson quickly put an end to the wholesale looting of Federal clothing, though not before a few soldiers left Manassas with a new pair of trousers or a jacket courtesy of the Federal quartermaster.[27]

After alcohol and food, clothing was one of the most desired objects for looting soldiers. The closing of Federal warehouses did not stop some soldiers from trying to get new garments. Trickling away from the warehouses, tents, and trains that contained U.S. Army and sutler supplies, some Confederates went after civilian property. Throughout the spring and summer hundreds of newly freed African Americans made it to Federal lines. Contraband camps formed throughout occupied Virginia, including one near Manassas. It is likely in this contraband camp that Trimble captured 200 African Americans earlier that morning. In addition to capturing the men and women, the men of Trimble's Brigade "got into the shanties" that made up the camp. Going through women's clothing, members of the 15th Alabama looked for new headgear to replace their nearly brimless hats. Soon "all such supplied themselves with women's hats and tied them on with the long red ribbons and trimmings attached." The combination of women's hats and dusty gray jackets presented one of the most unique sets of uniforms a Confederate soldier ever wore.[28]

As Taliaferro's and Hill's men raided Manassas, Ewell's Division remained at Bristoe Station, protecting Boswell's efforts to demolish the bridge over Broad Run. With Trimble's Brigade at Manassas, Ewell had three infantry brigades and an artillery battalion to guard the engineers. In addition to protecting the work against the railroad, Jackson warned Ewell not to be drawn into a potential general engagement. How Ewell wanted to deploy his men, Jackson left to his subordinate.

"Tricky Dick" Ewell formed most of his division perpendicular to the railroad, adjacent to the road the men had marched on a few hours earlier from

26 Casler, *Four Years in the Stonewall Brigade*, 107–108.

27 Moore, *Story of a Cannoneer under Jackson*, 109–110.

28 William Oates, *The War Between the Union and the Confederacy and Its Lost Opportunities with a History of the 15th Alabama Regiment* (New York, 1905), 135.

Thoroughfare Gap. Brig. Gen. Alexander Lawton deployed most of his Georgia Brigade near Bristoe Station. The Confederate line continued to Lawton's right with portions of Hay's Brigade of Louisiana Tigers, commanded this day by Col. Henry Forno. The seven Virginia regiments of Brig. Gen. Jubal Early's Brigade, supported by two regiments from Lawton's Brigade, anchored the far right of Ewell's new line. Interspaced throughout the new defensive position were the six artillery batteries assigned to Ewell's command. The flanks of the Confederate line at Bristoe were screened by the 2nd Virginia Cavalry.

Unknown to the enlisted men, Ewell hoped to use only a fraction of his force in fulfilling his mission. Worried about the vagueness of his orders, around noon Ewell sent a staff officer to Manassas for clarification from Jackson. Stonewall instructed Ewell "to feel their strength & if they were in force to fall back to Manassas—not to allow himself to become entangled." Hoping to avoid bringing his main line into a fight, Ewell gave Henry Forno instructions to form a small outpost further south. Forno was to both retard advances from Warrenton and give Ewell enough time to plan his response. The 60-year-old Louisianan quickly sent the 6th and 8th Louisiana about a mile and half south from Bristoe Station to sluggish Kettle Run. The Tigers' instructions were to skirmish with any Federals that might appear from Warrenton Junction but slowly fall back if the enemy appeared overpowering.[29]

Over the course of the first year of the war, Louisiana soldiers serving in the Army of Northern Virginia developed a fearsome reputation that matched their nickname: "Tigers." In particular, the 6th Louisiana developed a reputation as tough fighters in battle and undisciplined soldiers in camp. Recruited from the working classes of New Orleans, the 6th Louisiana contained enough recent immigrants to earn the nickname "Irish Brigade." A Virginian comparing his regiment to that of the 6th remembered, "The command was as unlike my own as it was possible to conceive. Such a congress of nations only the cosmopolitan Crescent City could have sent forth, and the tongues of Babel seemed resurrected in its speech; English, German, French, Spanish, all were represented, to say nothing of Doric brogue and local gumbo." The 469 men in the ranks represented nearly every nation in Europe. The more ordinary 8th Louisiana supplemented the force overlooking Kettle Run.[30]

Likely deployed on either side of the railroad bridge north of Kettle Run, the Tigers looked towards Warrenton Junction. A line of skirmishers forded

29 Jones, *Campbell Brown's Civil War*, 148.

30 Redwood, "Jackson's Foot-Cavalry at the Second Bull Run," *Battles and Leaders of the Civil War*, 2:535.

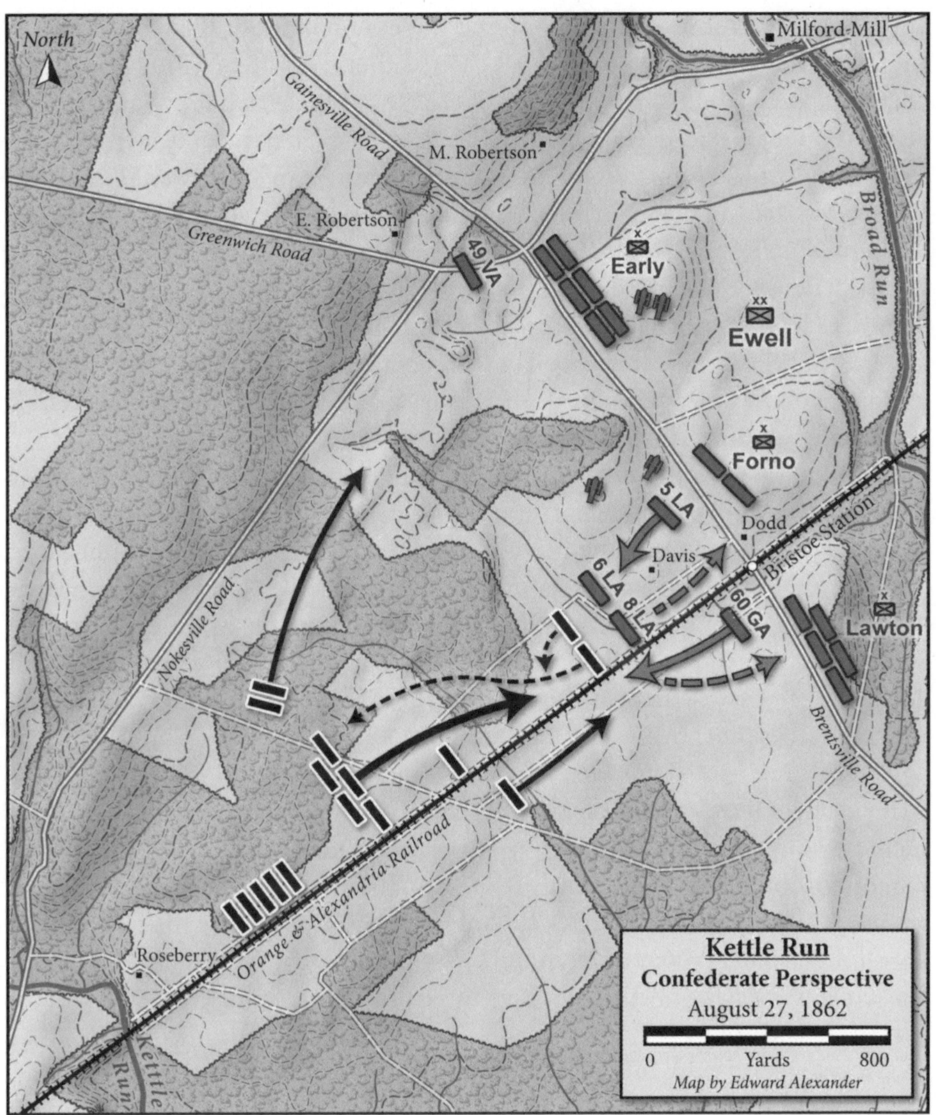

the stream and formed an ad hoc picket post. Soon a force of Federal soldiers of unknown size marched along the railroad. Clashing with the head of the approaching Yankee column, the skirmishers fell back towards the protection of the main battle line north of the stream. To Lt. George Wren of the 8th Louisiana, the crossing of Kettle Run "was about the tightest place we had ever been in. The act of retreating amidst a perfect hail storm of bullets was most alarming to me." Few of Wren's comrades were hit during the retreat and after the last man crossed, a detail set fire to the bridge. As the bridge crashed down into the water in flames, Forno ordered the commander of the 6th Louisiana to "fall back, skirmishing as he went." Retreating from Kettle Run, the Tigers finally stopped about 300 yards short of the main Southern line at Bristoe.[31]

Forno established a new defensive line in a small, dry creek bed edged with scrub brush and some small timber. Adding firepower to his forward line, Ewell ordered the 1st Maryland Artillery to a hill behind the Tigers. The linchpin in this new line, however, was a single regiment and artillery piece. Calculating that the Yankees would advance directly against Forno's men, Ewell ordered the 60th Georgia of Lawton's brigade accompanied by a cannon forward and parallel to the railroad. The final Confederate line resembled an L. An attacker would encounter heavy fire from the front and devastating fire on the flanks. The line set, soldiers from Louisiana, Georgia, and Maryland waited.

Around 2:00 p.m. the head of a Federal column arrived. Unaware of the Confederates directly in their front, the Yankees failed to take precautions, advancing in fragments. When the first regiment approached to within 50 or 60 yards of Forno, the Louisianans fired, followed by the 60th Georgia on their left. In the space of about 10 minutes the lead regiment was nearly destroyed. Serving in the 1st Maryland Light Artillery, Jonathan Scharf was thrilled at the developing scene. From behind Forno, Scharf saw "the damn colors of the Yankees advancing in lines of battles, with their flying rag before them. We know open our [guns] up them and, Oh! What a beautiful sight. We could see shot and shell plow through their crowded ranks and make long lanes, and we shouted with joy."[32]

Those not killed or wounded in the hurricane of fire "ran like turkeys." A second regiment arrived on the field but was driven to a small swell in front of the 8th Louisiana. Protected from the fire of both the Tigers and the Georgians, a prolonged firefight broke out along the battlefield, producing few casualties but much smoke.[33]

Approximately 15 minutes into the firefight with the concealed enemy, a new line appeared. Emerging from the woods that bordered the southern section of the battlefield appeared another Yankee regiment. The approaching line moved in fits and starts, with some parts appearing to struggle to remain abreast with the moving line. To an observant soldier, the small nuisances in the

31 George Wren Diary, Emory University; George P. Ring Diary, Tulane University, Howard-Tilton Library.

32 Tom Kelly, ed., *The Personal Memoirs of Jonathan Thomas Scharf of the First Maryland Artillery* (Baltimore, 1993), 37–38.

33 Jones, *Campbell Brown's Civil War*, 148.

enemy line, along with the number of officers, comprised the telltale signs of a brigade maneuvering. After a few moments finalizing the line's orientation, the Federals advanced and "with a yell attempted a charge upon our line, but before they had passed half across the field were met by a murderous fire from our ranks that caused them to halt."[34]

The infusion of an enemy brigade equalized the Union battle line facing Forno, but the Southerners still possessed advantages. Except for the one regiment laying behind the swell, most of the Union soldiers remained exposed in an open field. The slight streambed protected Forno's men from small arms fire. The 60th Georgia along the railroad poured a continuous fire into the enemy's right flank. After about 20 minutes of trading fire, the enemy sent two small regiments from its left to reinforce a deteriorating right flank. Protected by cuts and embankments along the track, the Georgians were likewise protected from much of the enemy's musketry.

The battle transformed into a contest of trading volleys with the enemy. Before leaving Jeffersonton on the 24th, each man in Jackson's command was issued 40 rounds for his musket. The few wagons accompanying Jackson's march consisted mainly of ambulances, medical supply wagons, and wagons carrying extra ammunition. Unless more could be captured, Jackson's Wing would be reliant on this supply for the foreseeable future. Forno's men fired a few volleys during the initial capture of Bristoe on the evening of the 26th. Before setting off to Kettle Run, Forno ensured that each member in the 6th and 8th Louisiana carried the standard 40 rounds on his person.

The skirmishing earlier by Kettle Run combined with the current battle reduced the ammunition in the Tigers' ranks to critical levels. During the fighting, Forno's two regiments fired nearly 36,000 rounds. Soon men were scrounging for extra ammunition in the cartridge boxes of the handful of killed and wounded that littered their line. Faced with the possibility that the main line might run out of ammunition, Forno faced a difficult decision. Detachments from the 6th and 8th Louisiana could be sent to the wagon train to retrieve more crates of ammunition to distribute to the men in the creek bed. This would take time. A more expedient option was sending in another regiment from his brigade to maintain fire on the Federals. Packing more men into a narrow creek bed produced confusion as the three regiments slowly degenerated into one large mass of soldiers.

The risk of the main line running out of ammunition forced Forno's hand. The 5th Louisiana soon advanced into the ranks of their comrades in the 6th and

34 Ring Diary, Tulane University.

8th regiments. The battle neared a tipping point by the time the 5th Louisiana arrived at the battle line. Within 30 minutes of engaging the enemy, the entire Confederate line began pulling back, evacuating Bristoe Station.

As the 5th Louisiana went in, the 60th Georgia began pulling out. The fire coming from the Georgians drew considerable attention from the enemy. Shifting regiments across the battlefield to eliminate the threat posed by the Georgians had thus far proved futile. A new Federal regiment appeared on the battlefield, marching up the flank of the Georgians and towards their rear. The left flank of the Georgians shifted their fire towards this new threat. Through the haze of the musketry smoke it appeared the enemy continued his advance before disappearing into a woodlot. Officers and men nervously scanned their left flank. The Federals soon reappeared and both regiments fired nearly simultaneous volleys. Appreciating their rapidly deteriorating position, the 60th Georgia abandoned the railroad and retreated to the safety of the main Confederate line. Amid the greatest danger of the day, an unlikely ally aided the Georgians. A newly arrived enemy force mistook the Federals firing into the retreating Georgians as part of the Confederate line and fired into the backs of their comrades a little further afield. During the five or ten minutes it took to rectify the situation the 60th Georgia escaped back to the protection of the main line.[35]

Another threat soon emerged on the other side of the line. A battery of artillery supported by at least two regiments of infantry appeared opposite the right of Ewell's main line. A small rise screened by trees prevented the artillery shelling the right and rear of Forno's position. Instead Ewell's main battle line became the center of attention. Shot and shell flew over the heads of the prone soldiers but soon the artillerists got the range and shell began to explode in both Early's and Lawton's brigades. The fight had now reached its culminating point.

Thus far Ewell gave Forno a free hand to conduct the battle as he saw fit. The largest contribution Ewell made to the battle was adding the firepower of the Georgians and the 1st Maryland Artillery to the fight. Keeping an eye out on the rest of the field, to an experienced commander such as Ewell, the Confederates now faced at least a division from Pope's army. The threat to both flanks warranted a decision. Ewell could either reinforce his forward line with more regiments, have the forward line fall back towards the main line, or initiate a withdrawal behind Broad Run.

35 David Donald, ed., *Gone for the Soldier: The Civil War Memoirs of Private Alfred Bellard* (New York, 1975), 130.

Fortunately, Ewell had clear orders from Jackson: defend the destruction of the railroad bridge over Broad Run, but do not bring on a general engagement with the enemy. The fighting had progressed well over two hours, allowing the engineers to complete their task. Holding explicit orders to fight a rear-guard action, Ewell had only one realistic choice: fall back towards Jackson at Manassas.

Disengaging from the enemy was hazardous. If the enemy learned of the evacuation, a sudden charge could throw the retreat into a route. Happily for the Confederates, during the day's fighting the Southerners appeared to severely hurt their enemy. When Forno evacuated his three regiments, a cheer emerged from the Federals. Content to claim victory by holding possession of the battlefield after such a bloodletting, the Federals were content to allow Ewell to pull back almost unmolested.

The fighting around Bristoe Station soon acquired the name of the battle of Kettle Run. Holding his division in reserve, Ewell had effectively held off a division of the enemy with just four regiments and a few cannons. The limited number of soldiers directly engaged in the fighting limited Ewell's casualties. During the fighting from Kettle Run to Broad Run, 34 soldiers were killed, 132 men were wounded, and 5 went missing. The majority of the wounded were evacuated via ambulance. Looking over the field, Forno estimated that the enemy lost about 80 killed and 200 wounded, with a disproportionate number of officers lost. If true, Forno not only succeeded in his mission but also mauled an enemy division in the process. Fulfilling his mission, Ewell traced the route Taliaferro and Hill took to Manassas Junction. When Ewell's men arrived most of the supplies had already been consumed, leaving slim pickings for his division. Around evening the tail end of Ewell's Division arrived, reuniting Jackson's Wing once again.[36]

As successful as this day had been, Jackson likely realized the dangerous strategic situation he faced. The battles of Bull Run Bridge and Kettle Run highlighted the stark reality that Jackson was in the middle of the Federal army. Although today's Federal attacks were weak and uncoordinated, Jackson could not expect his opponent to remain clumsy. If Jackson remained at Manassas for an extended time, he could expect attacks from both his front and rear and possibly having his link with Lee and the rest of the Confederate army severed. Staying at Manassas was not a realistic option for an experienced commander such as Jackson.

Jackson had only one viable option after reviewing the situation: move his wing west back towards the Bull Run Mountains. Positioning his command near

36 *OR* 12, pt. 2, 716–718.

the Bull Run Mountains gave Jackson the chance to attack a portion of the Federal army while it was in marching column. With luck, the Confederates could maul the Federals before they could properly react to the threat. Moving towards the mountains would also bring Jackson closer to the rest of Lee's army then taking Jackson's route to Thoroughfare Gap. To be successful, Jackson needed to sow confusion in Pope's mind about his destination. It was imperative that Jackson move from Manassas to his new position on the night of August 27–28.

Appreciating the necessity to move positions quickly, Jackson needed to decide what to do with the remaining supplies at Manassas. One of the principal reasons Jackson's Wing was in Manassas was the dearth of wagons needed to transport the supplies to Bristoe Station. A Virginian remembered that the Confederates "had no wagon train with us, [except] ordnance wagons, medical wagons, and ambulances." The additional 54 captured wagons greatly increased Jackson's logistical tail. He could now transport more supplies, but the wagons also slowed his command. Attempting to split the difference, the wagons would be used but then split up on the march to prevent a massive traffic jam on the road.[37]

The first order of business was the loading of supplies onto the wagons. As one soldier remembered, soon the "wagons are loaded with all that they can haul." Experienced with shortages, many soldiers were loath to see perfectly adequate piles of food and clothing burned for lack of transport. With the wagons full, some Southerners became creative. Food was deemed the priority over other comforts such as clothing and soon bags of food were collected and packed onto the backs of many of the horses pulling the wagons, artillery caissons, and cannon.[38]

The packing almost complete, soldiers were permitted nearly total access to the remaining stores. As one soldier remembered, everyone was "at liberty to take all they wanted except the sutler stores, which were kept under guard for the officers." After sifting through the piles of supplies looking for the last spoils of war, everything that remained was ordered destroyed.[39]

The resulting conflagration forever burned into the minds of those who witnessed it. As the head of Jackson's column started to move out of Manassas, detailed soldiers were instructed to set fire to the warehouses and trains left in town. A Georgian in Hill's Division gleefully told his wife "I witnessed the

37 Casler, *Four Years in the Stonewall Brigade*, 106.

38 Edgar, *My Reminiscences of the Civil War*, 84.

39 Casler, *Four Years in the Stonewall Brigade*, 107.

Although taken four months earlier during the first evacuation of Manassas by the Confederate army, destruction returned to the junction with Jackson's Wing. *Library of Congress*

burning" of the town and a "train of cars nearly a mile long." In a letter to his hometown newspaper a soldier estimated "We destroyed millions of property at Manassas. I counted 45 cars in one train crammed with every imaginable article of use or luxury." An astute artillerist wrote in a letter home "as the magnificent conflagration began to subside the Stonewall or 1st Division moved off towards the Battlefield of Manassas."[40]

40 Lowe and Hodges, *Letters to Amanda*, 24; *Lexington Post*, Sep. 11, 1862; Chamberlayne, *Ham Chamberlayne- Virginian*, 100.

Chapter 16

"Where Is Jackson"

Virginia: August 1862

While the volunteers in the Wisconsin and Indiana regiments drilled, squabbled, pressed their letter campaigns for promotions, and nursed troubled fears of what would come, outside events were occurring. With the Army of the Potomac inactive at Harrison's Landing near Richmond, there was a belief in Washington that the Rebels might attempt to concentrate in central Virginia. The burning question of the day was whether Confederate General T. J. Jackson, famous for his successful campaign in the Shenandoah Valley, and his command were again on the move and, where was he? As a result, elements of Rufus King's division were given the assignment to mount a series of marches and patrols to determine if the Confederates were already concentrating in central Virginia.

On August 5, General Gibbon led a foray to the Virginia Central Railroad. The column included the 2nd and 7th Wisconsin and 19th Indiana along with Battery B of the 4th U.S. Artillery, his old command, and elements of the 3rd Indiana Cavalry. "I think our force went out the telegraph road simply for the purpose of keeping off any force which might happen to be in the neighborhood of the railroad," Pvt. Hank Gaylord of the 19th Indiana wrote in a long letter to his hometown newspaper. There were several clashes with enemy cavalry the first day, he said, then, on the second day the weather turned hot and many of the infantrymen dropped out overcome by the heat. "When we got to the place where the artillery was stationed only 16 men were in ranks in our company and not over 150 or 200 in the whole regiment, the 2d and 7th Wisconsin regiments were no better off than the 19th."

The next day the Union force was ordered forward with the cavalry scouring the woods in all directions for four or five miles. "We marched till noon that day when the cavalry thought they saw signs of a considerable force getting in our rear," Gaylord reported. The cavalry skirmished on and off the rest of the day and into the evening. The next day they marched to Spotsylvania Court House and camped there one night before returning to Fredericksburg. "I don't know but we gained considerable by the expedition, but I can not see it in that light, as all of them were not able to go on with us the second day were taken prisoners, together with a train of forage wagons which came out after grain." Gibbon's losses were put at 59, most of them exhausted soldiers who were left behind and captured by Confederate cavalry.[1]

Another detachment under Colonel Cutler, including the 6th Wisconsin along with soldiers of the Harris Light Cavalry and a section of the 1st New Hampshire Battery, moved toward Frederick Hall Station. Cutler's force reached Frederick's Hall Station by the North Anna River, occupying the town, destroying Confederate supplies, and wrecking two miles of railroad track. By August 8, however, Gibbon's brigade was again assembled at Fredericksburg with not a lot to show for the two expeditions. Cutler's men boasted they had marched 90 miles in the heat over a three-and-a-half-day period.

The hot sultry August weather thinned the reconnoitering columns. Private William Ray of the 7th Wisconsin, left in camp due to a fever and severe outbreak of oak or poison ivy sores, watched his regiment march off on one reconnaissance. The regiment was not gone long, he wrote in his journal, when weary stragglers began stumbling into camp. One of them was a distraught Louis Kuntz, who brought news of a near escape from the Rebel horsemen and the capture of several Black Hats. He and a soldier from the 19th Indiana, he said, were played out and spent the night at a farmhouse. They were eating breakfast prepared by a woman at the house when a squad of Confederate cavalry rode up and surrounded a wagon full of worn-out boys from the 2nd Wisconsin that was just passing. Kuntz and the Indiana boy ran for it out of the house, but the Hoosier stopped when ordered and was captured. Kuntz made his way into the woods with bullets flying around him and hid out.

"He said all those along the road was taken prisoner & that not being a few," Ray wrote in his journal that night. "They took all of our provisions train but three wagons before coming up to this house. They just cleaned up everything that was behind the main body of troops." Later that night, it was learned, many of the supply wagons had been retaken.[2]

1 Nolan, *Iron Brigade*, 66–69; Otis, *Second Wisconsin*, 50–54; Hank Gaylord to *Steuben* [Angola, IN] *Republican*, Sep. 13, 1862.

2 Ray, *Iron Brigade*, 125–126. Kuntz was killed at Antietam Sep. 17, 1862. *Wisconsin Roster*, vol. 1, 560.

The regiment itself finally returned to camp on August 8. Ray described the scene in his journal: "A couple of the boys have come in bringing the news of the Regt coming in soon. Here some two or three more boys come. There some more. Well, they coming in separately, every man for himself. Here Cap comes with two or three more and they kept coming in for an hour." Ray gathered up buckets of water for the soldiers. "They complain of being tired & sore all over, some lame and some one thing and some another complaint. They have had plenty to eat but hard marching and not much rest and very little sleep." The soldiers threw themselves on the ground and slept for two or three hours only to awake up extremely stiff. "It being warm dry weathers all the time and the dust intolerable and scarcity of water and the excitement at times & doublequicking some, and altogether it was a wonder that some of our Co didn't die."[3]

After a day of resting and some preparation, the Black Hat Brigade was again given orders to "strike tents and fall in" and be prepared to march to reinforce a Union force under Gen. Nathaniel Banks which was some 80 miles away and facing a large Confederate force on the Rapidan River west of Fredericksburg. Some of the sick were sent off to Washington by train. In the 7th Wisconsin, there was a delay to fix a mix-up getting the knapsacks of the men loaded into wagons. A Wisconsin soldier said there was some grumbling about the haste. "McDowell was therefore hiked to saddle," he reported, "and the boys hustled out into line with bitter denunciations and a lame face, seriously deprecating the authority which allotted them no cessation of duty for recuperation."[4]

The 1,900 officers and men were soon on the road. The thick column moved quickly over dusty roads under a "scorching" sun and heat "like a great hot sponge, which sucked the moisture out of every poor of the soldier's body." The ambulances were quickly filled with "sick or given out men." Water was soon gone. "When a streamlet or spring was reached," one volunteer observed, "it was lined with eager soldiers scraping the muddle bottom with cups in order to provide for their exhausted canteens." The hours passed slowly, and the road had no end. Swept by rain at one point, the soldiers "were soon over shoe top deep with soft mud." The column halted for a time to wait out the wet weather. Private Chester Wyman of the 6th Wisconsin looked for a place for a quick nap. He found a rise in the ground and soon was asleep despite the rain. When he awoke, he discovered he was in a graveyard and sleeping on a grave.

3 Ray, *Iron Brigade*, 127–128; Otis, *Second Wisconsin*, 53–55.

4 Judson, letter, Oct. 21, 1877.

The column reached the Rappahannock River at Kelly's Ford at dusk. The bridge was out. Under a rising bright moon, the soldiers took off trousers, tucked up shirts, and holding muskets and cartridge boxes high, pushed waist deep into the river, stepping from stone to stone. Some of the soldiers without under drawers were naked from the waist down and the moonlight made their bare legs seem almost white. As the 19th Indiana passed over the river, one half-naked soldier presented himself to Colonel Meredith, who was sitting on his horse nearby watching. The soldier told the tall officer that he wanted to show off the perfect fit and durability of the "uniform" he had been wearing the past 22 years. Long Sol laughed out loud. The crossing was generally marked with friendly catcalls, an officer said, and "now and then, when a poor devil slipped from the stone and went, ca-souse, into the water, a great cry went up." On the other side, the soldiers marched a short distance, then halted to spread out wet clothes and sleep for the rest of the night. Distance marched: 20 miles.[5]

The night was somber. During the day, word reached the marching column that there had been a battle at Cedar Mountain "and that our folks was whipped and all kinds of rumors," one Badger wrote in his journal. In ranks and around the coffee fires, it was said that the large force of Confederates was apparently dispatched from Richmond to threaten the two Union divisions at Cedar Mountain. The Federals, expecting to be reinforced, attacked the larger Confederate force, and were defeated. The brigade of Wisconsin and Indiana men was part of a force rushed to Cedar Mountain.

When the Federal column arrived near the scene of the fighting, the battleground and flags of truce could be seen off to the south on high ground some distance away. In ranks, word spread that Union forces under Banks had been defeated and forced to retreat by Confederates under a "General Jackson," who was gaining a powerful reputation. Banks was outnumbered but attacked the Confederates anyway and after heavy fighting fell back to an earlier defensive position.

In the 7th Wisconsin, Private Ray, sick and exhausted, observed in his journal: "Well now we knew what the forced march was for and didn't regret it any although the complaints were loud about soreness and sleepiness." Wines and whiskey meant for medicinal purposes proved a problem. The officers

5 Otis, *Second Wisconsin*, 54; Ray, *Iron Brigade*, 128; Cheek and Pointon, *Sauk County*, 30; Chester A. Wyman, letter, May 28, 1918, private collection; Edward Bragg to Earl Rogers, Apr. 3, 1900, Jerome Watrous Papers, WHS; Gaff, *Bloody Fields*, 149. The number of 1,937 for Gibbon's brigade can be found in Alan Gaff, *Brave Men's Tears: The Iron Brigade at Brawner Farm* (Dayton, OH, 1983), 157. He credited the 2nd Wisconsin with 430; the 6th Wisconsin, 504; 7th Wisconsin, 580, and the 19th Indiana, 433.

drank up the spirits, Ray noted, and "doctors are so drunk they can hardly sit on their horses and they don't notice the poor fellows that are lying by the roadside panting and feeling as if they don't care whether they live or die for such is their feelings." Even the second lieutenant of his company was so tight that "he could walk and that was all and was perfectly foolish which I hated to see."[6]

The tired Wisconsin and Indiana men covered 45 miles and went into bivouac near the battlefield. It had been some of the hardest days so far, according to two of the Sauk County men: "Weather muggy, hot, no rest except to make coffee, wading streams, marching in mud very little rations (hardtack tasted good those days)." Other brigades in King's division were much thinned by worn out soldiers who fell behind. "Straggling became almost a mania, some regiments not being able to account for half their men," one Badger observed, adding: "Our regiments had comparatively no stragglers, not through the immediate influence of the officer alone, but a feeling of personal responsibility, each man for the man whose elbow he touched in ranks, and the responsive thought, 'I must not fail myself in the duty I demand of my comrade.'" General Gibbon rode ahead to look at the battlefield and "discovered evidence of a severe struggle, but from what I could learn it was not a very decisive one."

Captain Edward Brown in the 6th Wisconsin told his father in a letter two days later that General Pope "was so badly scared that on the night we arrived he caused all the stores everything belonging to the army to be shipped on the R.R. He expected to be attacked as Jackson was large reinforced." There was also some good news. The 3rd Wisconsin, which had been in the battle, was found camped alongside the roadway. As they approached, someone by a fire called out, "What regiment, boys?" Told it was the 7th Wisconsin, there was laughter, and a few cheers then questions about this man and who belonged to each regiment. "They were very glad to see us and us to see them. They said we were the only Wisconsin boys they had seen in the service. A great many found friends."

Brown also reported that the 3rd Wisconsin "suffered greatly in the fight but no mention is made of it. N.Y. & Penn Reporters monopolize all the glory for their own State troops, although they never do as well as the New England & Western troops—The marches made by our Regt. were the longest & most severe made this century. We cut off Jackson's Communications with Richmond & then marched here to help whip him, and the Sixth Wis. never even got a

6 Ray, *Iron Brigade*, 129.

Newspaper puff for it. Two New York Regts. who acted as our support 30 miles in our rear got all the newspaper Credit for what we did."[7]

Brown's obvious pride in the brigade's accomplishments is evident in the further detailed account he included:

> Our division arrived at this point [Cedar Mountain] just after the battle. We made a forced march to get here at that. Before that we had been out on an expedition to Frederick Hall Station on the Va. Central Rail Road. The Sixth Wis., did all that was done. The balance of the expedition failed. We tore up the track for miles and blowed up two Culverts, burned the Depot, and destroyed the commissary stores & other confederate property including 1,400 sacks of flour. . . . [W]e made a forced march of 39 *miles* crossing the branch of the Pamunkey, which was not fordable, going 10 miles beyond the Bridge over it. And only left a guard of 100 men who were tired out to guard it. On our retreat we burned the Bridge which was a wooden structure 150 long & 70 feet above the water. We think we did a big thing. We marched 102 miles in 3 ½ days, accomplishing a good deal. As above stated, had no support within 30 miles hardly slept or eat during the time, rested one night & half a day, were ordered peremptorily to march here.[8]

The regiments set up picket lines and established camps. That night, Sgt. John Johnson of the 6th Wisconsin, was making the rounds when he came upon a badly shaken Pvt. Dennis Kelly. "Sergeant," Kelly told Johnson, "I have seen ghosts of spirits." Kelly was a steady, young fellow and well known to the sergeant as being truthful. He told him to be quiet and he would examine the case. Johnson started in the direction of the field and marched directly to the nearest point where he found a dead body, "interred very shallow, and a phosphorescent light oscillating from the head to the foot of the corpse. And so it proved in every instance." Johnson puzzled over the cause and concluded it was a warm, sultry night and the reason for the light was due to some gas from the decaying bodies. Some of the corpses were covered so slightly, he noticed, that the head and feet protruded under the sod.

The battlefield was a horror for the untested soldiers as they looked it over the next day. "There is plenty of the Rebells that is barried So Shallow that their

7 Theron W. Haight, "King's Division: Fredericksburg to Manassas," *War Papers*, Vol. 2 (Milwaukee, 1896), 348; J. O. Johnson, "Army Reminiscences," *Telegraph*, Nov. 30, 1884; Gibbon, *Recollections*, 43; Cheek and Pointon, *Sauk County*, 30. Johnson served in the 6th Wisconsin.

8 Gibbon, *Recollections*, 43; George Eustice, letter, undated; Ray, *Iron Brigade*, 129; Brown to his father, Aug. 13, 1862.

hands & feet is Sticking out & Some places there is So many in one hole & since they have Swelled their Shoulders or hips are above the ground & the maggots are all over them. It creates a dreadful Smell. There is plenty of peaces of arms legs & all parts of men Scattered over the field," one of the 19th Indiana men wrote home. Two Wisconsin soldiers said the fallen soldiers were buried so shallow "that the tops of the trenches were moving like gentle waves with living corruption." They also could distinguish between the scent of dead animals and human beings in the state of decomposition. The human was very much more offensive than the animal. Private Hugh Perkins of the 7th Wisconsin wrote to a friend that "it looks hard to see men buried like a lot of hogs, 12 to 15 together. But I suppose they feel as well as though they [had] ever so nice a grave and coffin. We had nothing to brag about in this fight." Lieutenant John Shafer of the 19th Indiana wrote of "the piles of dead horses upon both sides, the remnants of arms, accoutrements and clothing, the fresh soil covering the remains of the fallen, were silent but melancholy evidence of the deadly conflict."[9]

The Black Hats spent a week near the battlefield, much of the time building cremation fires for the dead horses sprawled everywhere. The word making the round in ranks was that Confederate Jackson and his men had fallen back behind the Rappahannock River, and that General Pope reported to Washington that the enemy was "in full retreat towards Richmond, complete[ly] demoralized." One Wisconsin soldier complained bitterly that Pope compelled the army "to remain encamped more than a week during the hottest part of the year, on the battle field, subject to the overpowering stench of decaying horses and half buried bodies, when fifteen minutes march would have placed them in adjoining grove of timber where they would have shelter from the sun and have plenty of good water, and be removed from the filth and unwholesomeness of the battle field." A Wisconsin officer observed, "The battle field has its allurements and excitement but not so after it is over."[10]

Despite the stench and sickening work, however, appetites remained good. "Today the boys took everything they wanted if they could find it such as horses, mules, chickens, ducks & geese & honey which there was a plenty," Private Ray wrote in his journal, while another Badger reported that "the officers, though

9 Johnson, *Telegraph*, Nov. 30, 1884; Joshua Jones, letter, Aug. 18, 1862, *The Civil War Letters of Joshua Jones*, ed. Eugene H. Berwanger, *Indiana Magazine of History* (Sep. 1992): 230; Cheek and Pointon, *Sauk County*, 31; Dawes, *Service*, 56; "Letters of a Civil War Soldier," ed. Marilyn Gardner, prepared for syndication, Apr. 9, 1983, *Christian Science Monitor*, letter, Aug. 17, 1863; Gaff, *Bloody Field*, 150. Kelly would be wounded at Laurel Hill and die June 23, 1864. He was buried at Arlington National Cemetery. *Roster*, vol. 1, 526.

10 Young to wife, Aug. 10, 1862, *Dear Delia*, 86; Sullivan, *Telegraph*, Nov. 4, 1883.

against this, acted as if they didn't see anything. Only when it got to bad they raised hell with the soldiers." In one Badger company, the men simply said that "it was here not a question of what you should eat, but what you could get."[11]

The Wisconsin and Indiana boys were much changed from the awkward greenhorn patriots who tramped away from home in 1861. Just weeks before Cedar Mountain, in writing a friend, a Wisconsin officer explained that the "cowards have been sifted out of the ranks, and the huge talking men, the braggarts, and boasters have gone home. The men who are left are real warriors, and not the holiday party that you saw us when we went away." His 2nd Wisconsin was thinned by hard service, he said, but "I think what there are left of us are made of the 'real ould stuff'. I don't think it would be safe for any disease as the cholera, smallpox, or typhoid fever to attack us single-handed. Perhaps take the three combined they might make us sick—nothing more; for nothing short of a Minie [ball] can kill us, or we should have been dead ere this." Another Black Hat said that "we have some hard boys, I admit that; but when they get where there [is] any secesh they are not afraid."[12]

Gibbon's brigade crossed the Rappahannock near the Orange and Alexandria Railroad on August 20. "We had been hunting the rebels, and now we were trying to keep them away from us," one private wrote home. Gibbon found chaos: "Wagon-trains, Divisions, Brigades, and Regiments were all mixed up, apparently in the most inextricable confusion, nobody seeming to know where to [go] and where anyone else was, and there was such a total absence of all order and authority as to produce a most painful impression of the mind." The officers were slow to regain control and the soldiers could see troubling clouds of dust rising on roads opposite the river in such a way that "we could trace the advance of the rebel army." The next day a Confederate artillery battery swung into action and fired across the river. Union guns responded and soon silenced the opposing guns "showing a better practice and more accurate shooting."

The untested Western fellows "had never heard a rebel cannon before, but had been kept well posted about the 'black flags' and 'railroad' iron of the rebels by the warlike editors at home, and thinking that nothing else could make such unearthly screams, they said the 'greybacks were slinging railroad iron.'"

During all this, the 6th Wisconsin was marched behind the Federal guns in range of the Confederate artillery. As the line came into the open, the

11 Ray, *Iron Brigade*, 129; Cheek and Pointon, *Sauk County*, 31.

12 Kellogg, *Telegraph*, Sep. 26, 1879; Charles Dow, "Wartime Letters of Charles C. Dow, Co. G, 2d Wisconsin," in Otis, *Second Wisconsin*, 146 (originally in Wisconsin State register, July 5, 1862); Edwin R. Hancock, *Columbus* [WI] *Weekly Journal*, Jan. 22, 1862.

Confederates turned their fire full upon the regiment. The shells whizzed and burst over and around them, but the men marched steadily, keeping their places, new black hats held high and proudly. They soon learned that "a discreet and respectful obeisance to a cannon ball is no indication of cowardice."[13] A private in the 7th Wisconsin was distressed because he was cooking "some very fat pork" using his plate and a split stick when the order was given to fall back. It was the first salt meat he had had in the past week. A skirmish line of 6th Wisconsin men was thrown out at one point and shots exchanged. Several Rebels were wounded, and a lieutenant and two privates captured.

Toward evening, the 6th Wisconsin was again ordered to the river. A Rebel battery opened fire and Colonel Cutler halted and carefully, according to all regulations, established guides, and alignments before he would allow his soldiers to lie down. "You must get used to it," he said to the men around him. The cannonade did little damage, except for one bounding cannon ball which hit the colonel's mess chest and Cutler, who seemingly had been an indifferent spectator, ordered the regiment to "fall in" and he marched it about a length to one side, out of the line of fire. No one was injured. Two of the Sauk County boys noted that "the experience was valuable in showing the men that artillery fire was not so dangerous as they (or the officers) had anticipated." From the 19th Indiana, however, came the sad report that a shell killed two horses, including one owned by Lt. Col. Alois Bachman and the other "Bet," the fast mare which won all the races on the Fourth of July at Fredericksburg.[14]

The Black Hats received "several good shellings" over the next two days. On the 25th, King's division moved toward Warrenton but was slowed by enemy artillery and skirmishers. The next day, King's division was ordered to "march with the utmost haste" to Centreville. The marching Black Hats watched clouds of dust from beyond the river and said to one another that the Confederates believed to be under General Jackson had somehow gotten between Pope's Army of Virginia and Washington.

Word also reached the marching column that four days prior, Pope's wagon park had been attacked at Catlett's Station by Rebel cavalry which took prisoners and captured dispatches and baggage, including one of the commanding general's uniforms. The 21 wagons of Gibbon's brigade, however, had been successfully defended by the wagon guard along with the sick and lame soldiers left behind.

13 Cheek and Pointon, *Sauk County*, 36; Cook, *Telegraph*, Apr. 8, 1883; Dawes, *Service*, 46, 56–47; Sullivan, *Telegraph*, Oct. 21, 1882.

14 Dawes, *Service*, 57; Brown to his father, Sep. 5, 1862; Sullivan, *Telegraph*, Oct. 21, 1882; Cheek and Pointon, *Sauk County*, 35; Ray, *Iron Brigade*, 134.

The Wisconsin men had put up a small tent and were inside getting ready to sleep when the first shots were fired. "Blow out the lights," someone shouted. When they got out of their tents, several bullets passed over their heads, and someone raised the alarm: "Rebels! Rebels!"

The attack came at midnight during a thunderstorm and the 400 horsemen had to "climb over" a railroad track. At about three rods the Union soldiers under and around the wagons fired. The volleys by the 60 guards and a shower of stones thrown by the wounded and sick men turned back four attempts to rush the wagons although one cavalryman got close enough to slash the hand of one Badger with a saber.[15]

The view in the ranks involving the latest developments, however, was that all confidence in Pope's abilities was lost and it was "openly remarked in that McDowell was a traitor."[16] To add to the uncertainty was Gibbon's chance meeting with two Old Army friends—John Reynolds and George Meade. The two were just up from the Army of the Potomac as part of the reinforcements being sent to Pope. Meade said he had asked Pope what he was doing out at Manassas Junction, telling him, "This is no place for the army. It should fall back so as to meet the rest of the Army of the Potomac coming up and by superior forces overwhelm Lee." The general had little to say other than he had orders from Washington to hold the Rappahannock line for two days and by that time McClellan's men would be on hand. Pope sourly added that the 48 hours had passed and the "reinforcements had not arrived."[17]

The Western men now had been in the service for a year and some weeks. The long, uncertain road of civil war had first taken them to the sprawling Washington camps where McClellan purged the volunteer company command structures of the ill-prepared and immigrant officers and taught the men in ranks about soldierly bearing and military drill. The next stretch of the road was Fredericksburg in central Virginia where a new brigade commander—John Gibbon—made the independent and frisky backwoods boys wear leggings and white gloves and gave them a new uniform. The tall black hats made them

15 Dawes, *Service*, 57–58; Frank A. Haskell to his brothers and sisters, Sep. 22, 1862; *Wisconsin State Register*, Oct. 4, 1862; Cheek and Pointon, *Sauk County*, 32; *Soldiers and Citizens' Album of Biographical Record*, vol. 2 (Chicago, 1892), 722; Ray, *Iron Brigade*, 134. The account was that of Francis Deleglise of Co. E, 6th Wisconsin.

16 Sullivan, *Telegraph*, Nov. 4, 1883

17 Gibbon, *Recollections*, 47–48. Gibbon said the exchange between Meade and Pope demonstrated that Pope was "lacking in that sort of independence of character which not only prompts but enables an army commander to do on the spot that which he knows the exigencies require, independent of orders received from superiors at a distance and ignorant of the situation."

recognizable on drill field or in camp. They never took easy to the leggings or to the discipline, but Gibbon's steady training, they realized, turned them into better soldiers.

Indiana and Wisconsin now seemed far off and distant to the volunteers, with home a faded memory caught in a clutch of treasured letters and pictures. The soldiers were loyal to the other men around their cook fires and their company and even their regiment and the brigade. They still grumbled those days over the hated Gibbon and his Old Army ways and worried that the Lincoln administration would undo what had been accomplished with unnecessary political posturing and maneuvering. The volunteers were fiercely loyal to the Union, troubled about the whole matter of slavery and what to do about it, homesick, and worried the war might end without them getting a chance to strike a blow. The Westerners had marched here and there the past month, stood artillery fire, and now the long road, started so many months before, would take them past a rolling farm field not far from where the battle of Bull Run was fought in July 1861.

Chapter 17

"He Did Not Tell Ewell Where to Go"

Sudley Springs: August 28, 1862

The raid at Manassas became legendary in the Army of Northern Virginia. As important as the raid was, it involved only a third of Lee's army. Starting with Jackson's men in Manassas, Lee's army formed a crescent, with Lee and Longstreet south of the Rappahannock River and the rest of the army guarding Richmond. Depending on the movement of the Army of the Potomac, Lee faced the prospect of either reuniting his entire army or fighting the second major campaign in his career with just two-thirds of his strength.

Retaining the initiative over the Yankees, Lee decided to use whatever part of the army remained in central Virginia to suppress Pope. Using two-thirds of an already outnumbered army entailed risks, but Lee continued to sift through intelligence reports and believed he had an accurate picture of Federal positions and numbers. Reviewing captured letters, Lee pegged Pope's army at around 45,000, soon to be augmented by Burnside's men from Fredericksburg. The wildcard remained George McClellan and his Army of the Potomac. New reports of Fitz John Porter's corps of McClellan's army in Northern Virginia could presage a change of base of the main Federal army or it could just be a detachment, with McClellan and the rest of his army waiting at Harrison's Landing for an opening to the Confederate capital. Lee convinced himself that Porter was the advance of McClellan's army rather than just a detachment. The brigades of McLaws's and D. H. Hill's Divisions still around Richmond were ordered to be put in readiness to move to the Rappahannock river line.[1]

Prior to Richmond garrison marching to join the rest of the army, Lee detailed a portion of his staff to explore the feasibility of feeding and supplying a reunited Army of Northern Virginia in its namesake area. Although he

1 Dowdey and Manarin, *Wartime Papers of R. E. Lee*, 263.

expected difficulties in the beginning, Lee believed they would be "softened as we advance." The combined army could at least be reasonably fed and supplied. If it could not, there would be little reason to bring the rest of the army north from Richmond.[2]

Until McLaws and D. H. Hill returned to Lee, President Davis still had the possibility of recalling the nine brigades back to Richmond, if a new threat appeared. The time-consuming route from Richmond to the Rappahannock gave the president ample time to recall these troops if he deemed it necessary. The first leg of the journey required marching north of Richmond to Hanover Junction and the Virginia Central Railroad. Boarding trains, the divisions would journey over 40 miles to Gordonsville, transferring to the Orange and Alexandria Railroad for the short journey to Culpepper. From Culpepper McLaws and Hill had to march the remaining distance to Lee's army, depending on its current location. By 1862 the Southern railway system was deteriorating rapidly, with trains routinely traveling well under their prewar speed to minimize wear and tear on equipment and tracks. A conservative estimate of about a week's travel from Richmond to Lee's army meant that Lee could expect to fight the present campaign with the forces he presently had.

Expecting the eventual concentration of his army, Lee returned his focus to the Federals in northern Virginia. Following the August 24 meeting, Lee started to have reservations about the success of Jackson's flank march. Initially Jackson set off with a single cavalry regiment to both screen the marching column and to secure important crossroads and gaps crucial for the success of Jackson's march. On the night of August 25 Lee recognized his error in giving Jackson just one cavalry regiment. Summoning Stuart to his headquarters again, Lee instructed the young commander to "accompany the movement of Major-General Jackson, already begun" with his entire cavalry division. Lee's decision to concentrate his mounted arm with Jackson contributed to victories at Bristoe Station, Manassas Junction, and Bull Run Bridge, but stripped Longstreet of cavalry. It was imperative that Jackson both maintain a constant stream of couriers to the rest of the army to keep Lee abreast of the changing situations and hold important geographical areas in Confederate hands, especially the Bull Run Mountain gaps such as Thoroughfare Gap.[3]

As Jackson marched towards the rear of Pope's army, Lee instructed Longstreet to continue demonstrations along the Rappahannock River to pin

2 Ibid., 263.

3 *OR* 12, pt. 2, 733.

Pope in place. By the afternoon of August 26 it became clear that the Federals were withdrawing. Lee was anxious now to reunite his separated wings for a possible fight and gave Longstreet two options to get his men towards Manassas. Lee either wanted Longstreet to follow Jackson's wide flank march or "force a passage of the river." Reviewing a map, Longstreet worried that after crossing the river Pope had "numerous strongly defensive positions where a small force could have detained me an uncertain length of time." Taking a more conservative approach, Longstreet decided not to risk fighting a retreating enemy but instead to follow Jackson's route. The march would likely be devoid of enemy troops, but it would be hard on the men and take nearly two days to complete. The earliest Longstreet could get to Jackson would be August 28.[4]

Illuminated by the burning warehouses and trains, on the night of August 27 Jackson set off towards the Bull Run Mountains. After elements of his command fought two battles, Stonewall wanted to find a suitable defensive position closer to the rest of Lee's army. This necessitated a night march, something with which both Jackson and his men had little experience. Even in the best-managed commands, night marches usually proved a frustratingly confusing undertaking. Each officer needed to know not only his part of the marching column, but also that of the rest of the larger force to quickly resolve momentary confusion that could happen. Jackson continued his penchant for operational secrecy by keeping most of his subordinates in the dark. Campbell Brown remembered that Jackson "had not told Gen'l Ewell were to go, but he would send him a guide."[5]

The confusion on this night march is reflected in the after-action reports filed by the principal commanders months later. Since the march ultimately ended in the reunification of his command at the old Manassas battlefield, Jackson failed to detail the exact route of his command. It appears from reports that Taliaferro's Division moved first, just before dusk. The leading division typically enjoyed the best marching, and this night march was no different. Leaving Manassas Junction, Taliaferro headed west on the Sudley Road. After marching a little over five miles, the head of the column approached the old Manassas battlefield. Passing Henry House on their right, the men continued a little further on to the Stone House at the intersection of Sudley Road with the Warrenton Turnpike. Taking a left, the column headed in a southerly direction reaching the small hamlet of Groveton. After marching a little over 6 miles,

4 James Longstreet, "Our March Against Pope," *Battles and Leaders of the Civil War*, 2:517.

5 Jones, *Campbell Brown's Civil War*, 151.

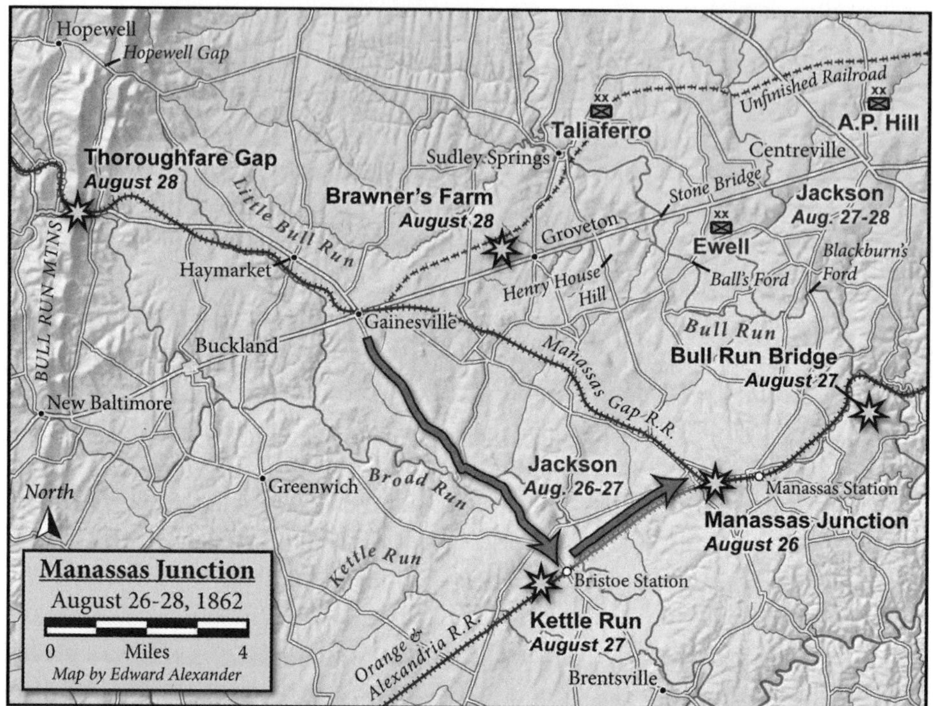

by midnight Taliaferro was in camp, with Bradley Johnson and his brigade of Virginians picketing the road leading towards Gainesville.[6]

A. P. Hill was next in the column, starting to move at midnight though the last of Hill's men didn't leave the junction until 2:00 a.m. Instead of heading west on Sudley Road, Hill trudged north on the Centreville Road. Crossing Bull Run at Blackburn's Ford, Hill continued north to the crossroads town of Centreville after marching 7 miles. Resting at Centreville that morning, by 10:00 a.m. an abandoned Hill decided to move his division southwards on the Warrenton Turnpike. Crossing Bull Run again near the Stone Bridge, Hill encountered a courier with a message from Jackson stamped 8:00 a.m. The note encouraged Hill to intercept the retreating Federals, a suggestion that Hill ignored. After reviewing a couple of captured Federal missives about attacking whatever Confederates might be found near Manassas, Hill decided to reunite with Jackson's command. Around afternoon most of Hill's Division arrived near Groveton after marching seven miles from Centreville, although Hill's artillery did not arrive until evening. The confusion in orders, and possibly a

6 *OR* 12, pt. 2, 644.

misinformed guide, nearly doubled the distance Hill covered, 14 miles compared to Taliaferro's 6 miles.[7]

After fighting the rearguard action at Bristoe Station, Ewell's Division once again found itself relegated to protecting the rear of Jackson's Wing. The evening of the 27th and the morning of the 28th portended a miserable day for Ewell's men. Wishing to get a head start and avoid the likely traffic jam that was bound to occur as the army attempted to leave Manassas Junction, Jubal Early moved his brigade of Virginians further north to the Bull Run Bridge battlefield. Located between Bull Run and Manassas, Early's men tried to get a few hours of sleep before another day of marching. Forno's Louisianans were expected to follow Early's men out of Manassas around midnight but marched around aimlessly looking for the Virginians. Soon Forno ordered his men to bed down, hoping to straighten everything out in a few hours when dawn allowed everyone to see easier.[8]

Ewell hoped to have his division on the road early on August 28 but was stymied by a missing brigade. Arriving from Bristoe Station, Ewell's division was now theoretically reunited. Ewell had Forno, Early, and Lawton well in hand but Isaac Trimble continued to be a problem. No one on Ewell's staff could locate the Marylander and Trimble seems to have continued to believe that he was detached from Ewell even though his commander was now at Manassas. Not wanting to lose a quarter of his division, Ewell remained in Manassas while staff members searched for the missing brigade. Finally, with dawn approaching, Ewell ordered his division on the road still missing Trimble.[9]

Ewell's staff continued to search for Trimble. Riding north on the Centreville Road, Campbell Brown found the Marylander preparing to ford Bull Run near Wilmer McLean's house, Yorkshire. Trimble had mistakenly followed A. P. Hill's division. Soon the head of Ewell's column approached Brown, and Trimble was ordered to fall in with the column. Fording Bull Run at Blackburn's Ford, Ewell's men marched through Fairfax County before heading south again. Recrossing the famous stream near the site of the Stone Bridge, Ewell's division continued on the Warrenton Turnpike towards Jackson's command near Groveton. By cutting cross-country in Fairfax, Ewell shaved off a few miles on his march, but his men still marched more than the six miles required.[10]

7 Ibid., 670; 674–675; 679; 700.

8 Ibid., 710, 718.

9 Jones, *Campbell Brown's Civil War*, 150–151.

10 Ibid., 151–152; Oates, *The War Between the Union and the Confederacy*, 137.

The confusion in the high command trickled down to the ranks. The frolic in Manassas buoyed spirits, but many men had not physically recovered from the march. Straggling presented a major problem throughout the day, and it appeared almost immediately. A few moments after leaving Manassas, John Casler and some comrades in the Stonewall Brigade strayed from their column. They soon lost track of their regiment and then their brigade and division. Momentarily resting at a road intersection, a nearby soldier claimed to Casler that the Federals were nearby and he better resume his march if he didn't want to be captured. An experienced soldier, the Virginian noticed that "some troops had taken one road and some the other, and I could not find out which one my brigade had taken." Unknown to him, Casler ended up following A. P. Hill's division to Centreville, reaching that hamlet around dawn.[11]

Straggling ensued in part due to the huge quantities of supplies many soldiers attempted to carry from Manassas. Weighed down with regular accouterments and weapons, soldiers also carried at least four days' worth of rations. Many experienced soldiers attempted to supplement their rations with yet more food. An officer in the 15th Alabama remembered that "after marching a mile or two the roadside was strewn with large boxes full or half full of crackers and pieces of bacon." Soldiers leaving the column to discard unwanted supplies or to investigate what these roadside boxes contained exacerbated the tendency of Jackson's troops to straggle.[12]

Jackson successfully reunited his wing near Groveton without damaging his command. After the campaign ended with a Confederate victory, the clouds of dust emitting towards Centreville were transformed by generals and later historians into a successful ruse that ultimately facilitated Confederate victory, since the Federals were supposedly confused about the destination of Jackson's command. The later success of the campaign complicates a critical examination of Jackson's night march.

Much of the blame for the confusion, historically, has been heaped on mistaken guides instead of Jackson himself. Jackson's insistence of operational secrecy put his command at risk of becoming separated and potentially destroyed in detail. The fighting on the 27th revealed Jackson's position between two large Federal armies and heightened the need to keep the Confederates concentrated. Jackson's decision to march towards the Bull Run Mountains was sound, but his reliance on guides instead of trusting his divisional commanders

11 Casler, *Four Years in the Stonewall Brigade*, 108.

12 Oates, *The War Between the Union and the Confederacy*, 137.

was negligent. Jackson's actions seem to highlight a continual lack of faith in his key subordinates, men who had shown skill and competence on battlefields from the Shenandoah Valley to Richmond. Not only had Dick Ewell grown up in the area, but most of Jackson's men were familiar with the area after camping in the vicinity for much of 1861–1862 after the first Manassas campaign. Jackson's commanders, and many of his men, knew the area, a fact highlighted by Hill's decision to march on the Warrenton Turnpike from Centreville to Groveton. Instead of outlining the day's march and trusting his subordinates to get to the concentration point in case of separation, Jackson instead created a scenario in which two-thirds of his soldiers wandered aimlessly for a good portion of the day.

Jackson's location during the march is hard to determine. His after-action report is concise about the movement towards Groveton and many of his staff officers likewise are vague in their later writings. It seems that Jackson accompanied Taliaferro's division. If Jackson remained at Manassas Junction, it is reasonable to assume he would be aware of Hill and Ewell marching in the wrong direction almost immediately after exiting Manassas.

The separation of Jackson's command for the first half of the 28th opened the possibility of his wing being destroyed in detail. The main enemy force at the battle of Bull Run Bridge emanated from Fairfax County, a fact known to Jackson while he was still in Manassas. Allowing two divisions to march blindly in an area of a known enemy force was a recipe for a meeting engagement near Centreville. But Jackson's luck held. The confusion he sowed in his command resulted in avoidable miles many of his men were required to cover. The nickname "Jackson's Foot Cavalry" proved popular in his command, showing that the men took pride in their ability to cover long distances on foot. Even Stonewall's men had a physical breaking point, however, and Jackson needlessly drove his men towards it. From Jeffersonton to Manassas the Southerners marched over 60 miles in 3 days and enjoyed only a few hours of sleep each night. The march to Centreville not only added pointless miles but also robbed many of critical rest, especially when a fight was likely in the near future.

Chapter 18

"A Rude Baptism of Fire"

Virginia: August 28, 1862

It had been a hot and dusty day in late August 1862 and the Western soldiers marched on short rations. As the column neared Warrenton, Gen. John Gibbon sent riders ahead to have food placed along the sidewalks so his men could pick it up as they passed through the town. When he reached the intersection, however, he found it "packed with troops, and trains slowly making their way forward, but everything else seemed to be hurried and confused." The hungry soldiers could see "wagon-loads of hard tack and pork" being burned, but when they halted in the street and began to stuff haversacks with the waiting food, Gen. Irvin McDowell, on a nearby porch, saw them.

Gibbon went to the general to explain the situation but was turned away with a sharp order to keep his column moving. The hungry soldiers were obliged to turn their backs on the much-needed food. Scarcely had they cleared the town than the road was found so blocked up in front that progress became terribly slow. After marching till long after dark the brigade bivouacked for the night only five miles beyond Warrenton.

Gibbon did manage to load some boxes of hardtack and bacon on the caissons and limbers of Battery B, but there was not enough food to go around. "The officers know how to take care of themselves. Nobody worries about us. They care very little," a Badger wrote with bitterness in his pocket diary.[1] A Wisconsin officer wrote home: "This Country is all woods & hills & they lay in ambush for us everywhere. I am afraid Pope is not equal to the task before him."[2]

1 Gibbon, *Recollections*, 47–48; Dawes Service, 58–59; Ludolph Longhenry, diary, Aug. 18, 1862, private collection.

2 Douglas S. Freeman, *Lee's Lieutenants*, Vol. 2 (New York, 1943), 102–107; Gaff, *Brave Men's Tears*, 43–54; Nolan, *Iron Brigade*, 72–79; Brown to his father, Aug. 19, 1862.

General John Hatch's brigade of Rufus King's division was the first to move the morning of August 28, followed by Gibbon's four regiments and Battery B. King's two other brigades and their attached artillery and wagons followed. The column was well spread along the Warrenton Turnpike with about a mile interval between the brigades. The division's senior brigade commander, Hatch, was in charge because King was ill. The general was seen by the marching soldiers standing wan and disheveled by a log fire and in ranks it was whispered he was drunk.[3]

Almost as soon as the brigade got on the road, Gibbon was halted by stopped wagons. It went that way most of the day, march and halt, march and halt, the soldiers soon out of sorts in the heat and dust. They passed through Gainesville where the men found "a cluster of two or three houses where the Manassas Gap railroad crosses the turnpike," then finally turned down a lane branching to the right. They marched a mile and were halted. Orders were given to form a line of battle and then countermanded. The brigade remained halted in this position for several hours and in ranks the soldiers were busy speculating as to what was going on and what was to be done. The men stacked arms and began to boil coffee paying no heed to the distant sound of artillery fire.

A large body of Confederate prisoners passed and some of the Wisconsin and Indiana men came out for a look. The Johnnies were dirty and much used-up. They said they were some of Jackson's men and they had not been able to keep up. One weary Rebel looked over the Wisconsin men with their knapsacks and profusion of belts and accoutrements. "You uns is pack mules, we uns is race horses," he told them. "All old Jackson gave us, was a musket, a hundred rounds and a gum blanket, and he 'druv us so like hell,' that I could not stand it on parched corn."[4]

After a time, seeing no immediate end to the halt, Gibbon ordered beef cattle being herded with the brigade to be killed and eaten. But marching orders came before the meat could be distributed. In the 19th Indiana, one soldier said, hunger forced "many of us [to] cut off chunks and [eat] them warm and raw."[5]

At 4:00 p.m., orders came to return to the Warrenton Turnpike and go on to Centreville. The dispatch rider told the soldiers around him that the Confederates were apparently at Centreville and that King's division was being told to "move rapidly" along the roadway and be ready to bag Jackson in the morning. That

3 In fact, King was suffering from an epileptic seizure.

4 Dawes, journal, undated; Dawes, *Service*, 45–47, 59.

5 Gibbon, *Recollections*, 56; Gaff, *Bloody Field*, 155.

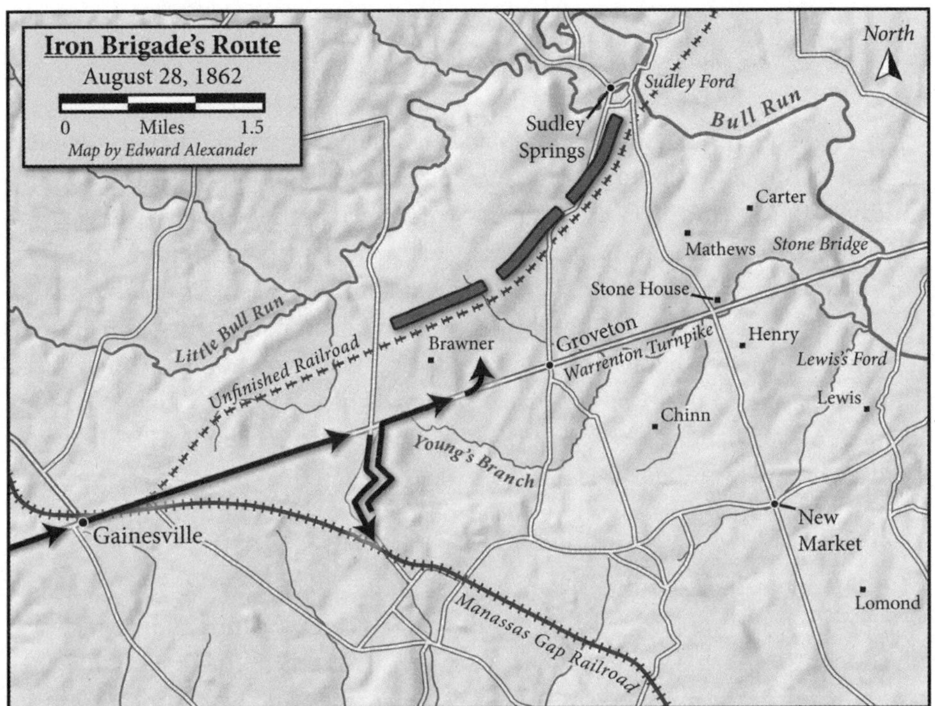

word quickly spread down to the ranks and the tired soldiers marched back up the lane. At the turnpike, they found McDowell and King looking ahead with field glasses. Hatch's brigade deployed skirmishers and moved forward behind the thin line moving over the fields north of the turnpike. No enemy was discovered, however, and Gibbon's brigade filed onto the road to follow Hatch. The 6th Wisconsin was in the lead, followed by the 2nd and 7th Wisconsin, the 19th Indiana, and the guns of Battery B.

There was little apprehension as the column moved along the turnpike. The soldiers chatted and joked in the usual manner. To the north, some distance ahead, they saw a farmhouse and outbuildings and then the turnpike passed through woods where the road had been excavated leaving a three-foot embankment. As they passed near the trees, the soldiers looked ahead for some distance over the flat country, part fields and part woods. The horizontal rays of the setting sun cast long shadows ahead of the moving soldiers, flashing now and then on the bright musket barrels. At one point, a brass band far off played "the jolly notes of a popular soldier song, and here and there in the ranks the marching men took up the chorus":

Johnny stole a ha-a-am,
And didn't care a da-a-a-m.[6]

The band fell silent and the singing gave way to the usual murmur of voices and the thump and clanking of the moving column. Gibbon on his small horse rode near the leading 6th Wisconsin, moving ahead as the regiment was clearing the wooded area to ride to a gentile rise just north of the Warrenton Turnpike. For a time, the marching soldiers watched a lone horseman on the distant ridgeline. Then one private saw more horses and thought at first the animals were pulling army wagons and wondered what they were doing in the woods. The horses turned to reveal they were pulling artillery pieces. "That don't look like any of our batteries," a Wisconsin soldier said to a friend, who shook his head and sharply replied, "See here! We have been in the service over a year and except a few skirmishes, we have never been in a fight. I tell you, this damned war will be over and we will never get into a battle!"

Gibbon recognized the distant artillery was going into battery. He called to an orderly, "Ride back and bring up Battery B on a gallop." The order was no sooner given when the far-off artillery fired two shots. The first hissing shell whooshed over the marching 6th Wisconsin, and men and officers neatly bowed away from the sound. The shell exploded harmlessly in the woods south of the turnpike. The enemy battery followed with more shots, fired in quick succession. For a long instant, the Wisconsin men seemed ready to bolt, and then Colonel Cutler's steady voice called out, "Battalion, halt! Front! Load at will! Load!" The soldiers responded instinctively to the commanding voice heard on so many drill fields. Ramrods clanked as the men pushed the lead bullets down the muzzles of their rifle-muskets. Two more artillery rounds came. One knocked a horse over against the fence and the other just missed two officers of the 2nd Wisconsin. "Lie down," Cutler ordered, and the Badgers hugged the embankment as more "shells came quick," sweeping the area and exploding with a clap of thunder and smoke. Gibbon thought the enemy artillery was trying to delay the column.[7]

Down the roadway at a run came the six bronze guns of Battery B kicking up clods of dirt and stones as the heavy smoothbores were pulled forward by

6 Alan T. Nolan, "John Brawner's Damage Claim," *Giants in Tall Black Hats*, eds. Sharon Vipond and Alan Nolan (Bloomington, IN, 1998), 1; Edward Bragg to Earl Rogers, Apr. 3, 1900, Edward Bragg Papers, WHS; George Fairfield, diary, Aug. 28, 1862; Cheek and Pointon, *Sauk County*, 37.

7 Dawes, *Service*, 60; A. R. Bushnell, "How the Iron Brigade Won Its Name," *Grant County* [WI] *Herald*, undated clipping, Watrous Papers, WHS; Brown to his father, Sep. 5, 1862; Cheek and Pointon, *Sauk County*, 37–38; *Telegraph*, May 6, 1888; Otis, *Second Wisconsin*, 250; Sullivan, *Telegraph*, Nov. 4, 1884; Gibbon, *Recollections*, 51–52; *Telegraph*, Sep. 7, 1884.

the wide-eyed, straining artillery horses. The guns passed along lines of men crouching against the side of the road. There was a partial rail fence along the road and several infantrymen from the 6th Wisconsin jumped forward to kick it aside, assisted by one of the contraband cooks who struggled with his pack of pots and pans. The guns rolled through the gap to the knoll where Gibbon was waiting and the soldiers saw him swing his arm to show where he wanted them placed, calling out, "Into battery, here!" The guns were swung around with a practiced style, the trails dropped, the gunners moving into position. The battery opened with a terrible roar, the blasts flattening the grass in front of the muzzles and filling the air with smoke.

One of the soldiers in the 2nd Wisconsin pressed in the huddle against the embankment glanced up to see the general talking with his adjutant, Capt. John P. Wood. Wood ducked his head when a shell passed overhead, and when the private again glanced back he was surprised to see Wood standing in the road where an instant before he had been mounted—his horse had been blown from under him. The shaken captain looked up and the private heard him say, "Pretty well done, general." Gibbon nodded his head and responded, "That's War."[8]

Another artillery bolt careened through the six guns of Battery B cutting off the tail of one of the bay battery horses, giving him "a deep cut across the rump." The wounded horse was named "Tartar" and his adventures became entangled into the lore of the Black Hat brigade.[9]

8 Sheldon E. Judson, letter, Oct. 1, 1871, T. C. H. Smith Papers, Ohio Historical Society.

9 James Stewart, letter, Dec. 8, 1889, quoted in Buell, *Cannoneer*, 30–31. Tartar, with his bobtail, became well known. After the war, one veteran said, his small children asked him over and over at bedtime for the "horse story," and he admitted he might have romanced it and changed a fact or two. The truth was just as interesting. Tartar entered the service at Fort Leavenworth, Kansas, in July 1857 just before the battery started on the Utah expedition. The horse was abandoned at Green River, Utah, a short time later when taken sick with distemper. The following spring, two Indians brought him back to the battery. The shell at Second Bull Run carried away Tartar's tail, cutting him on both flanks. When the army retreated the next day, Tartar was left behind and turned out into a small pasture. The next morning, Tartar was again found with the battery horses, having jumped the fence. Sometime late in the war, during a review attended by President Lincoln, Tartar again attracted attention. As the battery passed the reviewing stand, Lincoln smiled and remarked to the generals around him, "This reminds me of a tale." Lincoln's son, Tad, who had accompanied his father, was much taken with Tartar. Tad was mounted on a pony and followed the battery pestering Lt. James Stewart to trade horses. "I told him I could not do that, but he persisted in telling me that his papa was the President, and would give me any horse I wanted in trade for Tartar. I had a hard time to get away from the little fellow," he said. Tartar was wounded again at Fredericksburg in 1862 and again left behind, only to show up on a Federal cavalry picket line a month later. Stewart said when he was promoted and transferred to the 18th Infantry in 1866 Tartar was still in harness with Battery B, in the tenth year of "his honorable and distinguished service."

Chapter 19

"A Very Formidable Barrier"

Thoroughfare Gap: August 28, 1862

As Jackson's scattered command trudged towards the old Manassas battlefield, Lee, Longstreet, and the Right Wing of the Army of Northern Virginia were on the move. Pulling away from the Rappahannock River line, Longstreet's Wing snaked westward. Approaching Jeffersonton from the southwest, an artillerist in the Donaldsonville Cannoniers was shocked by the damage the war wrought to the area. "On our route we see signs of the Yankee Ravages, churches completely destroyed, all the benches and fixtures inside broken up and Yankee names written in prominent places." Entering Jeffersonton the same Louisianan was disgusted by the "poor deserted hamlet."[1]

Concentrating this wing on August 26, Longstreet's men followed Jackson's route. A soldier in the Texas Brigade remembered that day's march as "the longest and most fatiguing march we have ever made." Members of the Donaldsonville Cannoniers had to stop their march early on account of the "great many straggling soldiers that had fallen out." That evening Longstreet's men bedded down near Orlean.[2]

As Jackson's men trudged into Manassas Junction, Longstreet resumed the march. The 12-mile march between Orlean and Salem proved uneventful though the ubiquitous Virginia dust continued to cover men, horses, and wagons. At Salem, Lee's earlier decision to send Stuart and all his cavalry with Jackson caused an unanticipated delay in Longstreet's march. A few squadrons of Federal cavalry bumped into the Confederates but quickly retreated eastwards

1 Michael Marshall, *Gallant Creoles: A History of the Donaldsonville Cannoniers* (Lafayette, LA, 2013), 94.

2 Richard McCaslin, ed., *A Soldiers Letters to Charming Nellie* (Knoxville, TN, 2008), 41; Marshall, *Gallant Creoles*, 94–95.

back towards Warrenton. Deploying on the fields outside of Salem, Federal cavalryman continued to watch the Confederates. Without cavalry of their own to either drive back the enemy or determine if they were a detachment or the head of a sizeable Federal force, the Confederates cautiously deployed. After an hour of light skirmishing, the Federals withdrew, and the march resumed.[3]

Soldiers quickly started to spread rumors about the cause for the halt. One rumor swirling through the ranks of the Texas Brigade pinned the delay on a Federal spy. According to Pvt. Joseph Polley of the 4th Texas, "the story, as I heard it" involved a Federal officer dressed as a Confederate courier. Approaching a part of the Confederate column, the messenger ordered a general to halt his command on orders from Longstreet. Obeying the order but smelling a rat, the unnamed general held the courier until Longstreet himself appeared. Inquiring if it was General Longstreet ordering the halt, the courier answered in the affirmative. A staff officer asked if the courier knew what Longstreet looked like, and after the courier said he did know, Longstreet asked if the general was present. When the messenger said he was not present, Longstreet ordered the spy arrested and "then detail an officer and six privates to carry him to that tree over yonder and hang him—he is a spy." Like all good army rumors, the men spreading it hadn't seen anything with their own eyes but many were certain it was true.[4]

After the Federal cavalrymen left, Longstreet's men resumed the march towards the Bull Run Mountains. Marching 5 miles from Salem, once the column reached White Plains around evening Longstreet ordered his men to bed down for the night. Over the course of August 27th, the Right Wing of the Army of Northern Virginia marched 16 miles, a pace slower than Jackson's but still a trying experience for the soldiers. Encamped at White Plains, Thoroughfare Gap was an easy 5 miles away. If Jackson required it, Lee seemed certain that he could reunite the Army of Northern Virginia on August 28.[5]

That evening Lee sent President Davis a cable on the progress of the campaign. Jackson had been successful in not only breaking the railroad at Bristoe Station, but Trimble had captured Manassas Junction. Ominously, Jackson's men had encountered soldiers from the Army of the Potomac. Lee requested that the President "expedite the reinforcements ordered," namely McLaws and D. H. Hill. Lee seems to have understood that Longstreet's delay

3 *OR* 12, pt. 2, 564.

4 McCaslin, *Soldiers Letters to Charming Nellie*, 42.

5 *OR* 12, pt. 2, 564.

at Salem stemmed from a lack of accompanying cavalrymen. Recognizing this, Lee finished his message: "I particularly require Hampton's Cavalry."[6]

Lee's telegraph to Davis highlights his constant communication with Jackson's Wing on the other side of the mountains. Jackson routinely sent Lee updates on the progress of his operations and any new information that he acquired. Critically, Jackson relayed information that he fought against elements of the Army of the Potomac at both Bristoe Station and Bull Run Bridge. Lee for his part updated Jackson on the progress of Longstreet's Wing. The most direct route between Jackson and Lee continued to be Thoroughfare Gap. In his memoirs Longstreet posits that these communications "reported it clear," convincing Lee that Longstreet's men could easily access the critical gap early the next morning.[7]

Leading the column on the 28th was a man developing into one of Lee's best commanders. A native South Carolinian, Maj. Gen. David Rumph "Neighbor" Jones had been a brigadier general in the Confederate army since June 17, 1861. Displaying solid competence during the Peninsula campaign, in the reorganization of the army Jones received a division in Longstreet's Wing. Commanding his division for over a month, Jones had yet to lead it in battle.[8]

Jones's responsibility on this day was the occupation of Thoroughfare Gap. The unexpected appearance of Federals at Salem the previous day continued to delay the progress of Longstreet's column. Still without cavalry, Longstreet devised a way to temporarily convert some of his infantrymen into the role of cavalry. The lead brigade, Georgians under Brig. Gen. George "Tige" Anderson, remained in column on the road while the 9th Georgia cleared an area about 400 yards in advance of the main line. Anderson instructed Col. Benjamin Beck to send "his best officer with his company 200 yards in front" of the rest of the 9th Georgia with instructions "to be very careful that we were not ambuscaded or surprised." Just prior to starting the march Anderson discussed his tactical set up with his wing commander, which Longstreet "heartily approved."[9]

Leaving White Plains that morning, the careful advance guaranteed few surprises from an enemy force. The caution taken by Longstreet's Wing reduced the speed of its march to Thoroughfare Gap, but the rapid communication between Jackson and Lee continued to portray the gap as free from any Federals. Altogether Longstreet and Lee did not want to have the same surprise

6 Dowdey and Manarin, *Wartime Papers of R. E. Lee*, 265–266.

7 Longstreet, *From Manassas to Appomattox*, 173.

8 Warner, *Generals in Gray*, 163–164.

9 Neal Griffin, "Thoroughfare Gap, and the Second Battle of Manasses," http://www.sumtercountyhistory.com/wbts/2MANASS.htm, accessed Nov. 14, 2020.

they encountered a few hours ago near Salem. By 3:00 p.m. the 9th Georgia approached the gap.

Less than 500 feet wide, Thoroughfare is the largest gap in the Bull Run Mountains. The mountains south of the gap are a series of four hills and valleys with no suitable gaps for an army crossing. North, the mountain ridge rises over 1,000 feet, with some peaks cresting above 1,200 feet. Broad Run, a stream emptying into the Potomac, created Thoroughfare Gap and later drove industry in the area. Through the gap ran a road from the tidewater area near the Potomac River to the Shenandoah Valley known as the Valley Road. Paralleling the road ran the tracks of the Manassas Gap Railroad, the road Joe Johnston had used 13 months before to transport his men to the first battle of Manassas. The war had so severely damaged the railroad by 1862 that it was now practically abandoned. Situated to the east of the gap proper, first the Beverly family and then the Chapmans operated a five-story stone mill powered by Broad Run. The poor, rocky soil in the vicinity limited the number of farms in the immediate area.

Expecting the gap to be unoccupied, Colonel Beck sent an urgent message to his brigade commander that he had encountered dismounted Federal cavalry in the gap and was currently skirmishing with them for its possession. Forwarded up the chain of command, this information sent shockwaves throughout Longstreet's Right Wing. The continual stream of couriers lent credence to the belief that the gap remained open. The terrain nearly guaranteed a small force of Federals could hold back Longstreet and Lee for hours while the rest of the Federal army focused on Jackson. Reopening communication with Jackson became the first priority, with the capture of Thoroughfare Gap a close second.[10]

Brigadier General George "Tige" Anderson now assumed responsibility for opening the most direct avenue to Jackson. The native Georgian had pursued an unconventional path into the prewar army. Leaving college early to fight in the Mexican-American War, in 1855 Anderson received a direct commission into the U.S. Army. At the outbreak of hostilities, Anderson became the colonel of the 11th Georgia before assuming command of a brigade at the Seven Days' battles where he saw modest combat. On August 28, 1862, Anderson was still developing into one of Lee's hard-hitting brigadiers.[11]

Consolidating his strung-out regiment, Colonel Beck soon had the 9th Georgia moving through the gap, routing the dismounted cavalrymen. Technically the Confederates now had possession, but ownership was soon

10 Longstreet, "Our March Against Pope," *Battles and Leaders*, 517.

11 Warner, *Generals in Gray*, 6.

challenged. Past the fleeing troopers, Beck saw what he supposed to be about a division's worth of Federal infantry forming up for an attack. With his regiment in hand, the 9th Georgia took a defensive position near the Chapman Mill. Fighting against a larger force, Beck remained near the mill until the enemy started to extend around both flanks of his regiment. If the Georgians remained in their current position, they faced either destruction or capture from the advancing enemy. Beck gave the command to fall back, fighting about 100 feet to the protection of the narrowing gap itself.[12]

Hearing musketry, Anderson double-quicked his brigade to Beck's assistance. As the Georgians arrived, Anderson's brigade expanded to the north with the 1st Georgia Regulars on the left of Beck, followed by the 7th Georgia, 8th Georgia, and 11th Georgia anchoring the left flank. Once his entire brigade finalized its deployment, Anderson ordered each regiment to send out two companies as skirmishers. With five regiments, Anderson's order put 10 companies, or an *ad hoc* regiment, in front of his line.[13]

The advance of the skirmish line signaled a change in the Confederate battle plan. From a fighting withdrawal, Anderson's men prepared for a limited counterattack. A skirmisher in front of the 8th Georgia infantry remembered the vegetation in front of his regiment as "a cluster of vines and briers well-nigh impenetrable." Ordered to advance, the Southerners struggled to navigate the area as best they could. The men deployed in a loose skirmish line four paces away from comrades, which proved an easier formation to maneuver large numbers of soldiers than the common battle line.[14]

Protecting the main line, Anderson's skirmishers advanced towards the enemy. In addition to vines and briers, the skirmishers encountered thick undergrowth of cedar trees. Rockslides on Bull Run Mountain were not uncommon, though confined to only certain locations. Soldiers navigating these areas found "a very formidable barrier" consisting of "a perpendicular wall of five or six feet that was very difficult to scale."[15]

Determining that the skirmishers had advanced far enough, Anderson ordered his main line of five regiments forward. Negotiating the terrain in loose skirmish line was difficult. Moving over the same area in compact battle lines verged on the impossible, but as one Georgian remembered "soldiers must know

12 Griffin, "Thoroughfare Gap, and the Second Battle of Manasses."

13 *OR* 12, pt. 2, 594.

14 B. M. Zettler, *War Stories and School-day Incidents for the Children* (New York, 1912), 100.

15 Ibid., 101.

no obstacles." The cedars, vines, and brush soon squeezed men out of formation, forcing them to reform as best they could on the move. Moving along the actual gap itself, Beck's regiment and the 1st Georgia Regulars had an easier time. Further on the left of the line, the steep slopes of the mountains forced some soldiers to climb on "their hands and knees to reach the enemy."[16]

Positioned between the main body of Anderson's brigade and the enemy towards their front, skirmishers tried to fulfill their responsibilities of locating the enemy and reporting its location up the chain of command. Climbing a mountain forest, some Georgians became lost and started to wander aimlessly in search of the Confederate line, including 19-year-old Berrien Zettler. The 8th Georgia private quickly lost contact with his company but continued to advance, halting every few steps to catch his breath on the climb up the mountain. Wandering around a few moments, Zettler stumbled across his comrade, Samuel Baldy. In the dark forest ahead of them, the 19-year-old heard the jingle of canteens carried by a soldier on a water detail. The unknown man had also seen the two Georgians. Aiming his rifle at the canteen carrier, Baldy prepared to fire but was held by Zettler, who said "Don't shoot; it may be one of our men." Asking for his company, the distant soldier shouted he belonged to Company A. Still suspicious, Baldy shouted for the man to next identify his regiment. When the soldier yelled 11th Massachusetts, Baldy immediately fired. Owing to the underbrush, neither Baldy nor Zettler saw the Bay Stater fall.[17]

Not wishing to draw fire on themselves, the two Georgians decided to fall back down the mountain, hoping to find an officer to report the encounter. Reaching the bottom, the men bumped into General Anderson who inquired about the size of the force they met. A veteran soldier, Zettler figured that the canteen detail predicted a regiment of Federal infantry up ahead. The report of a single regiment ahead of the 8th Georgia so exasperated the general that he scolded the young Georgian: "You were frightened to death, and don't know what you saw."[18]

A few moments after this exchange, Private Zettler realized that his experience on the mountain was similar to the rest of his unit. By ones and twos men trickled down to the bottom of the mountain after becoming separated from the main line and stumbling upon the Federal line. Unlike Baldy, few chose to fight the Federals and instead retreated down the mountain to report

16 Ibid., 100; *OR* 12, pt. 2, 594.

17 Zettler, *War Stories*, 101.

18 Ibid., 102.

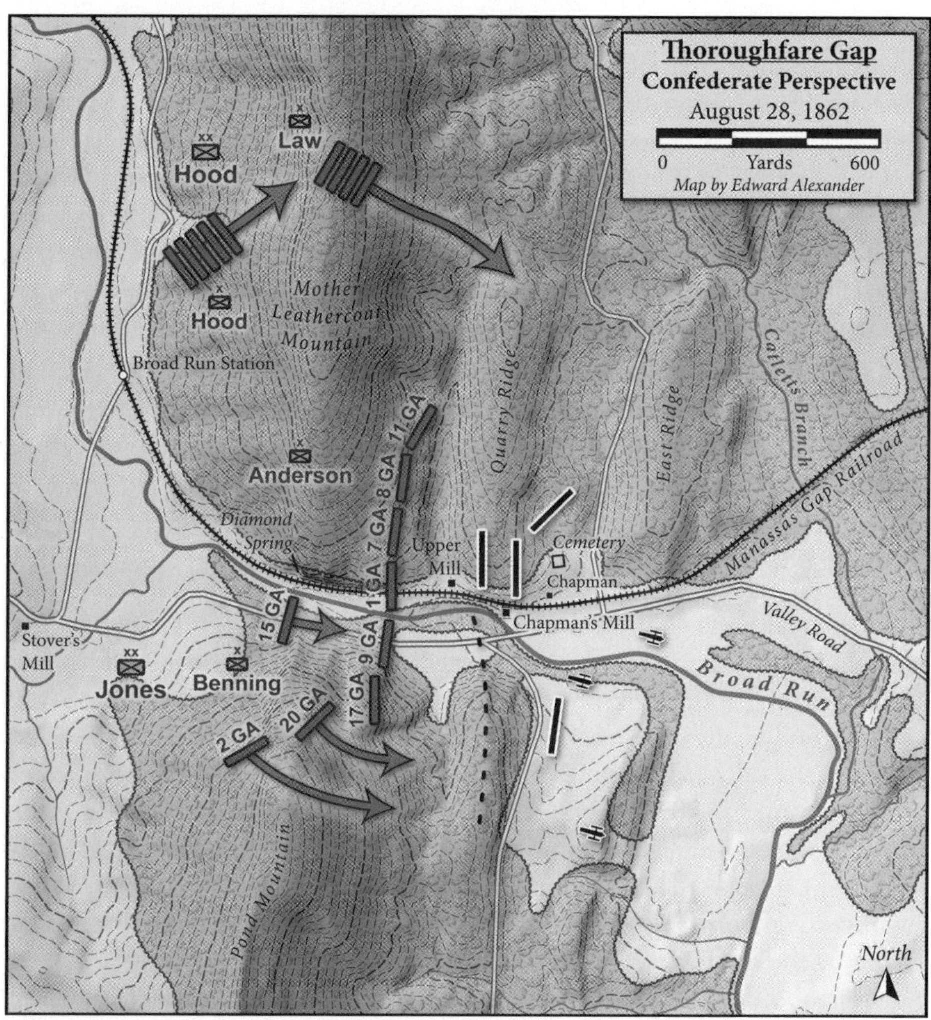

encounters with the enemy. Hearing multiple soldiers report a single regiment ahead, Anderson quickly became frustrated by the incomplete intelligence he was receiving. Hoping that the appearance of a lieutenant would finally provide a clearer picture, Anderson became irate when the officer replied to his inquiry of enemy strength with "Well, General, we came upon them very unexpectedly—." Cutting the subaltern off, Anderson snarled "Yes, and they stampeded you like they did the boys; so you know nothing. Get your men together, sir, and go back and stay there until you know something definite."[19]

19 Ibid.

The majority of Anderson's Brigade imitated the experience of the 8th Georgia. Finding that all five regiments reported the enemy in their front, Anderson knew he faced at least an enemy brigade. Although all of Anderson's regiments reported contact with the enemy, only the 1st Georgia Regulars engaged the Federals beyond an initial skirmish. Unlike the regiments farther to their left, the soldiers in the 1st Georgia Regulars formed a battle line closer to the gap. Arriving near a ditch, the Regulars instinctively fell into it since one Georgian remembered they had trained "to take advantage of everything when engaged with the enemy." Seeing a Federal battle line a few yards away, the Georgians opened up a blistering musketry fire.[20]

The fight between the barely visible Federals and 1st Georgia Regulars soon settled into a deadly rhythm. After a few volleys, the Federals charged, throwing the Regulars out of the protective ditch. Pushing past the ditch, the Federals advanced over a small ridge and into the waiting muskets of the rallying Georgians. A quick volley sent the Federals back and the Confederates counterattacked, regaining their old position in the ditch. The fight seesawed between attack and counterattack at least three times. At one point the charging Federals claimed they were the 8th Georgia and then later friends, with some Regulars yelling "Damn all such friends."[21]

Returning to the ditch after the last counterattack, Capt. John Patton walked the line of the Regulars steadying his men. Stepping over prone men, one soldier became mesmerized by the sight of the officer's act of bravery in the face of the nearby Yankees. The enemy remained so close by that Captain Patton easily fired his pistol into the enemy ranks. Firing all six rounds of his revolver, the captain brought down five Federals, killing an enemy captain, two privates, and wounding the rest.[22]

"Neighbor" Jones needed to gain possession of Thoroughfare Gap immediately. Anderson's brigade had yet to drive the Federals away, so Jones committed another brigade to a battle that had thus far been confined to the gap itself and the mountain to the north. Jones planned to extend his line to the south and outflank the Federal left. If the flanking mission failed, at least the Federal line would be forced to extend, thinning out the enemy's position and increasing the odds of a breakthrough.

20 Richard McMurry, ed., *Footprints of a Regiment: A Recollection of the 1st Georgia Regulars 1861-1865* (Atlanta, 1992), 60.

21 Ibid., 61.

22 Ibid.; *OR* 12, pt. 2, 594.

Marching directly behind Tige Anderson, Toombs's Brigade arrived onto the battlefield about an hour after its start. Nine days earlier Longstreet placed Brig. Gen. Robert Toombs under arrest for "usurpation of duty" stemming from some confusion about picket duty along the Rappahannock River. Once the march began, Toombs remained under arrest and unable to command his brigade of four Georgia regiments in person. Until the charges against Toombs could be resolved, the senior regimental commander assumed command.[23]

At war's end Henry Benning emerged as one of the best brigade commanders in an army that had produced a stable of brilliant brigadiers. By 1863 "Old Rock" Benning and his brigade of Georgians were regarded as some of the best shock troops in the Army of Northern Virginia. But that all remained in the future. The start of the flank march during Toombs's confinement elevated the former lawyer to acting brigade commander. The battle of Thoroughfare Gap proved to be Benning's baptism under fire.[24]

When the head of Benning's brigade, the 20th Georgia, entered the gap it immediately received "shot and shell on the south side from two or three batteries, so situated as to sweep much of the railroad and more of the turnpike on that side." Benning's soldiers' natural desire to slide to the south to get out of range of screaming artillery shells merged with Jones's wish to extend the division's line further to the right. Unknown to the Georgians at the time, their part of the battlefield was not one large mountainous ridge like Anderson's men negotiated. Instead, south of the Gap Pond Mountain is an undulating ridge with four main peaks and valleys. The vines and rocks were similar to the north, but regiments could disappear and suddenly reappear.[25]

Artillery fire continued to fall near the 20th Georgia until a portion of Pond Mountain obscured the line of sight of the enemy cannoneers. Struggling to get his entire regiment into position, Maj. James Waddell threw out one of his companies into skirmish line with orders to race to the summit of the mountain as the rest of the regiment struggled behind them.

Arriving on the mountain crest, Waddell's skirmishers saw a blue skirmish line less than 40 yards away. Driving the enemy away, Waddell found himself in an uncomfortable position. Down the slope towards the base of the mountain, the major saw Federal artillery accompanied by "two full regiments of infantry" in support. Holding the high ground, the Georgians could rain a plunging fire

23 Ulrich Phillips, ed., *The Correspondence of Robert Toombs, Alexander H. Stephens, and Howell Cobb* (Washington, D.C., 1913), 604.

24 Warner, *Generals in Gray*, 25–26.

25 *OR* 12, pt. 2, 580.

onto the Yankees from the relative safety of the mountain. Unfortunately for Waddell, most of his men still carried smoothbore muskets. In close quarters, such as the men of the 1st Georgia Regulars were discovering, a smoothbore musket produced tremendous damage with its .69 caliber musket ball and three small buckshot ripping through an enemy line. At any distance over 100 yards, however, the erratic flight of the ball decreased accuracy to the point of near uselessness. Major Waddell found himself in a tactically enviable position but with severely limited firepower.

Of nearly 500 men in the ranks, only 60 soldiers in the 20th Georgia possessed modern rifle muskets that had the range to be effective against the Federals. Commencing a long-range harassing fire with their rifle muskets, Major Waddell ordered most of his regiment to take cover among the rocks during the retaliatory artillery bombardment the riflemen stirred up. Aiming at the largest target available to them, the Georgian sharpshooters killed or wounded all the horses assigned to the opposing enemy artillery. Dragged off the battlefield by hand, once the artillery withdrew, a lull appeared on the front of the 20th Georgia.[26]

Lieutenant Colonel William Holmes and his 2nd Georgia soon aided Waddell's men in silencing the Federal artillery. Marching directly behind the 20th, upon arriving on the battlefield Benning ordered Holmes's command to follow Waddell up Pond Mountain. The mountainous terrain produced confusion. Moving through brush, briars, and the Manassas Gap Railroad, when Holmes arrived at the previous location of the 20th Georgia he found the place vacated. Unknown to him, Waddell decided he could no longer wait for the 2nd Georgia to arrive and advanced up the mountain alone. Failing to find the regiment he was instructed to form up on, Holmes "consequently halted there for directions." Eventually the 2nd Georgia pulled into line next to the 20th and aided in throwing back the artillerists.[27]

Neighbor Jones now had two of his three brigades deployed on the battlefield, but less than 2 hours of sunlight remained, and the Federals still held the gap. With nearly his entire command either deployed or approaching the battlefield, Jones decided the time had come to push the enemy away from the gap in a division-sized assault. Brigadier General Thomas Drayton's mixed Georgia and South Carolina brigade would lead in a direct assault up the gap, supported by Benning's brigade on their right. Before Drayton's men had formed, Jones

26 Ibid., 591–592.

27 Ibid., 581.

observed the Federals falling back. Not wanting to miss the opportunity, Jones ordered an immediate advance. Fading sunlight obscured the battlefield as the Georgians and South Carolinians advanced over only token opposition to finally gain full possession of the gap. After gaining Thoroughfare Gap, the Federals were able to successfully withdraw owing to the "intense darkness and ignorance of the fords over the creek in my front [which] prevent pursuit." At 6:46 p.m. sunset ended the battle, nearly 3 hours after the 9th Georgia first entered Thoroughfare Gap.[28]

The afternoon of August 28 proved frustrating for James Longstreet. Instead of easily passing through the Bull Run Mountains and reuniting the Army of Northern Virginia, Lee's Old War Horse found himself fighting an enemy at a place that should have been under Confederate control. As Jones's Division wrestled Thoroughfare Gap back, Longstreet's remaining divisions stood idle on the road, waiting to pass the mountains and resume the march. Though Jones appeared to be gaining the upper hand, the battle had not progressed fast enough for Longstreet. The longer the Federals held Thoroughfare Gap, the longer Jackson remained separated from the rest of the Confederate army.

Marching behind Jones's Division was the smallest division in Lee's army. Containing just two brigades, Brig. Gen. John Bell Hood's small division had some of the best regiments in the army. For about a month Hood had the unusual task of commanding both his brigade and division after the nominal commander transferred away from Lee's army. This unusual command situation was mitigated by the complete faith Hood had for his old brigade of Texans and Georgians. The other brigade in Hood's Division, a mix of Alabamians, Mississippians, and North Carolinians, was in the capable hands of Col. Evander Law.

To help Jones open the gap, Longstreet ordered Hood's two brigades to follow a "foot-path over the mountain to turn the enemy's right." Chaplain Nicholas Davis of the 4th Texas remembered the foot-path as "a narrow defile, only sufficiently wide to admit a line of men in double files, with high mountains and long slopes on either side." The terrain forced Hood's brigades to string out several hundred yards on the path. After judging himself to be sufficiently over to turn the right flank of the Federal defenders, Hood ordered his men to advance. By the time Hood's men started their descent, the setting sun began to cast long shadows on the eastern face of the mountains. Encountering no

28 Ibid., 579.

enemy, when his soldiers reached the base of the mountain, Hood ordered his tired men into bivouac.[29]

Further along in Longstreet's column stood the Alabamans, Floridians, and Mississippians of Brig. Gen. Cadmus Wilcox's Division. After Longstreet ordered Hood to turn the Federal right flank, he decided to send Wilcox's three brigades on a further flanking movement north towards Hopewell Gap. Located three miles north of Thoroughfare Gap, Hopewell Gap served locals as another passage over the mountains. A narrower gap than the one to the south, Hopewell Gap contained only a small, twisting farm road hardly conducive on which to operate a large army. If Jones and Hood could not force away the Federals at Thoroughfare Gap, Wilcox was to "turn the right, and attack the enemy in the rear."[30]

While Wilcox's mission was framed as part of offensive operations against Thoroughfare, Confederate possession of Hopewell Gap reestablished communications between Jackson's Wing and the rest of Lee's army. Wilcox's brigades also opened a secondary line of retreat for Jackson in case he needed it while Longstreet fought for Thoroughfare. If that disaster befell Jackson and he was forced to retreat to Hopewell Gap, he would be forced to abandon most of his wagons and cannons. The primitive road network filing through Hopewell Gap could not cope with both thousands of soldiers and hundreds of wheeled vehicles. Thoroughfare Gap thus remained key for Lee and the safety of his army.

Ultimately overshadowed by skirmishing that boiled over into full-fledged fighting near Groveton, the fight for the possession of Thoroughfare Gap threatened to derail what had so far remained a successful Confederate offensive. Realizing that he made a mistake in the initial division of his cavalry, Lee sent most of his mounted force to operate with Jackson in his march towards the Federal rear. Once Jackson's mission was accomplished, by severing the Orange and Alexandria Railroad at Bristoe Station and Manassas, Jackson allowed Stuart to take most of the Confederate cavalry on a raid north through Fairfax County. A single cavalry regiment was expected to keep open the line of communications between Jackson and Lee in addition to scouting for Federal infantry coming from Warrenton.

As a semi-independent commander in the Shenandoah Valley earlier in 1862, Jackson did not need to worry about keeping his lines of communication clear. Only during the march between Winchester and Cross Keys in May/June 1862 did Jackson fear being cut off from the rest of the Confederate

29 *OR* 12, pt. 2, 564; Donald Everett, ed., *Chaplain Davis and Hood's Texas Brigade* (Baton Rouge, LA, 1999), 110.

30 *OR* 12, pt. 2, 564.

Longstreet's Wing marching through Thoroughfare Gap to rejoin Jackson near Manassas.

Battles and Leaders

army. Through hard Confederate marching, Federal mismanagement, and luck, Jackson's command had beat a delayed Federal effort to cut him off near Winchester. Through the rest of the Valley campaign, Jackson always had multiple lines of retreat available to him. It now seemed that Jackson failed to grasp the necessity of keeping his lines of communication open even though he was almost cut off earlier in 1862 at the first battle of Winchester.

Once Jackson crossed the Bull Run Mountains he reverted back into a version of his Shenandoah style: a semi-independent commander focused on the offensive. In the Valley campaign, Jackson used his cavalry under Turner Ashby to harass his opponent. A few months later with Stuart, Jackson returned to a style in which his mounted force remained committed to harassing the enemy instead of keeping his line of communications secure. At times Jackson became so focused on the offense that prudent measures fell by the wayside. His failure to keep Thoroughfare Gap open for Lee and Longstreet added unnecessary hazards to his command. If his wing got into trouble, Jackson risked converting the defeat of his command into the possibility of its destruction. Only Longstreet's rapidity in opening up Thoroughfare Gap (and securing Hopewell Gap as a back-up crossing) saved Jackson's command from the threat of total annihilation, if Pope proved able to respond quickly and forcefully against Stonewall. By dusk, a juncture of Lee's army had still not occurred. Unknown to Lee, Jackson decided to focus on his front instead of his rear and fight a portion of the Federal army at a small crossroads town called Groveton.

Chapter 20

"Horse Artillery or Something More"

Brawner Farm: August 28, 1862

The general rode into the nearby woods to watch the effects of his battery's fire. The division had been under scattered shellings most of the day and he was now convinced it was just Confederate horse artillery and not something more. Confederate cannons could also be heard firing on the two rear brigades of King's division. General Abner Doubleday's brigade marching behind General Gibbon moved up along the pike to crowd in behind the cover of the small woods. Battery B's accurate shooting soon slowed the fire of the first Rebel battery.

Doubleday came up and joined Gibbon. The two old artillery officers watched the artillery exchange for a time, then Doubleday said he thought the Rebel battery could be captured. "By heaven, I'll do it," Gibbon said. He then sent an aide back to bring up his most veteran regiment—the 2nd Wisconsin under the trusted, fellow West Pointer, Edgar O'Connor. Gibbon rode back to meet the regiment coming at the double quick in column through the woods. The general was heard to call out "Where is Colonel O'Connor?" The colonel responded, "Here I am General at the post of duty."[1]

Back on the roadway, the other Wisconsin and Indiana men huddled along the embankment. One 7th Wisconsin man watched in astonishment as one of the brigade aides, Lt. Frank Haskell, jumped "his horse over the fence and rode up toward the battery to reconnoiter the enemy's position, and then turn and walked his horse back as calmly as though there was not a rebel within a thousand miles."

1 John Gibbon in a speech to the Iron Brigade Association at Lancaster, WI, in 1884; Sheldon E. Judson, letter, Oct. 1, 1871, Earl Rogers Papers, Wisconsin Veterans' Museum, Madison; King, *War Papers*, 2:212.

Colonel Edgar O'Connor, 2nd Wisconsin
Brett Wilson Collection

Watching as the 2nd Wisconsin regiment stood up to advance, a disappointed man in the 6th Wisconsin said out loud to the men around him, "What luck! There is the Second in again before us." The 2nd Wisconsin moved by the left flank and disappeared into the woods as a ragged cheer was lifted by the three other regiments. Bloodied at Bull Run—the men bragged so long about it!—the regiment went forward.

In the woods, Gibbon told the regimental officers that it was probably just a cavalry battery on the ridgeline and "if we can get you up quietly we can capture the guns." The order was to move into the open field, form a line of battle, fire a battalion volley, and then advance at the double quick to capture the guns. In a clearing north of the woods, the regiment formed and at least one man in ranks worried about presenting a "well dressed line" to the remaining regiments.[2] Two companies were pushed forward as skirmishers and eight companies followed, closed on the flags and marching abreast. As the skirmishers advanced the Confederate artillery went silent. No enemy was sighted as the line moved up a gentle slope.

The 2nd Wisconsin was marching in line of battle by the left oblique and nearing the farm buildings. As it came to the top of a slight ridge, it was hit in the flank by musketry from a nearby ravine filled with tall grass. O'Connor wheeled to the right, watching as his skirmishers chased a scattering of Rebels toward the ridge line. At the top of the slope, O'Connor halted his regiment and gave the order to "Fix Bayonets." That was no sooner done when the colonel saw his skirmishers coming back on the run and a thick line of Confederate infantry "three lines deep" pouring out of the wood line. In ranks, the Badgers were surprised and alarmed to see the flags of at least five Confederate regiments. The Wisconsin regiment halted and waited. Suddenly the "bullets came thicker than

2 Judson, letter, Oct. 1, 1871.

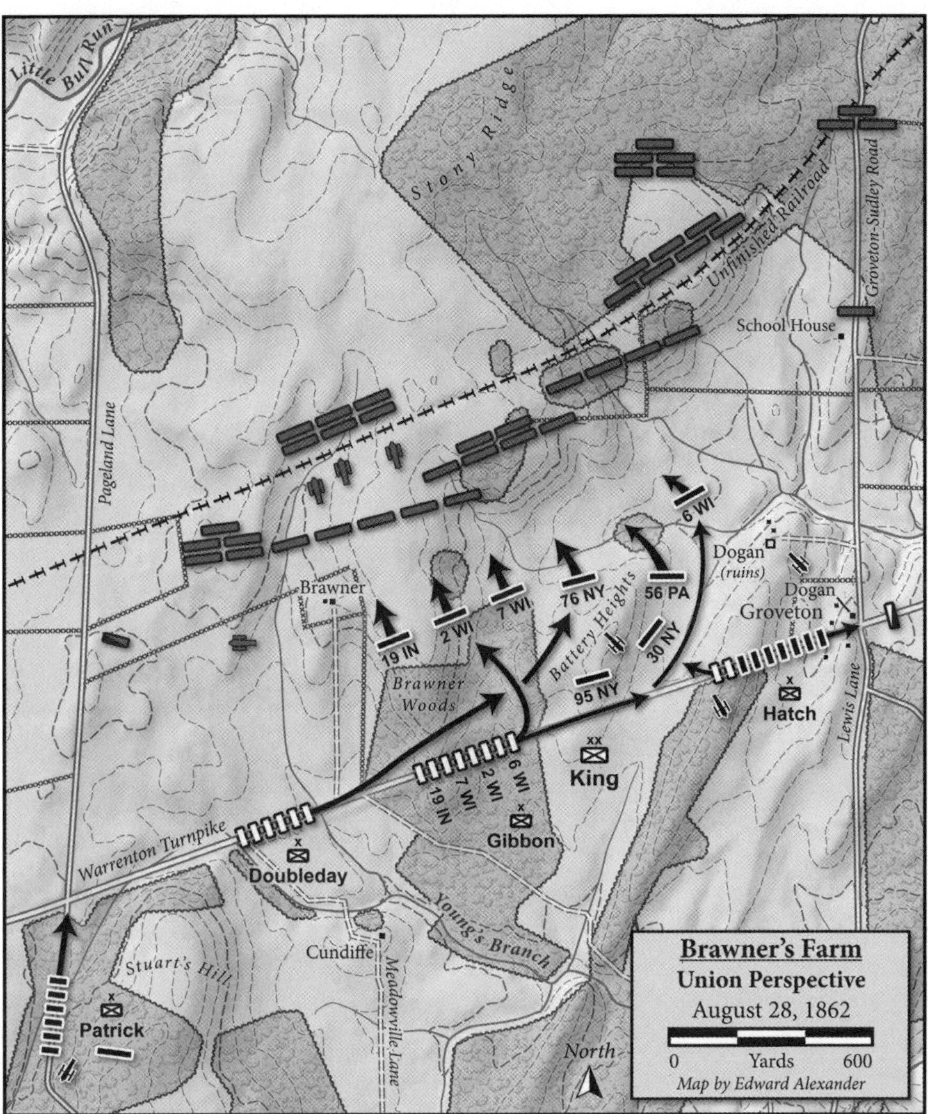

rain" and it seemed the whole regiment would soon be annihilated. Officers and men alike realized with a jump of the heart that they had found what the whole army had been seeking the past several days—the feared "Stonewall" Jackson and his Confederates. To a watching soldier in the leading brigade a mile ahead, the rip of distant musketry made a sound "like that of hailstones upon an empty barn."[3]

3 Bushnell, *Herald*, undated; Cheek and Pointon, *Sauk County*, 38; Sullivan, *Telegraph*, Nov. 4, 1883; Cornelius Wheeler, journal, Aug. 28, 1862, Cornelius Wheeler Papers, WHS; King, *War Papers*, 217; Dawes, *Service*, 60; *Telegraph*, Sep. 4, 1884; Gibbon, *Recollections*, 53–54.Harries, in Otis, *Second Wisconsin*, 251; Thomas Allen, letter, Sep. 4, 1862, *Civil War Times Illustrated*, Nov. 1962, 32–33; Theron W. Haight, "Gainesville, Groveton and Bull Run," in *War Papers*, 2:361; Judson, letter, Oct. 1, 1871. Wheeler wrote: "The regiment met a heavy body of the enemy's infantry; here for nearly twenty minutes, until succored by the other regiments of the brigade, the Second Regiment alone sustained and checked the whole of 'Stonewall' Jackson's division, under one of the intensely concentrated fires of musketry probably ever experienced by any troops in this or any other war."

Chapter 21

"Move Your Division and Attack the Enemy"

Groveton: August 28, 1862

Located thirty miles south of Washington D.C., Prince William County, Virginia, runs from the Potomac River through the rolling hills of the Piedmont to the Bull Run Mountains. Established in the eighteenth century, Prince William County witnessed enormous change in the nearly 100 years between the American Revolution and the Civil War. The tobacco economy centered on the Potomac slowly migrated westward as fields became exhausted from overproduction.

Attracted to cheaper land, pioneers of western Prince William settled the rich piedmont area in hopes of creating productive farms to support growing families. By the early nineteenth century, the tobacco economy in Northern Virginia had experienced decades of slow decline necessitating a switch from tobacco to grains and wheat. The agricultural shift soon produced an excess of enslaved labor that correlated with dwindling farms. For most of the nineteenth century, Prince William County continued to lose population as many residents moved to other sections of the state or to new parts of the country.

The small crossroads community called Groveton reflected this decades-long trend. Located at the intersection of the east-west Warrenton Turnpike and north running Groveton Road, Groveton was originally a small parcel of land within hundred-acre land grants given to wealthy Virginia landowners during the colonial period. After the American Revolution the Dogan family bought much of the land in the immediate vicinity. The original owner, Henry Dogan, named his new farm Peach Grove, soon transmuted to Groveton and the name of the surrounding community.

The road network that developed around Groveton brought prosperity to the area during peace. In wartime it facilitated easy movement for armies. The northern road linked Grovetown with the community of Sudley Springs while

The modern Brawner Farmhouse from the Warrenton Turnpike during the first half of the 20th century. *Library of Congress*

a narrow farm road linked the area to the many small communities in central Prince William County. More than anything else, the major east-west road running through Groveton spurred growth. Unlike most roads in northern Virginia, the Warrenton Turnpike was a private road constructed with a layer of logs to keep the road surface in working order year-round. The roadbed's construction allowed for fast and easy movement from Gainesville to the west and Centreville to the east.[1]

Unbeknownst to the Dogans and their neighbors, Groveton is part of an 80-mile long, 20-mile-wide geological area known as the Culpeper Basin. Created from millions of years of geological movement, much of the basin contains sedimentary rocks such as sandstone, siltstone, and shale. Battlefield geologists E-An Zen and Alta Walker describe the terrain containing the sedimentary rocks as "gently rolling land surfaces, with open, nearly flat hilltops dissected by ravines that cut into the soft bedrock." Other sections of the Culpeper Basin were created by a large body of magma that cooled and formed distinct geological features. Depending on the varying speed that the magma cooled, different rocks formed distinct ridges. South and east of Groveton, many of the hills contain a foundation of sandstone and siltstone. The hills that played a prominent role in the first battle of Manassas, Henry House, Bald, Buck, and Matthews Hills, as well as Chinn Ridge, are all nearly the same height, 270 to

1 Benjamin Ford and Stephen Thompson, *Archaeological Investigations Associated with the Fauquier and Alexandria Turnpike* (Charlottesville, VA, 2013).

290 feet because "the 'hills' are remnants of a flat area, underlain by the same geologic formation of siltstone and shale, dissected and distinguished by ravines cutting down through the area."[2]

North of Groveton runs a long narrow ridge angled to the northwest locals called Stony Ridge. Unlike the hills a few hundred yards away, the slow cooling lava creating Stony Ridge produced a different rock, diabase. "Harder and more resistant to erosion than are the sedimentary rocks into which it intruded, [diabase] forms steep ridges which rise above the surrounding sedimentary rocks." Unlike Henry House Hill, Stony Ridge rises nearly 340 feet. The difference in the rock foundation is not only distinguishable in the varying ridge heights. The softer sandstone and siltstone produce soil easily tilled in agriculture compared to the rocky soil found in diabase areas. Reflecting the different soil composition, by the 1860s most of the sedimentary rock areas were farms while the diabase areas remained wooded.[3]

The road network and terrain influenced Jackson's decision about how to deploy his men on August 28. The fiasco of the night march from Manassas to the old battlefield area strung out Jackson's Wing during the march and into its subsequent deployment. Jackson's lead division under Taliaferro, experiencing an easy march, deployed along Stony Ridge to the northeast of Groveton. Jackson's other two divisions, having marched unintentionally in a roundabout route to Centreville, arrived at the old battlefield later and more dispersed than Taliaferro. Ewell's Division deployed onto Taliaferro's left on Stony Ridge covering the Groveton-Sudley Road. Hill's Division extended Jackson's line along the ridge to Sudley Road and the outskirts of the old Manassas battlefield. A small reserve near Sudley Church formed in Jackson's rear.

Once Jackson's men arrived at their positions, the Confederate line extended over two miles with the right flank under Taliaferro closer to the Warrenton Turnpike while the left flank angled away from the road. The Southern position along Stony Ridge was nearly perfect. Lying atop the diabase ridge, the Confederates were on some of the highest ground in the immediate vicinity and its thick woods easily camouflaged the resting soldiers. Running towards the northwest, Stony Ridge paralleled the Warrenton Turnpike for most of Jackson's line. The Southerners found themselves watching one of the major road networks in the area, one that promised to be used by the Federal army, along a hidden height.

2 E-An Zen and Alta Walker, *Rocks and War: Geology and the Civil War Campaign of Second Manassas* (Shippensburg, PA, 2000), 15–21.

3 Ibid., 15.

The Stony Ridge position did contain some defects. Jackson's three divisions fell short of Bull Run. Likewise, Jackson's right flank was in the air. Without an anchor on either end, Jackson needed to remain vigilant against having his position turned. Since Jackson did not have enough soldiers to anchor his flanks, he also lacked a large reserve available to stabilize the line if a portion buckled under assault. The strong defensive position also lacked a direct route to Lee and Longstreet at Thoroughfare Gap. With Bull Run to his rear, if defeated Jackson faced the possibility of being cut off and destroyed in detail. Finally, the very strength of the Stony Ridge position posed problems. Federal soldiers marching along the turnpike could march past without seeing Jackson. If Stonewall desired to spring a trap on a marching column of Yankees, he would be required to move his infantry off the ridge closer to the turnpike, where the terrain balanced out between the defender and the attacker.

Colonel Bradley Johnson found himself responsible for the protection of the Confederate right flank. The 33-year-old native Marylander was one of several political officers who continued to command brigades in Lee's army after the Peninsula campaign. A lawyer from Frederick, Maryland, Johnson was a powerful Democrat in the Old Line State prior to the war. After the outbreak of hostilities Johnson raised a company of pro-Confederate Marylanders for the Southern army, soon expanding into a regiment. Forging an excellent combat reputation with Jackson in both the Valley and Peninsula campaigns, the1st Maryland was one of a handful of regiments that the Confederate War Department allowed to be discharged after its one-year enlistment period expired. Temporarily without a command, Johnson quickly found himself in command of a brigade of Virginians in Taliaferro's Division.[4]

The Marylander controlled three infantry regiments, one battalion, and two batteries of artillery during the early morning hours of August 28. After reaching the intersection dominated by the Stone House at the old Manassas battlefield around midnight, Taliaferro ordered Johnson due west on the turnpike towards Groveton. While Jackson's men continued to stream towards the Manassas battlefield, Johnson picketed the roads leading from the west and south. Arriving at Groveton, Johnson pushed one regiment south along the Groveton Road while another continued west along the Warrenton Turnpike towards Gainesville. The rest of the brigade remained at Groveton as a reserve in case either regiment bumped into the enemy.[5]

4 Warner, *Generals in Gray*, 156–157.

5 *OR* 12, pt. 2, 664.

A half-mile west of Groveton, Johnson's pickets bumped into Company K, 1st Virginia Cavalry, tasked with guarding the area around Gainesville. After talking with Capt. George Gaither, commander of the cavalry and yet another native Marylander in Lee's army, the two Marylanders came to agreement on how to fulfill their mutually supporting missions. The cavalry agreed to travel further west on the turnpike and form a series of vedettes (mounted pickets) while the infantry set a reserve in their rear.[6]

Shortly after dawn, approximately 7:30 a.m., Captain Gaither reported a column of Federal cavalry advancing from Gainesville. Keeping his men hidden, Gaither's troopers surprised and captured a Federal courier. On the courier's person the cavalrymen found a dispatch from Pope to Generals Sigel and Reynolds ordering them to concentrate at Manassas Junction. The dispatch even detailed the exact routes both were to take to Manassas. Sigel was to march to Manassas "from Gainesville with his right resting on the Manassas Gap Railroad; Reynolds, also from Gainesville, to keep his left on the Warrenton Road; and King's division to move *en echelon* in support of the other two." Provided that the two Federal officers obeyed this order, the two Federal columns would drift apart from another after passing through Gainesville, with Sigel heading on an easterly axis while Reynolds and King moved to the northeast.[7]

Possessing critical knowledge about the Federal march, Johnson ordered both the courier and his dispatch first to Taliaferro's command and then up the chain of command to Jackson. Apparently there appeared some questions about the veracity of the captured message from Jackson's headquarters since Johnson ordered Captain Gaither to "report to Major-General Jackson in person the contents of the dispatch." Instead of trotting eastward on the Warrenton Turnpike, Gaither decided to take a circuitous route, ultimately ending in Gaither, bumping into a Federal patrol, getting captured before he reached Jackson.[8]

The rationale for Captain Gaither's decision for a roundabout route to Jackson's headquarters was never examined by either his contemporaries or subsequent historians. Meeting with Johnson's infantryman in the early morning hours, Gaither knew of the presence of Taliaferro's Division at Groveton. The most direct route from his position southwest of Groveton and Jackson's Wing was the Warrenton Turnpike. A short trot on the pike would easily have brought Gaither to Jackson's headquarters. It seems that the Confederate detour into Fairfax not

6 Ibid., 664.

7 W. B. Taliaferro, "Jackson's Raid Around Pope," *Battles and Leaders of the Civil War*, Vol. 2, 507.

8 *OR* 12, pt. 2, 664.

only had the potential to confuse the Federal army but also confused portions of the force operating with Jackson. Gaither proved to be an intelligent man, later in the war being appointed as a Confederate agent in Europe, so his decision to move on any route other than the Warrenton Turnpike is hard to comprehend. All the other routes between Gainesville and Groveton angled towards Manassas before side roads linked a traveler back to the Warrenton Turnpike and the old Manassas battlefield. Potentially both Johnson and Taliaferro lacked knowledge of Jackson's position, forcing Gaither to wander around the area looking for the wing headquarters. If a cavalry captain could not locate Jackson with the full support of a brigade and division commander, August 28 did not portend to be a good day for Confederate command and control.

The captured directives detailing the route for Sigel, Reynolds, and King to concentrate at Manassas seemed to be clear to everyone but Jackson. Still marching north of Bull Run in Fairfax, at 10:00 a.m. A. P. Hill received a message from Jackson dated "battle-field of Manassas, 8:00 a.m." that the Federal army was in full retreat. To keep pressure on the enemy, Jackson ordered Hill to advance to the Bull Run fords blocking Pope's army from McClellan. The timing suggests that Jackson's conclusion about Pope's army came from the captured note. Gaither's men captured the courier around daybreak,7:30 a.m. on August 28, 1862. While it is unlikely that Gaither's report had reached Jackson in this short time, it seems that the news was spreading throughout his command. Hill disregarded the order to cover the Bull Run fords because he had also seen reports of the captured Federal orders and "deemed it best to push on and join Jackson."[9]

Jackson's interpretation of the Federal marching order was not a concentration of Pope's army but rather a retreat toward McClellan. In his after-action report submitted in April 1863, Jackson still seemed confused and it is worth citing:

> My command had hardly concentrated north of the turnpike before the enemy's advance reached the vicinity of Groveton from the direction of Warrenton. General Stuart kept me advised of the general movements of the enemy, while Colonel Rosser, of the cavalry, with his command, and Col. Bradley T. Johnson, commanding Campbell's brigade, remained in front of the Federals and operated against their advance. Dispositions were promptly made to attack the enemy, based upon the idea that he would continue to press forward up on the turnpike toward Alexandria; but as he did not appear to advance in force, and there was reason to believe that his main body was leaving the road and inclining toward Manassas Junction, my command was advanced through the

9 Ibid., 670.

woods, leaving Groveton on the left, until it reached a commanding position near Brawner's house.[10]

Jackson believed elements of Pope's army would march down the Warrenton Turnpike towards Alexandria but Taliaferro, Hill, Stuart, and Johnson all understood the captured note ordering a concentration at Manassas. If Jackson rejected the majority consensus of his subordinates and thought Pope would march east on the Warrenton Turnpike, Jackson's 8:00 a.m. order to Hill moving his division to cover the Bull Run fords is likewise confusing. At the time Jackson wrote his order, Hill's Division was beginning to assemble near Centreville. If the Federals were indeed marching on the turnpike, Hill could best block the most direct route between Pope and McClellan at Centreville. Covering the Bull Run fords would open the way for Pope and McClellan to link up.

As Captain Gaither began his futile ride to Jackson, Bradley Johnson began deploying his brigade against a sizable Federal column he knew to be approaching. On paper his brigade was a formidable force. The grueling battles Johnson's Virginians fought at Shenandoah, Peninsula, and Cedar Mountain had whittled his regiments down to a hardened core of veterans. The brigade leadership had nearly been annihilated. A private later remembered that the brigade contained only one field officer, Maj. John Seddon, commanding the 1st Virginia Battalion. The 21st Virginia and the 42nd Virginia were both commanded by captains while the remnants of the 48th Virginia was led by a lieutenant. All told, Johnson had only 600 men in his brigade.[11]

Preparing his brigade for the coming fight, Johnson ordered the 1st Virginia Battalion and the 48th Virginia south of the turnpike along the Groveton Road under the overall command of Major Seddon. Deploying over half his infantry units south of the road, Johnson hoped to detect and prevent any enemy force turning his left flank and throwing his line into confusion. Back along the turnpike, Johnson ordered Capt. John Penn and the 42nd Virginia east along the turnpike as skirmishers while Capt. William Witcher and the 21st Virginia remained in reserve.[12]

Needing to add firepower to his diminished line, Johnson had available a total of six artillery pieces. In addition to four smoothbore cannons from an unknown battery assigned to his brigade, Johnson obtained the service of two rifled cannons that had somehow been assigned to the 1st Virginia Cavalry for

10 Ibid., 644–645.

11 Worsham, *One of Jackson's Foot Cavalry*, 122; Gaff, *Brave Men's Tears*, 43.

12 *OR* 12, pt. 2, 665.

its mission to reconnoiter the enemy. The four smoothbores remained in reserve while the rifled guns deployed north of the turnpike near a farmhouse occupied by the Brawner family.[13]

Like the community of Groveton a few hundred yards to the northeast, the Brawner farm contained a rich history extending to the Revolutionary era. Originally part of large land holdings of the wealthy Carter family, over the first half of the nineteenth century different families purchased or sold parcels of land depending on economic fortunes. By the 1850s George Douglas owned less than 350 acres of land centered on a house he christened "Bachelor's Hall," although puzzlingly he was married at the time. After Douglas's death in 1856, his wife rented out the house and the farm to the Brawner family.[14]

The "Bachelor's Hall" farm centered on the main building and its associated outbuildings. Set about a third of a mile from the Warrenton Turnpike, "Bachelor's Hall" was likely a two-and-a-half story house. Set on a stone foundation bookended with two brick chimneys, the house was a prominent landmark for travelers on the turnpike between Groveton and Gainesville, as it was easily seen from the turnpike. Only an observant sightseer could make out the handful of outbuildings scattered around "Bachelor's Hall."[15]

Like many Prince William farmers in the late antebellum period, the Brawners did not own the land on which they lived and farmed, although the family did own an enslaved hand. The 300 acres of the Brawner farm classified as "improved land" produced 48 bushels of wheat (1.4 tons), 300 bushels of corn (10.5 tons), 100 bushels of oats (1.6 tons), two bushels of grass seed, and 12 tons of hay in 1860 though by 1862 only a fraction of the farm was likely in peak production. As productive as the Brawners were, approximately 1/3 of their crop went to the Widow Douglas in addition to the $150 annual rent.[16]

To protect valuable crops from being damaged by roaming pigs (including the Brawner's nine pigs), the family maintained a series of fences scattered across their farm. Immediately north of the turnpike stood a fence that ran along a farm lane connecting the house with the main road. Another series of fences separated the farmland into smaller, more manageable fields. Yet another fence separated the main fields from the house, creating approximately one acre of

13 Ibid., 665.

14 "Manassas National Battlefield, "Environmental Assessment Rehabilitation of Brawner Farm House" (Washington, D.C., 2005), 10–11.

15 Judith Earley and Kay Fanning, "Manassas National Battlefield, Brawner Farm Cultural Landscapes Report," (Washington, D.C., 2005), 20.

16 Ibid., 37–38.

enclosed workspace immediately around the house. Finally, another fence stood on the property to define the boundaries for the orchard that probably stood to the southwest of the house.[17]

The final landmark on the Brawner farm was the 35 "unimproved" acres that were mainly wooded. Commencing near the farm lane, the edge of the woodlot paralleled the turnpike for approximately 1,500 feet before turning in a 90-degree angle and running an additional 700 feet and rounding back towards "Bachelor's Hall." From a birds-eye view the woods, which locals called "Brawner's Woods," looked like an L on its side.[18]

After deploying his section of rifle artillery on a ridge slightly north of the Brawner farm, Johnson tweaked his brigade's dispositions. The 21st Virginia remained in reserve but closed with the artillery to act as its reserves. The 42nd Virginia remained along the turnpike but moved to the cover of the Brawner Woods.

A little before 11:00 a.m., clouds of dust were spotted coming from Gainesville, signifying a large force approaching Johnson's position. To buttress support for the artillery, Johnson moved the 48th Virginia north of the turnpike leaving only the understrength 1st Virginia Battalion picketing the road between the Brawner farm and Manassas. When the 48th Virginia settled into its new position, Johnson gave permission to the section commander to open fire.[19]

As the artillery boomed, a sergeant in the 21st Virginia witnessed the Brawner family race for safety. John Worsham remembered seeing a woman exit the house "bareheaded" alongside an enslaved woman. Between the two women was a child, "crying loudly." Worsham and his comrades momentarily forgot about the Federals and instead focused on the civilians, watching them as they "crossed the pike, climbed over the fence, and went directly south through the fields, and were soon lost to sight." The soldiers chuckled that in their excitement the women did not close the door to the house.[20]

The Confederate shells were not producing amusement in the Federal ranks. After a few shots, the artillerists soon had the range of the Federals and quickly dropped several shells into the turnpike. A puff of white smoke mixed with dust showed that one shell fell directly onto the massed Federals on the turnpike. After the Federals abandoned the turnpike, a Confederate soldier with

17 Ibid., 20–21.

18 Ibid., 87–90.

19 *OR* 12, pt. 2, 665.

20 Worsham, *One of Jackson's Foot Cavalry*, 123.

binoculars saw the results of that one shell: eight killed or wounded soldiers scattered across the road.[21]

Johnson saw a battery of Federal guns deploy south of the turnpike supported by what looked like a full brigade of infantry in battle line. Within moments smoke belched from the opposing artillery but no shells fell amongst the Confederates. At first some of the experienced Confederate artillerists thought their opponents were having trouble finding the range of the Southerners. After a few more rounds it became clear that the Federals had deployed a battery of smoothbore guns that were operating beyond their maximum range. The Confederates enjoyed the interlude, firing methodically without danger from their counterparts.[22]

Realizing their smoothbores didn't have the range to hit Johnson's guns, the Federals brought up a battery of 10-pound Parrot guns. Soon Federal shells began to fall amongst the Confederate position. Worse, elements of the Federal infantry were observed shaking into a loose skirmish line and advancing towards Johnson. Anxious that he lacked strength to combat the developing Federal presence north of the turnpike, Johnson ordered Major Seddon to ready the 1st Virginia Battalion to abandon its position south of the road and join the rest of the brigade near the Brawner farm.

Shifting Seddon's battalion proved the key moment in the early afternoon's skirmish. Besides shelling the Confederates, the Federals apparently refused to use the visible infantrymen in an attack. A lull appeared over the field with both Johnson and the Federals watching one another. Once Seddon's men were in north of the turnpike, Johnson decided to clear the enemy from the road. His opponents put up light skirmishing as the Virginians approached the roadbed. Once at the turnpike, the Southerners discovered the reason behind the slackening enemy fire. The Federals were moving off the Warrenton Turnpike and onto Pageland Road which ran south of Groveton. After concentrating his entire brigade north of the turnpike, Johnson was now blind to events south of the road. Although it appeared that the Federals were marching towards Manassas on Pageland Road, there also stood the possibility that the enemy was trying to turn Johnson's left flank. To prevent being cut off from the rest of Jackson's Wing, Johnson decided to abandon the Brawner farm and return to Groveton.[23]

The lunchtime skirmish near the Brawner farm produced hardly any Confederate casualties but a few close calls. A soldier in the 21st Virginia lying

21 Alonzo Hill, *Our Boys: The Personal Experience of a Soldier in the Army of the Potomac* (Philadelphia, 1866), 371.

22 *OR* 12, pt. 2, 393.

23 Ibid., 665.

prone near the artillery had the heel of his shoe taken off by a passing Federal shell but otherwise left him unharmed. Unbeknownst to anyone in the ranks, the battle of Brawner farm had begun. By the end of the night scores of Southerners would find they did not possess the luck of that fortunate Virginia soldier.[24]

Johnson was perplexed that he did not receive instructions from his divisional or wing commander when the artillery signaled the start of an engagement. Some of Bradley Johnson's Virginians started to worry that they were forgotten by the high command. Returning to Groveton, Johnson found a courier waiting for him with orders to report directly to division headquarters and General Taliaferro. Before he could find his commander, J. E. B. Stuart ordered Johnson's brigade to a nearby skirt of wood and "formed the brigade into line of battle, stacked arms, and lay down in position."[25]

Stuart's insertion into the infantry chain of command portended the possibility of unneeded confusion. Commanding the Army of Northern Virginia's cavalry as a major general, normally Stuart reported directly to Lee. If Lee deemed it advantageous, he could and sometimes did, assign elements of Stuart's cavalry to work with his wings. If Stuart joined one of these detachments away from the main army, the cavalryman reported to the local wing commander until Lee arrived on the field and returned the chain of command to its standard arrangement. Stuart supposedly reported directly to Jackson while Ewell, Taliaferro, and Hill took charge of most of his infantry. Typically, orders to the infantry, except in extraordinary circumstances, emanated down from divisional headquarters to brigade and later regimental commanders.

As a major general, and thus the ranking officer on the field, Stuart possessed the authority to order Johnson's brigade. Stuart's decision to move the infantry to cover and allow them to rest in case the fighting flared up again later that afternoon was sensible. The process of that movement, though, could be dangerous. By breaking the chain of command, Stuart caused a situation in which Taliaferro lost contact with a sizable portion of his division. Although he was eventually brought into the loop about its position, if this happened again Taliaferro's authority over his men would not only be degraded (important to a new commander getting to know his men and vice versa) but in the case of an emergency the scattering of commands could result in piecemeal movements that almost always resulted in unnecessarily higher casualties.

24 Worsham, *One of Jackson's Foot Cavalry*, 122.

25 *OR* 12, pt. 2, 665; Worsham, *One of Jackson's Foot Cavalry*, 123.

As Johnson skirmished with the Federals near Groveton, it appears that the captured Federal courier note from earlier in the morning finally reached Jackson. According to Taliaferro:

> Johnson's messenger, bearing the captured order, found the Confederate headquarters established on the shady side of an old-fashioned fence, in the corners of which General Jackson and his two division commanders were profoundly sleeping after the fatigues of the preceding night, notwithstanding the intense heat of that August day.[26]

Taliaferro remembered that Jackson "called no council to discuss the situation disclosed by this communication, although his ranking officers were almost at his side; he asked no conference, no expression of opinion; he made no suggestion, but simply, without a word except to repeat the language of the dispatch, turned to me and said, 'Move your division and attack the enemy'; and to Ewell, 'Support the attack.'"[27]

After receiving the captured order, Jackson had two choices about how to react to this new development, attack or remain on the defensive until Lee and the rest of the army arrived. Characteristically Stonewall chose the boldest.

Remaining on the defensive posed both benefits and problems for Jackson's Wing. Marching from Manassas Junction to the old Manassas battlefield took longer than expected and even at noon Hill's Division was just now arriving on the field after being on the road for nearly 12 hours. Unless responding to a dire emergency, Hill's Division needed at least a few hours' rest before it could be considered reasonably combat effective. Until the soldiers could rest, Jackson temporarily lost the use of his largest division. If Hill needed to be moved to another part of Jackson's line, it might very well take the rest of the day for Hill's men to arrive. Remaining on the defensive promised a day of rest for his men, allowing them to engage the enemy with more physical strength when the time for battle finally arrived.

If Hill's odyssey made his command a spent force, Jackson still had two divisions nearby that could be used. Arriving on the old battlefield that morning, Taliaferro and Ewell both possessed commands that had the opportunity to rest and recuperate from the efforts of the past few days. Taliaferro's rawness in command of his division seemed offset by the competent commanders of his brigades. Ewell, on the other hand, possessed both a rock-solid record as

26 Taliaferro, "Jackson's Raid Around Pope," *Battles and Leaders*, 2:507.

27 Ibid., 508.

a divisional commander and a team of skilled brigade commanders. An air of confidence existed in these two divisions that allowed for daring decisions.

Besides being blessed with experienced subordinates, Jackson also had a command full of soldiers and officers familiar with the local terrain. Returning to the fields where he earned his nickname and the baptism of fire for many of his men, Jackson seemed confident the local terrain would not be an issue. Unlike his performance around Richmond where he slowly groped around unfamiliar territory and upset Confederate battle plans, Jackson and many of his men were familiar with the local roads, hills, and valleys and seemed confident that familiarity offset a still incomplete picture of enemy dispositions. Tired as he and his men may have been, Jackson had enough confidence both in his officers and men and in the knowledge of the terrain to bring battle.

The events of the past two days also contributed to the choice to attack. From Bristoe Station, Manassas Junction, and Bull Run Bridge every time Jackson's men found and engaged the enemy, the Confederates had emerged triumphant. Johnson's skirmishing with the Federals may have led Jackson to the belief that the enemy had located Jackson's Wing and that the Federals may return to attack him. Attacking soon, before the Federals concentrated around him, presented Stonewall an opportunity to attack in strength and defeat them.

Finally, the proximity of Lee and the rest of the Army of Northern Virginia likely assured Jackson that if any disaster fell upon his command, sizable reinforcements were nearby. Jackson assumed that Thoroughfare Gap remained in Confederate hands, allowing the army to concentrate quickly if the need arose. Confident in his men, his knowledge of the terrain, the proximity of the rest of Lee's army, and his innate aggressive disposition to resolve contingencies, Jackson decided to attack. As the ranking officer on the field, the decision to attack ultimately rested on Jackson.

A little after noon, orders arrived for both Taliaferro and Ewell to move their divisions in preparation for an attack. Starting near Sudley, Taliaferro marched west through the woods surrounding the unfinished Manassas Gap railroad. The Stonewall Brigade led the column followed by Taliaferro's mixed brigade of Alabamians and Virginians, while Starke's Brigade of Louisianans brought up the rear. After marching about two and a half miles from Sudley, Taliaferro stopped his division in the woods to the west of Groveton. Ewell's Division immediately followed Taliaferro.[28]

Arriving at their new position along Stony Ridge, the enlisted men attempted to rest while their officers conferred. A staff officer remembered, "the

28 *OR* 12, pt. 2, 656.

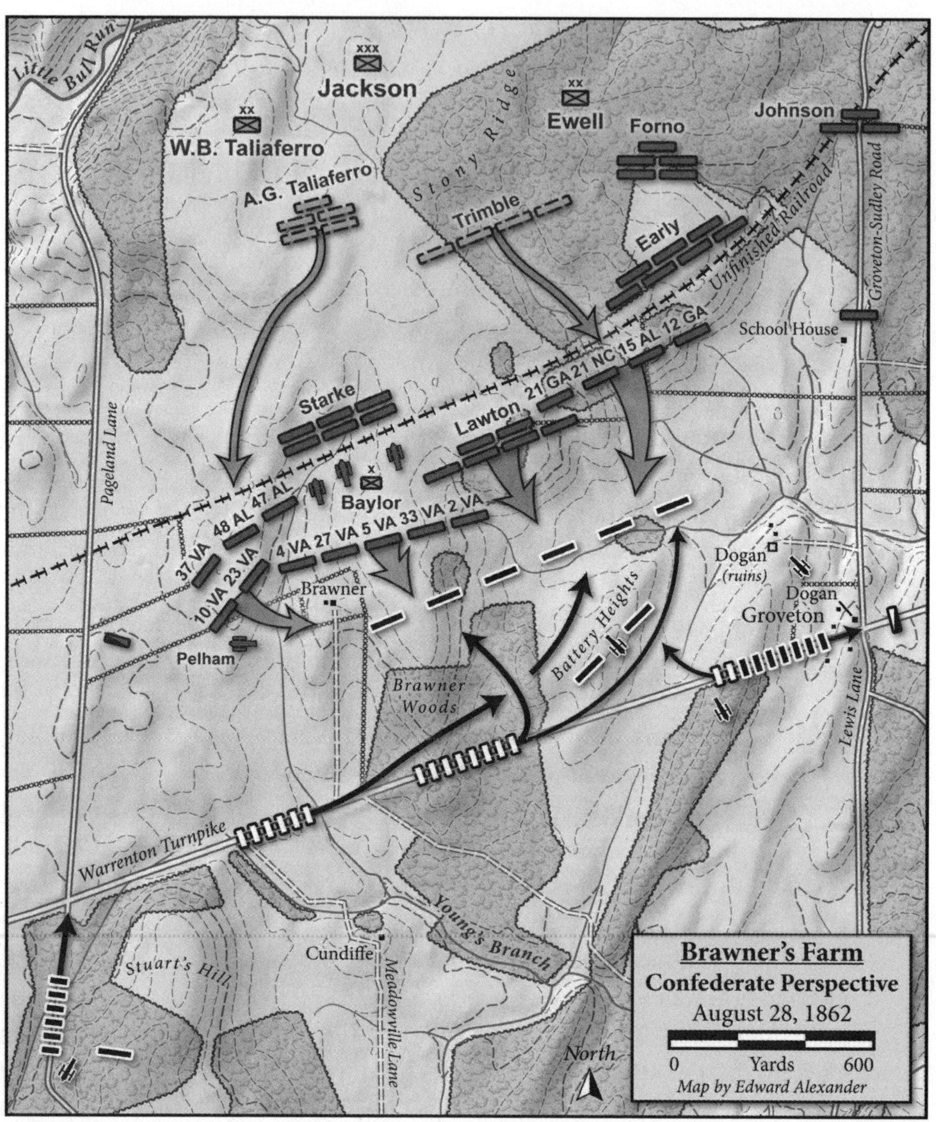

Brawner's Farm
Confederate Perspective
August 28, 1862
0 Yards 600
Map by Edward Alexander

men were packed like herring in a barrel in the woods." Stacking their arms, the soldiers were allowed to rest with the order that music and shouting be strictly forbidden. However, "the men had no restrictions as to laughing and talking in an ordinary voice, and the woods sounded like the hum of a beehive in the warm sunshine of the August day."[29]

29 Blackford, *War Years with Jeb Stuart*, 117.

Jackson's decision to attack the Federals near the Brawner farm appeared to be for naught. By the time Taliaferro had his division in position and ready to attack, the enemy that Johnson had skirmished with earlier began to pull back from the Warrenton Turnpike. As the skirmish line approached the turnpike, Taliaferro saw columns of the enemy turn off the turnpike onto Pageland Road towards Manassas Junction. The Federals were marching *away* from the Confederates.

Before following Stuart's orders, Johnson decided to finish his little battle, ordering his two rifled pieces to open fire on the Federal column on the road. Soon after the artillery resumed firing Johnson received an order from Jackson to pull his brigade further north along Stony Ridge. Around 4:00 p.m. officers bellowed "Right face! Double quick! March!" Marching away, Johnson observed a line of Federal infantry and cavalry skirmishers closely following his brigade. Annoyed at this pursuit, Johnson ordered Lt. Virginius Dabney to attack the Federals with the 48th Virginia (all 21 soldiers present that day). The Federals were content to let the Virginians leave in peace after this company-sized attack forced the Federals back towards the turnpike. Resuming the march, Johnson's men were astonished to find Jackson's Wing formed up in the woods. Recognizing their earlier duty picketing the Warrenton Turnpike, Jackson slid Johnson on the left flank of his new position serving as a link to Hill at Sudley, promising to keep the brigade out of the coming fight "if he could avoid it."[30]

Johnson's withdrawal ushered in a lull as the Federal column marched out of sight. While most of the enlisted soldiers talked and gambled the afternoon away, some soldiers became interested in fulfilling the inner man. Unlike the majority of Jackson's Wing, Ewell's Division missed most of the feast the previous day at Manassas. After guarding the rear at Bristoe Station, by the time they arrived at the railroad junction many of the warehouses had already been put to the torch. Some enterprising (and likely hungry) troops visited a nearby farmhouse in search of delicacies. While not approaching the quality and quantity of the food found at Manassas, the farmhouse treats served to break the otherwise monotonous army fare. Returning to their units in the tree line, some of the soldiers met "Tricky Dick" Ewell riding his line inspecting both his troops' position and the potential battlefield. Briefly chatting with the soldiers, Ewell joked "that a canteen of buttermilk was a delicacy not to be

30 *OR* 12, pt. 2, 665; Worsham, *One of Jackson's Foot Cavalry*, 125–126.

despised on such an evening by the commander-in-chief," and asked for the men to fetch him a quaff.[31]

The soldiers interrupted Ewell as he prepared himself for a potential fight. The right of Jackson's new line contained the three brigades of Taliaferro's Division (Johnson's Brigade detached further down the line on the left and unlikely to be called to action). To the left and rear of Taliaferro, Ewell formed his division. Settling his men in, Ewell made the decision to split the division in two for the coming fight. The two brigades closest to Taliaferro's Division, Early's Virginians and Hay's Louisianans, were left to the direction of Jubal Early. Ewell's remaining two brigades, Trimble's mixed brigade and Lawton's Georgians, remained under the direct supervision of the division commander. This unusual arrangement mitigated the command-and-control problems that the woods of Stony Ridge presented. Couriers moving laterally through the forest were forced to negotiate trees, slowing down the transfer of messages, and even presenting the possibility of couriers getting lost in the forest. As a seasoned commander, Ewell appreciated the fact that the battlefield was a fluid place, with important opportunities for decisive action sometimes appearing for a few precious moments. To capitalize on mistakes the Federals might make, Ewell entrusted half his command to his most able subordinate. Instead of waiting for a courier to arrive giving Early permission from Ewell to take an action that could be vital to the course of the battle or the safety of his command, Ewell trusted his subordinates to make the correct decision in real time, something that Jackson failed to implement with his key subordinates.[32]

Jackson as a subordinate contrasted starkly with Jackson the commander. Leading a quasi-independent force in the Shenandoah Valley in 1861–1862, Jackson technically reported to Joe Johnston when the Valley District was subordinate to the Department of Northern Virginia. Practically, however, Jackson was given wide discretion over how he conducted the troops in his command, provided that he fulfill the broad objectives set by his superiors in Richmond and the main Virginia army. This relationship survived when Robert E. Lee assumed command of the Army of Northern Virginia around Richmond. During both the Peninsula campaign and later in central and northern Virginia, Lee allowed Jackson latitude in how he accomplished the objectives with which he was tasked. It is important to remember that after the disappointing performance during the Peninsula campaign Lee included his key subordinates

31 Taliaferro, "Jackson's Raid Around Pope," *Battles and Leaders*, 2:508.

32 *OR* 12, pt. 2, 710.

in his informal councils to discuss the campaign and the role each commander was expected to play in it. Before the march to Manassas, at Jeffersonton, Lee met with his three key subordinates to review the current situation the army faced and how each officer was expected to perform. Thus, Jackson was given not only what his role was in the overall campaign but also the expectations and objectives that the other elements of the army had.

As a commanding officer Jackson's command style could at times be enigmatic at both the operational (campaign) and tactical (battlefield) levels. Command problems at the operational level had been recently demonstrated in the wing's march from Manassas Junction to its defensive position by the old Manassas battlefield. Before leaving the railroad junction Jackson failed to confer with Taliaferro, Hill, and Ewell about the immediate next steps in the campaign. If Jackson had conferred with his divisional commanders, the unnecessary detour to Centreville by a substantial portion of his command would have easily been avoided. All three divisions contained both officers and men that had spent months in the area between the first battle of Manassas in July 1861 and the evacuation of northern Virginia in March 1862. If the division commanders knew their destination, they would have taken the necessary steps to get their commands on the right track when it was discovered they were marching in the wrong direction on the night of August 27–28.

Adding to an already problematic command style, Jackson appeared confused about Federal intentions, even after reading the morning's captured dispatch. Arriving near Stony Ridge, Taliaferro was perplexed to see "that the enemy had abandoned his intention of attempting to cross at Sudley and was moving off to the right of the Turnpike." Why should Taliaferro expect the Federals to advance along the Warrenton Turnpike towards Sudley? Surprisingly, Jackson held a mistaken view of his opponent's movements. In his after-action report Jackson admitted "dispositions were promptly made to attack the enemy, based upon the idea that he would continue to press forward upon the turnpike toward Alexandria."[33]

Earlier in the day Hill's instruction to block the Bull Run fords implied fighting. Jackson intended to attack Pope as he marched along the Warrenton Turnpike before he could join McClellan in Fairfax County. Jackson expected the main Federal column to remain on the turnpike. While Hill held up the column along Bull Run, the rest of Jackson's Wing would roll up the exposed column. As we have seen, by 10:00 a.m. Hill had heard enough of the reported

33 *OR* 12, pt. 2, 644, 656.

captured note to ignore an order from his prickly superior and move his division away from Bull Run towards Sudley.

Earlier in the month before the fighting at Cedar Mountain, Hill had run afoul of Jackson. For Hill to ignore an order from Jackson just weeks after upsetting Stonewall meant that either Hill remained impetuous, as he had been under Longstreet, or Hill felt that the situation had changed to such an extent that Jackson's orders were outdated. That the sometimes irascible Jackson allowed the matter to drop afterwards (a few months earlier Stonewall had filed charges against Brig. Gen. Richard B. Garnett for his actions at the first battle of Kernstown and started court-martial proceedings months later) suggests that Jackson realized his mistake and wished for the matter to quietly drop.

The delay incurred from Stuart maneuvering Johnson's Brigade further added to the confusion. Jackson either ignored the information in the captured Federal note or remained fixated on fighting a Federal force attempting to cross Bull Run, or perhaps, Jackson assumed the Federals would remain on the Warrenton Turnpike before turning on Sudley Road and continuing the march to Manassas. Since Jackson had both local troops raised in the area and a large portion of a command familiar with the area, he would have been aware of the other routes available to a force marching from Warrenton to Manassas Junction that did not include marching through the old Manassas battlefield. Regardless, Johnson was on his way to report to Taliaferro of Federals leaving the Turnpike and turning onto Pageland farm (likely in the brigadier general's mind potentially outflanking his position). It appears that communication between Johnson and Taliaferro was almost nonexistent since the division commander lacked news that the Federals were already marching off the battlefield on Pageland Farm Road.

Stuart attempted to keep Jackson appraised of Federal movements. Privy to information about the captured dispatch, Stuart requested permission to take the portions of his command near at hand and advance towards Haymarket. Knowing that large numbers of Federals were about to pass through Haymarket, and not hearing from Longstreet and Lee, Stuart's objective in moving towards the hamlet was to "establish communication with him."[34]

Departing the turnpike, Confederate troopers approached Haymarket "by a by-path." A quick reconnaissance of the area exposed "a large force there prepared for attack." Before Stuart decided on a course of action, firing

34 Some regiments such as the 1st Virginia Cavalry were engaged in picketing some of the local roads while much of Fitzhugh Lee's brigade was then on an expedition towards the city of Alexandria, so Stuart had pieces of two brigades.

from the Bull Run Mountains revealed Longstreet's battle for possession of Thoroughfare Gap. Worried about the delay of the rest of the army near the gap, Stuart decided to skirmish with elements of the enemy near Haymarket. Although outnumbered by his opponent, Stuart gambled that skirmishing with Federal soldiers near Haymarket prevented them from being inserted into the Thoroughfare Gap fight. With luck, Longstreet's men would be coming from the mountain soon.[35]

Stuart's presence in Haymarket reduced Jackson's cavalry to a handful of worn-out cavalry regiments in desperate need of rest. Lacking mounted pickets, the Warrenton Turnpike in front of Taliaferro and Ewell remained open but with Stuart supposedly in Haymarket, Federals approaching Jackson's position from the west would logically first have to battle Stuart. The sounds of battle coupled with the inherent ease of travel for mounted soldiers mitigated against Jackson's infantry finding themselves surprised by Federals along the turnpike.

Skirmishing with the enemy and trying to reopen communication with Lee and Longstreet, Stuart somehow preserved enough presence of mind to inform Jackson of Federal troop movements along the Warrenton Turnpike. Soon, couriers raced eastward carrying news that portions of the Federal army were marching along the turnpike from Haymarket towards Groveton. When the first cavalryman reached Jackson's headquarters, the news awoke the general from a brief nap. As his surgeon, Hunter McGuire, recalled years later, "General Jackson sprang up and moved rapidly towards his horse, buckling on his sword as he moved and urging the greatest speed on all around him, directing Ewell and Taliaferro to attack the enemy." The battle of Groveton was about to resume.[36]

35 *OR* 12, pt. 2, 735.

36 Hunter McGuire, *An Address by Hunter McGuire, M.D., Medical Director of Jackson's Corps at the Dedication of Jackson Memorial Hall, Virginia Military Institute* (Richmond, 1897), 12.

Chapter 22

"The Woods Are Full of 'Em"

Brawner Farm: August 28, 1862

Colonel Edgar O'Connor of the 2nd Wisconsin felt that he still had something to prove given lingering questions about his loyalty to the Union, which centered on gossip that his marriage to a Southern wife and West Point education made him friends with individuals serving in the Confederate army. Adding to his difficulties was a lingering bronchial illness that required the colonel to give his commands in a whisper to an aide who then repeated them in a loud voice.[1]

O'Connor had less than 430 men in his line, but many of them were veterans of Bull Run, and he had held his regiment steady before in the face of what seemed to be an advancing Confederate brigade. To the watchers on the turnpike, the small Wisconsin regiment alone in an open field seemed doomed as the thick enemy ranks swept toward it with loud yells. Then the front-rank soldiers in black hats knelt as though bidding the enemy to come on. For the past year, the Wisconsin men had boasted and told tall tales of what it meant to stand fire and one observer believed that "if fifty brigades, instead of five, had burst upon them, there were men in those stubborn ranks that would never have yielded an inch." Holding their pieces with a tighter grasp, one said, they expressed their "impatience with low mutterings in such honest, if not classic phrases, as 'Come on, God damn you,'" and they waited.[2]

Finally, at about 150 yards, the Badgers clearly seeing the hats and caps of the Rebels, O'Connor whispered the order to an aide and his blue line exploded with a crash of smoke and noise. It was the first of three volleys. When the

1 A 19th Indiana soldier who saw O'Connor during the battle Aug. 28, 1862, at Gainesville said: "I thought I never saw a handsomer man." Stine, *Army of the Potomac*, 132.

2 King, *War Papers*, 273.

Johnnies halted at a rail fence to take cover some 80 yards away, the Wisconsin boys raised a yell. The shooting was now steady with the men on both sides firing as fast as they could reload. The Wisconsin boys finally found the battle for which they had so yearned.

Now aware he probably had found the main Confederate force, Gibbon ordered the 7th Wisconsin and 19th Indiana forward. The 2nd Wisconsin was heavily engaged, and it was almost 20 minutes before the 19th Indiana came up on the left. The dusk light was already dimmed by powder smoke as Col. Sol Meredith brought his 420 men in line of battle at the double-quick. "Boys," he called to his regiment at one point, "don't forget that you are Hoosiers, and above all, remember the glorious flag of our country!" The colonel was mounted on a big horse behind the regimental flags, and he called, "Forward, Guide center, Double-quick, March!" The line lurched forward with a yell, advancing on the farm buildings just ahead. At the summit of the ridge, the Hoosiers climbed or knocked down a rail fence. They had just resumed the advance carrying their muskets at "Trail Arms" when a Rebel regiment hidden by a fence and some haystacks fired into them at a range of 75 yards. The musketry fight began in earnest. The arrival of the Indiana men eased the heavy enemy fire being poured into the 2nd Wisconsin.

The 580 men of the 7th Wisconsin came up on the right of the embattled 2nd Wisconsin. Colonel William Robinson marched his regiment in column through the 300 yards of woods and formed a line of battle. The colonel had been sick and unfit for duty for several weeks but left an army ambulance and climbed on his horse to honor a promise to his men that he would be with them in a fight. The 7th Wisconsin's flank companies advanced too far and were bowed forward and had to be halted, about faced, and marched back to correct the alignment. It was during this maneuver that Pvt. William Ray was hit. Three men in his company were already down when a ball struck the back of his head, spinning him around "like a boy's top" and he fell with his feet in the air. When he came to his senses, he rolled to his knees and crawled a few rods, then walked to a little gully where he laid down to rest, but the "balls fell around like hail striking very close so that wouldn't do."[3]

Lieutenant Colonel Lucius Fairchild of the 2nd Wisconsin, wearing a shirt with the sleeves rolled up and sword in hand, came up in the smoke and confusion to the 7th Wisconsin. "For God's sake colonel, deliver your fire up to the left. We are all cut to pieces, and the enemy are advancing on us." Robinson was a stiff-mouthed Vermonter who had served in the Mexican War.

3 Gaff, *Bloody Field*, 156; Ray, *Iron Brigade*, Aug. 28, 1862.

Colonel William Robinson, 6th Wisconsin
Howard M. Madaus

Sick or not, he calmly looked over the situation, ordered, "Battalion! Change front forward on tenth company! By company, left wheel—March! Forward—March!" Company after company came into alignment along the foot of a slope, and the men poured in their fire as "cool as if shooting rabbits" into the enemy's lines along the edge of the woods. The enemy line faltered in disorder, then fell back as the Wisconsin men lifted a cheer heard over the gunfire.[4]

All three regiments were now heavily involved with the Rebel lines expanding to the left and right as other units moved up. Gibbon sent an aide to the 6th Wisconsin waiting at the turnpike. The young officer was a bit excited. It was Captain Wood. An artillery bolt had knocked his horse out from under him in the first minutes of the firing. Somewhere, the men in the regiment observed, he found a remount and now, still pale and shaken, they heard him call out, "Colonel, with the compliments of Gen. Gibbon, you will form your regiment by battalion front, advance and join on the right of the Seventh, and engage the enemy." Wood looked around in wild fashion, and then blurted, "Colonel, for God's sake, go over and help the Second. They are being cut to pieces."

Cutler was sitting on the rail fence by the roadside watching the fight with his field glasses. "Yes," he said, "the woods are full of 'em. Get ready boys, for the fun is coming."[5] Cutler looked the situation over again, and then told the men around him, "We can not let our comrades be slaughtered in that manner." The Badgers pulled down portions of the fence along the north side of the roadway and formed on the brow of the ditch. The regiment was dressing its line when three soldiers ran up with rifle-muskets and belts in hand. Foot-sore and broken down by hard marching, the three had been in the ambulances but ran

4 Alexander Gordon, Quiner Scrapbooks, Correspondence of the Wisconsin Volunteers, 1861–62, Vol. 4, 13.

5 *Telegraph*, Sept. 4, 1884.

Lieutenant Colonel Edward Bragg, 6th Wisconsin. *Lance J. Herdegen*

to join their companies at the first fire.[6] They found their places and the 6th Wisconsin moved into the open field with full regimental front and step and "guide left" as regular as if on parade.

Major Dawes marched to his first battle "with something of the feeling that one would hurry to save a friend from peril." His mare was caught up in "the fierce excitement" and "ran up the bank and leaped a fence like a squirrel." The 6th Wisconsin had 500 men in ranks, and it pushed forward rapidly over the open field. Cutler was on his large dark bay, well known to all the men as "Old Prince." Lieutenant Colonel Edward Bragg's pure white horse was skittish and unmanageable in the noise and confusion. Dawes felt a "feeling of intense horror" when he cleared the bank and saw the 2nd Wisconsin "gallantly struggling and staggering under the fire of not less than six regiments of the enemy." To his right, Bragg, unable to control his horse, dismounted and went forward on foot.[7]

The regiment moved down a sloping meadow, drifting away from the right flank of the 7th Wisconsin, and then started up the slope to the wooded ridge. Slightly to the left of the unit's immediate front and extending a long distance to the left the men could see in the early dusk a flickering line of fire and to the far left was a similar line of fire. It was the opposing Confederate and Union lines and they could see "the fight was an exceedingly hot one."[8]

6 The three were Pvts. Harry Dunn of Menekaunee, John Burus of Oakfield, and William Campbell of Mauston. Burus died May 7, 1864, of wounds at the Wilderness; Dunn was mustered out at the end of his three-year enlistment, and Campbell would resign his commission as first lieutenant Oct. 11, 1864. *Wisconsin Roster*, vol. 1, 513–514, 533.

7 Gaff, *Brave Men's Tears*, 73; Cheek and Pointon, *Sauk County*, 38; Marsh, *Telegraph*, Jan. 16, 1886; Fairfield, diary, August 28, 1862; *OR* series 1, vol. 12, part 2, 382; Dawes, *Service*, 61; Dawes, journal, undated. Dawes later wrote in pencil on his journal that he wrote it in 1862 and 1863.

8 *Telegraph*, May 6, 1888.

Major Rufus Dawes, 6th Wisconsin
Lance J. Herdegen

About 40 rods into the field and half-way to the wood line, Pvt. "Mickey" Sullivan looked back and saw Cutler "sitting on his big horse as straight as a rod." It was the young Irishman's first time under fire, and he was feeling "a queer chocking sensation about the throat," but then the soldier in the rear rank stepped on his heel. He instantly turned to him angrily to demand if there was "not room for him to march without skinning my heel." The jawing and fussing went on until Cutler called "Halt!" and Sullivan looked ahead to see a heavy column of the enemy marching by the flank. It was moving to envelope Gibbon's line and was unaware of the approaching Wisconsin regiment.

Cutler called: "Sixth regiment, Ready! Aim—Aim Low, Fire!" The regiment delivered a sharp and crashing volley and the Confederate column, which turned to form a line of battle, melted away, presenting "the appearance of a skirmish line that had rallied by fours, there being only groups left, here and there." But another line moved up in the smoke and gathering darkness and both sides stood and fired at each other at less than 100 yards. It was now almost dark, and a "sheet of fire" could be seen from both lines. The Wisconsin men could hear the orders given by Confederate officers. "Charge bayonets, forward—double quick—march!" The Johnnies started "yelling like demons" and advanced but the Badgers "gave yell for yell" while wildly firing. Sullivan fired 20 rounds from his cartridge box when the second Confederate line fell back only for a third line to replace them, and the Black Hats again renewed the frantic volume of their fire.[9]

9 Sullivan, *Telegraph*, Nov. 4, 1884; Willie W. Hutchins, letter cited In *Brandon* [VT] *Monitor*, Oct. 10, 1862, "Our Rifles Spoke," Keith Bohannon, ed., *Civil War Times*, Apr. 2019.

Private J. P. "Mickey" Sullivan, 6th Wisconsin. *Pat and Robert Sullivan*

The 6th Wisconsin was at the base of a slight ridge and was well to the right of the make-shift Union line of three regiments. Heavy battle smoke painted the sun blood red as it dropped behind the hills. The steady and united fire of the four regiments was throwing the "rebels into complete confusion" as they fell back to the woods behind them. The brigade line gave a loud cheer. Dawes observed that the 6th Wisconsin was on low ground and the gathering darkness gave it an advantage as the Confederates overshot their line. He also realized there was open space for a thousand men between his unit and the other three regiments to the left.[10]

10 Dawes, journal, undated.

Chapter 23

"Could Not Brook the Idea of Quitting"

Brawner Farm: August 28, 1862

August 28 dawned near Groveton with Johnson's Brigade aiding the 1st Virginia Cavalry skirmish with detachments of Federal patrols. After fighting in the late morning threatened to boil over into a major battle, peace returned as the Confederate line pulled back towards Stony Ridge. By the time Ewell and Taliaferro arrived with their divisions ready to fight, the enemy had disappeared. Resting in the hot woods north of the Warrenton Turnpike, countless Southerners expected a peaceful end to the last Thursday in August.

Unknown to most, Stuart's message to Jackson promised one final opportunity for a Confederate attack. Decades prior to the widespread adoption of daylight savings time, dusk settled over Groveton around 7:15 p.m. By the time couriers raced to divisional and brigade commanders the sun was nearing the horizon. The window to effectively attack was rapidly closing.

After the initial fury of action in preparation to attack, most Southern infantrymen settled in for a lazy afternoon. Unlike the previous summer, the army was now made up mainly of veterans, especially its commanders. While mistakes could still be made, a level of professionalism had settled over the army in the 13 months since the armies first met by Henry House Hill. While most soldiers rested, some unfortunate few found themselves detailed as a loose set of picket posts established between the Brawner family's house and the turnpike. If the enemy appeared, these pickets quickly became an impromptu skirmish line, retarding the Federals until the main battle line appeared.

After the earlier attack fizzled, Jackson ordered his chief of artillery, Col. Stapleton Crutchfield, to "move the whole of the artillery force" from near Sudley Spring to the new Confederate position north of Groveton. Leaving five cannons behind to protect both a critical ford and Jackson's wagon train, Crutchfield proceeded towards the right flank of the new line. However, "owing to the difficulty of getting artillery through the woods," Jackson "did not have as much of that arm as I desired at the opening of the engagement." Initially three batteries of Maj. Lindsay Shumaker's battalion provided the only artillery support for Taliaferro's brigades near the Brawner farm.[1]

Shumaker's three batteries unlimbered about a quarter mile further away from the Warrenton Turnpike than Johnson's cannon in the morning skirmish, with the Louisianans of Starke's Brigade serving as support in a nearby unfinished railroad bed. Unlimbering on the right of the new artillery line were the men of the Danville Artillery commanded by Capt. George Wooding. Wooding's Battery was divided into two sections, one containing two obsolescent 6-pound model 1841 cannons and the other armed with one 3-inch Ordinance Rifle and a 10-pound Parrott rifle.

To the left of the Danville Artillery, Lt. Joseph Carpenter's Alleghany Artillery pulled into position. Unlike his neighbors, Carpenter's artillerists manned modern cannon, thanks to the Federals. Less than 48 hours earlier, Carpenter's men traded their older guns for four new pieces captured at Manassas Junction. Like Wooding's Battery, the Alleghany Artillery was mixed with one section composed of two 12-pound Napoleons while the other section was armed with two 10-pound Parrott rifles. Before the third battery could navigate the wooded terrain and deploy, the head of a new Federal column appeared on the turnpike.[2]

Although positioned slightly further to the rear than Johnson's earlier artillery line, most of the Southern guns easily possessed the range to fire on the Federal column approaching the crossroads intersection of Pageland Lane and the turnpike. The only problem with the new line came from Wooding's Battery. The section of 1841 6-pounders lacked the range to effectively reach the road.

Though a quarter of Major Shumaker's available guns sat passively at the start of the fight, the remaining guns picked up the slack. After a few near misses, the Southerners soon obtained the range. Engaging the Federals was not without risk. Firing diagonally to the southwest, some of the artillery shells whistled over the heads of the Confederate infantrymen acting as skirmishers along the turnpike. Rounds falling short could accidentally strike some unfortunate infantrymen, although the loose formation of the skirmishers coupled with the skill of the veteran cannoneers lessened the possibility of friendly fire. Using shells with notoriously fickle fuses, the skirmishers were more likely to be hurt from a shell exploding prematurely.

1 *OR* 12, pt. 2, 651, 645.

2 Keith Bohannon, *The Giles, Alleghany, and Jackson Artillery* (Lynchburg, VA, 1990), 22.

Luckily the limber chests of Carpenter's and Wooding's batteries possessed shells with proper fuses. Instead of exploding among the Confederates, the shells detonated over the Federals. One soldier on the receiving end of the barrage remembered the Confederate artillerymen's skill. "The shot and shell fell and burst in our midst every minute, striking the fence, exploding in the middle of the road." With the turnpike hazardous to life and limb, the head of the Federal column quickened its pace to get out of range while other elements began to deploy and take cover.[3]

From the heights near Brawner farm, some of Shumaker's officers observed Federal artillery unlimbering south of the turnpike. Once in position, the Federal artillery engaged in counterbattery fire. After a handful of shells began to land near his line, Shumaker's third battery galloped up. Captain William Poague's Rockbridge Artillery, a mixed battery of rifled and smoothbore guns, added additional weight to the developing artillery duel.

A loose skirmish line was all that protected the Federal artillery harassing Shumaker's three batteries. When the main target for the Confederate cannoneers began to disappear as the Federal column left the road, the rationale for the artillery line receded. Both Jackson and Taliaferro issued orders maneuvering the three batteries to a new position towards the extreme left of Jackson's line. Once in position Shumaker's artillery poured a destructive enfilade fire upon the Union guns.[4]

As the artillery moved to its new position, its supporting infantry also received orders to move. After Taliaferro and Ewell settled into their new positions near Stony Ridge, Jackson's line stretched nearly two miles from the Brawner farm northeast towards Sudley Springs. Ordinarily a line of that length would have been easy for Jackson to manage, provided the line occupied relatively flat and open ground. Jackson's new line along Stony Ridge, however, was both thickly wooded and hilly, hindering Stonewall's ability to command his men. In anticipation of a fight, in the afternoon Jackson designated Ewell as his right-wing commander, composing both Ewell's and Taliaferro's divisions. As the ranking divisional commander in Jackson's Wing, Ewell had seniority over Taliaferro. More importantly, Ewell was one of the few commanders that had Jackson's trust. The day before while Jackson took his two junior divisional commanders with him to Manassas, Stonewall purposely gave Ewell the difficult job of guarding the Confederate rear at Bristoe Station. Managing an

3 *Rochester Union and Advertiser*, Sept. 11, 1862.

4 *OR* 12, pt. 2, 652, 657.

outstanding operation at Bristoe, Jackson trusted Ewell completely, a difficult feat to accomplish as a subordinate to Stonewall.

In the narrative he wrote after the war, Campbell Brown succinctly wrote "Gen'l Jn to Gen'l E. to complete his arrangements, then take charge of the right wing (his own & Taliaferro's Divn) & advance." In his after-action report of the campaign he submitted eight months after the battle, Jackson wrote more about the fighting around Manassas Junction on August 27 than the fight by the Brawner farm the next day. For his part Taliaferro is silent in his report of the battle about any temporary command reorganization prior to the evening assault. In early 1863 Jubal Early finally found enough time to sit down with his staff officers to reconstruct to the best of his abilities an after-action report for Ewell's Division. Assuming command of the division in the midst of the battle, Early tried to account for the actions and movements of Ewell's Division. Since Ewell never submitted a report of his own for the second Manassas campaign, historians have been forced to rely on Early's attempt to piece together the division's role in the late August fighting. Until reaching the point when Early assumed actual command of the division, the report is a good summation of its travels but lacks any attempt to contextualize or rationalize command decisions that Early naturally wasn't part of.[5]

Subsequent histories of fighting around Brawner farm generally tend to ignore the likelihood that Ewell was nominally in charge at the start of the battle. The lack of references for the *ad hoc* command arrangement in the *Official Records of the War of the Rebellion* naturally made subsequent historians dismissive of Campbell Brown's account. Although he eventually became Ewell's stepson, the majority of Brown's Civil War narrative is corroborated by other pieces of historic documentation. Brown's account then, can be viewed as an accurate depiction of Ewell's high command. Brown's account of Ewell commanding the right wing of Jackson's forces also makes military sense. The broken terrain promised difficulty communicating between Jackson's Wing. In the absence of timely orders, the competence of Jackson's subordinates could be the difference between defeat and victory. In command for barely three weeks, Taliaferro had demonstrated competency as a divisional leader, but many in Jackson's command still referred to the division as Jackson's Division. Placing Ewell in nominal command of Taliaferro's men added a steady, veteran hand at the outbreak of battle.

Frustrated earlier by the disappearance of the Federals opposite Johnson, Jackson became anxious when Shumaker's batteries engaged this new enemy

5 Jones, *Campbell Brown's Civil War*, 154; *OR* 12, pt. 2, 644–645, 656–567, 710–711.

column. If Jackson wanted to attack a portion of Pope's army, this was his last chance to do it this day. A two-division attack emanating from Stony Ridge should easily sweep the enemy off the turnpike. The question remained whether there was enough daylight left to materially damage the enemy.

Speed and overwhelming strength were essential for success. Thus far the renewed fighting indicated that the new enemy column was opposite the Brawner farm and Taliaferro's Division. Ewell's Division remained farther to the east, apparently facing no Federal force immediately in their front. With approximately an hour of daylight left, shifting Ewell's Division closer to the Brawner farm would consume precious minutes and still not guarantee that the division would engage the enemy. Instead of repositioning his men, Ewell seems to have determined on a frontal attack *en echelon*.

Taliaferro's men would advance straight towards the Warrenton Turnpike and engage whatever force they encountered. Taliaferro's goal was to either drive the enemy in his front if he had enough strength, or failing that, to fix the enemy in position. After Taliaferro's men were engaged, Ewell's men could then move towards the turnpike. If Taliaferro found the enemy too strong to defeat himself, Ewell's men would threaten the right flank of any Federals fighting against Jackson's old division. Ewell's plan presented the probability of delivering a one-two knockout blow to the Federals along the turnpike.

A good plan considering the constraints facing him, Ewell's dispositions were not perfect. After stepping off from Stony Ridge most of Taliaferro's men encountered a "gently undulating" field that was "quite open" and did not pose much of a problem for his brigades. Towards the left, in front of Ewell's Division, the terrain abruptly changed. Much of Ewell's men faced "a ravine [that] ran down towards the pike, full of small trees & old-field pines." An *en echelon* attack meant Ewell's Division would be engaged later, since navigating the difficult ground might delay the division's insertion in the battle, forcing Taliaferro's men to take the brunt for a longer period of time.[6]

Leading the dusk attack in Taliaferro's Division was probably the most famous Confederate unit in 1862. Thirteen months earlier and just two and a half miles to the east along Henry House Hill, then Brig. Gen. Thomas J. Jackson led his five regiments in a series of vicious charges and counterattacks that became the basis for Jackson's legend. Promoted soon after, Jackson's nickname transferred to his original command, now known as the Stonewall Brigade. Molded by Jackson in both camp and on the battlefield, the men of the Stonewall Brigade retained a deep-seated respect, if not love, for their eponymous commander who

6 Jones, *Campbell Brown's Civil War*, 155.

reciprocated feelings of mutual esteem by ensuring his old brigade remained in his ever-increasing command in 1862.

Close association with Jackson brought attention and high casualties to the Stonewall Brigade. After Jackson's promotion in late 1861, Richard Garnett assumed command of the brigade. A popular officer with the rank and file, Garnett's actions at the first battle of Kernstown in March found him at odds with Jackson. Under arrest after the Confederate defeat, Garnett was replaced by Charles Winder, who led the Virginians through the rest of the Valley campaign and the later fighting around Richmond. Contrasting with both Jackson and Garnett, few men in the brigade looked up to the native Marylander. Not a few enlisted soldiers half-joked about killing Winder in battle. The malcontents need not have complained, after a Federal artillery shell mortally wounded Winder just a few weeks later at Cedar Mountain.

A solid, competent volunteer officer, when the regiment reorganized in April 1862, William Baylor found himself unanimously elected colonel. Leading his men through the Valley campaign and the fighting around Richmond, Baylor's effective leadership found commendation by official praise from Winder, not an easy laurel from the notoriously prickly general.[7]

After the demise of his brigade commander on August 9, Baylor assumed command of the Stonewall Brigade, the first time a colonel commanded the brigade. Initially a temporary solution, less than a week after Cedar Mountain the field officers of the brigade petitioned the general to make the appointment permanent. Complaining that all previous brigade commanders "were brought from other commands," the officers thought that Baylor "is in every respect qualified to lead and command the Brigade." Appreciating his contribution both on the drill field and the battlefield, the Staunton lawyer held "the confidence of the officers, and men, and his appointment as Brigadier, would be altogether acceptable."[8]

An experienced regimental commander enjoying the full support of his subordinates, Baylor had been in command only a short time during Jackson's flank march and skirmishing against the Federals north of Manassas Junction the previous day. The fight developing at Brawner farm would be Baylor's first major battle commanding not just a brigade, but one possessing arguably the best reputation in the entire Confederate army.

7 John Johnson, *The University Memorial: Biographical Sketches of Alumni of the University of Virginia* (Baltimore, 1871), 222–225.

8 *Staunton Spectator*, Dec. 9, 1862.

Whittled down by constant campaigning and fierce battles, the entire brigade on August 28 barely reached the strength of one of its regiments a year earlier at the first battle of Manassas. Approximately 875 soldiers stood in line before advancing towards the Brawner farmstead, with individual regimental strengths falling in three distinct categories. On the high end stood both the 5th Virginia and the 33rd Virginia with about 250 men in each regiment. Both the 2nd Virginia and the 4th Virginia mustered approximately 140 and 180 soldiers respectively. The 27th Virginia held the dubious distinction of being one of the smallest regiments in Lee's army at Manassas. Prior to the fighting at the old Manassas battlefield, the regiment struggled to field 65 men, just over half the authorized strength of a single infantry company.[9]

Arranging his brigade's front, Baylor put his two medium sized regiments on his flanks, with the 2nd Virginia forming the left end of the line and the 4th Virginia on the brigade's right. The diminutive 27th Virginia held the right center of the line, as the 33rd Virginia filed into its left between the 2nd and 27th. The 5th Virginia slid in between the 27th and 4th. Without the aid of a skirmish line in front, every member of the Stonewall Brigade advanced towards the Warrenton Turnpike as part of the main line. In its current trajectory, the right flank of the brigade (4th Virginia) was poised to brush against the Brawner farmhouse. The only impediments to the road appeared to be a few sections of farm fencing that divided the gently rolling farm fields. Near the Brawner house stood more substantial Virginia rail fencing.

Advancing over the Brawner family's rented farm, Baylor's Virginians saw a Federal skirmish line to their front, perhaps sent out to either harass or even capture Shumaker's batteries before they redeployed. About 75 yards from the Brawner farmhouse, the Stonewall Brigade received its first enemy volley. Out in the open, the veteran officers and men of the Stonewall Brigade recognized that the fence line was the only shelter from enemy fire in the immediate vicinity. The weight of the musketry and artillery fire directed at his regiment temporarily halted the colonel of the 33rd Virginia. Noticing his commander's pause, a captain asked if there were any orders for the regiment. Over the din of battle Col. John Neff bellowed "None; go to the fence and do whatever you may regard as necessary to be done." With that, the 33rd Virginia and the rest of the

9 *OR* 12, pt. 2, 661, 663–664. All regimental reports, save the 5th Virginia, include both an approximated initial strength and casualties. The report for the 5th Virginia only includes the total number of casualties in the regiment for the duration of the battle. During the battle the regimental casualty rate in the Stonewall Brigade ranged from 42 percent to 55 percent. Assuming the 5th Virginia sustained an average rate in the brigade, approximately 240 men would likely have been found in the ranks on August 28th.

Stonewall Brigade swept the field towards the fence line, like a wave careening towards a beach.[10]

Living in Clarke County, Virginia, prior to the war, Thomas Gold enlisted in the Clarke Rifles in the spring of 1861 at the age of 16. The teenager proved to be a natural leader, rising to the rank of sergeant before being captured at the first battle of Kernstown on March 23, 1862. A prisoner of war at Fort Delaware, Sergeant Gold missed much of the carnage his comrades witnessed in the first half of 1862. Paroled just three weeks before, Gold rejoined the 2nd Virginia, bringing his company's strength up to 23 men and officers.

Receiving the initial Federal volleys, Gold and his comrades immediately responded with a volley of their own, "firing as we advance." The unauthorized firing released the tension and anxiety inherent in coming under enemy fire and also hopefully decreased the rate of fire from that enemy, which initially came "thick and fast." Firing their muskets, the Southerners contributed to the cloud of smoke that limited Gold's view of the battlefield. With the "smoke hanging low" both sides soon lost sight of one another, firing only at flashes of the enemy's muskets. While soldiers continued to fall in the charge towards the fence line, the increasing clouds decreased the accuracy of everyone's musketry. In a few moments, Baylor's regiments reached the fence and redoubled their fire at the Federal line that now stood less than 70 yards away. The Virginians were so close, some could hear the commands of the Federal officers opposite them.[11]

The musketry smoke descending over the battlefield obstructed Baylor's ability to see how the battle was progressing. The sounds of battle could be just as helpful to Baylor to estimate how his brigade was faring in this fight. Aided by the flashes of Federal musketry in the smoke, the sound of the battle soon indicated that the Stonewall Brigade outnumbered the Unionists. Providing he acted before enemy reinforcements could reach the field, Baylor might even be able to outflank the emerging battleline. In front of the 4th Virginia, and thus the right flank of his brigade, stood the Brawner farm complex. If the 4th Virginia could advance to those buildings, not only would the Federals in front of the Stonewall Brigade be exposed to a deadly flank or enfilade fire, but the men would have even better protection from enemy musketry.

The 4th Virginia advanced towards the buildings without its nominal commander. Immediately following the death of General Winder at Cedar

10 *Biographical sketches of the graduates and élèves of the Virginia Military Institute who fell during the war between the States* (Philadelphia, 1875), 404.

11 Thomas Gold, *History of Clarke County, Virginia and its connection to the War Between the States* (Berryville, VA, 1914), 178.

Mountain, Col. Charles Ronald left his regiment to command the Stonewall Brigade. Apparently, Ronald received information that his tenure commanding the brigade would be a brief one, since he subsequently helped write the petition to get Colonel Baylor command of the brigade. After Baylor's elevation to brigade command Ronald normally would have returned to the command of the 4th Virginia. Instead he turned command of the regiment to Lt. Col. Robert Gardner and Maj. William Terry to take a leave of absence just prior to the campaign.

Leaving the protection of the fence line, the 4th Virginia raced towards the Brawner buildings that soon overflowed with Virginians. Quickly filling the outbuildings, the rest of the regiment took cover behind yet another fence line. Once in position Gardner's men fired at "the flash of the other's guns." After pouring a few volleys into the exposed left flank of the regiment facing the rest of the brigade, soldiers on the far right flank of the 4th Virginia and closest to the turnpike thought they heard and saw signs of another regiment emerging from the road. Gardner's men now were the ones threatened with being outflanked.[12]

Gardner and Terry hastily shifted their men in anticipation of this new threat to their flank. Reorganizing the regiment back into a line of battle, the center near the main house and the right flank resting "on some outbuildings," the 4th Virginia prepared itself. Within moments a "heavy fire of rifle and musketry" fell upon the regiment. Refusing to fall back, the men took what cover they could and were determined to hold this new Federal regiment at bay.[13]

Casualties soon mounted for the 4th Virginia in their fight for the Brawner farm, including their 38-year-old major. A lawyer from Amherst County, William Terry had marched off to war as captain of the Wythe Grays, which soon became Company A of the 4th Virginia. After serving the first year of the war as a company commander, the regiment elected Terry as major in April 1862.

During combat a regiment was broken into two wings. While the colonel retained overall command, the lieutenant colonel and major each took command of a wing. Commanding large numbers of men, all the members of the field and staff remained mounted. As battle smoke began to obscure the enlisted men on the battle line, the field and staff officers literally sat above the smoke. Giving them a better view of the field, remaining mounted on a horse also made these officers easier targets for the enemy. Soon Federal lead found Major Terry as one round struck his left elbow, and another hit him in his side. Carried away from

12 Casler, *Four Years in the Stonewall Brigade*, 109.

13 *OR* 12, pt. 2, 661.

the line to an aid station, Terry's wounding left Warner the single senior officer left with the 4th Virginia.[14]

The casualties suffered by the 4th Virginia weren't confined just to the field and staff officers. Brothers Robert and John Peck grew up in privilege in the shadows of the Blue Ridge and Alleghany Mountains of Montgomery County. The sons of a banker, the Peck boys grew up in one of the wealthiest households in their community. At the outbreak of the war, Robert and his younger brother left their school to join the Montgomery Highlanders. Although they had the local connections for commissions in other units, the Pecks decided to remain in their company as privates when it became Company E, 4th Virginia. Surviving 13 months of combat and disease, the luck for the brothers broke at Groveton. Twenty-year-old Bob Peck went down "by a ball passing through the left leg above the knee" which somehow was classified as "not a very severe wound." To add to his misery, a spent musket ball hit him on the inner leg near his knee, "but the bone not broken."[15]

Eighteen-year-old Ed Peck was wounded while he was likely lying prone. A minie ball entered Ed's left arm near his armpit, traveling up near his collarbone, traveling so deep that the surgeon was unable to "find exactly where it lodged." Unsurprisingly the younger Peck's "arm is a good deal swollen, but it seem to be subsiding."[16]

More Montgomery Highlanders fell fighting near the buildings. Twenty-year-old David "Tob" Robinson fell after a musket ball shattered his hip while 21-year-old Charles Carden, 38-year-old Adam Cunningham, and 19-year-old Sgt. Joseph Henderson were likewise all wounded. As terrible as their wounds were, they counted themselves lucky compared to their two comrades killed in the fight: 22-year-old Andrew Cromer and 20-year-old Miles Adams.[17]

Later that evening after the fighting ended, company commanders conducted roll calls to determine the number of casualties before compiling a list sent to Gardner for a tabulated regimental loss. Formulating ten reports highlighted the severe beating the 4th Virginia took around the Brawner buildings. Going into the fight with about 180 officers and men, 60 enlisted men were either killed or wounded. Soldiers expected more from their company officers than their non-commissioned officers, which is reflected in the respective casualties: 11 officers

14 Jack Welsh, *Medical Histories of Confederate Generals* (Kent, OH, 1999), 212.

15 U.S. Federal Census, 1860.

16 Glenn McMullen, ed., *The Civil War Letters of Dr. Harvey Black* (Baltimore, 1995), 17–18.

17 McMullen, *Letters of Dr. Harvey Black*, 17.

were either killed or wounded compared to 5 NCOs. The 4th Virginia was not the Harmless Fourth on August 28.[18]

To the left of Gardner's regiment, the rest of the Stonewall Brigade likewise took heavy casualties in the fight along the fence line. The largest regiment in the brigade, the 33rd Virginia, went into the fight under the leadership of Col. John Francis Neff. The 28-year-old graduate of the Virginia Military Institute joined the "Lousy Thirty-Third" as the regimental adjutant in January 1862, quickly rising to command the regiment after the deadly spring and summer fighting. With Neff leading a regiment in the main Confederate army, his father thought he had sent enough sons into the army. When John's younger brother became eligible for the draft, the elder Neff, a practicing Quaker, paid for a substitute to take the young man's place.[19]

Rejecting the rest of his family's pacific ways, Colonel Neff emerged as a capable regimental commander, when he was present on the battlefield. A falling out with Brigadier General Winder earlier in the Valley campaign culminated in charges filed against the colonel. Relieved of command until a court-martial could convene and clear up the situation, Neff continued to follow his men. A few weeks earlier at Cedar Mountain, stripped of his authority and his sword, he nonetheless accompanied his men into combat. His voluntary decision to follow his men "inspired them with an ardor and enthusiasm . . . they had never manifested before in so eminent a degree." Soon after Winder's death, Baylor restored Neff back to command.

Joyfully rejoining his regiment for the second Manassas campaign, the combination of the Virginia summer, hard marching, and lack of sleep took a hard toll on Neff. After battling his superior to regain the command of his men, when the regimental surgeon suggested he temporarily take a leave of absence to recover his health, Capt. David Walton remembered the colonel "could not brook the idea of quitting even temporarily his position under the circumstances." On the morning of August 28, the regimental surgeon again begged Neff to report to a nearby field hospital after feeling his pulse. The surgeon's pleas again fell on deaf ears. Owing to his poor health, or in spite of it, Neff abandoned his horse and planned to accompany his regiment on foot, knapsack strung on his back.[20]

Reaching the fence line, Neff's regiment, like the rest of the Stonewall Brigade, settled into a prolonged firefight with the Federal infantrymen in

18 *OR* 12, pt. 2, 662.

19 John Neff, "Family History," Manassas National Battlefield Park [hereafter MNBP].

20 *Biographical sketches of the graduates of the Virginia Military Institute*, 404.

their front. Under the weight of heavy enemy fire, most of the veterans took advantage of whatever cover they could. John Casler, a 23-year-old private in the 33rd Virginia, remembered his regiment "was behind an old fence, and would lie down, load and fire, and it seemed that every one who would raise up was shot." Casler's company, the Potomac Guards from Frederick County, Virginia, went into battle with 17 men and lost in the fighting 5 killed, 5 wounded, and 1 missing but presumed to be dead, a casualty rate of 65 percent.[21]

The fence line fight became a test of endurance once the men reached the protection of the line. In the confusion of the fighting, no one in the 33rd saw Colonel Neff fall. The first indication that something had happened to the colonel occurred between dusk and the end of the fight when the surviving company officers began to inquire about the whereabouts of their commander. Apprehension fell over the survivors when no one remembered the colonel encouraging the men in their fight, as was his custom. Lighting candles, officers and men searched the field for signs of Neff. Ignoring a slight wound, David Walton joined in the search. Walking back towards the area where Neff initially encouraged his men towards the fence, Walton found the colonel's corpse. Struck in the head by a musket ball "just below the left check bone—passed out of the right ear," Neff likely was killed instantly. The grim discovery of Neff's body brought the total number of killed and wounded in the 33rd Virginia to approximately 100 officers and men.[22]

The men in the 2nd Virginia were likewise sustaining heavy casualties holding the left flank of the brigade. The Stonewall Brigade enjoyed exceptional regimental commanders on August 28, including Col. Lawson Botts. The 37-year-old commanding officer briefly served as one of John Brown's defense attorneys after the latter's aborted raid on Harpers Ferry in 1859. This controversial client did not diminish Bott's standing in his hometown of Charles Town. He was elected captain of a local militia company that so revered him that they made their unit's name the Botts Greys. Demonstrating clear leadership skills, after mustering into the Confederate army Botts quickly rose to major and later to colonel.

Reaching the fence line, the men of the 2nd Virginia "returned the fire promptly and vigorously" of the enemy line facing Botts's regiment. Through the smoke, Capt. John Nadenbousch, a 38-year-old former miller leading the Berkeley Board Guards, saw the Federal infantry behind a fence and near the

21 Casler, *Four Years in the Stonewall Brigade*, 109.

22 David Walton letter, 33rd Virginia file, MNBP; *OR* 12, pt. 2, 663.

edge of part of the Brawner Woods. In the firefight with this portion of the enemy line, the 2nd Virginia's musketry sent a portion of the enemy line into the woods. Seeing this partial retreat, Colonel Botts quickly ordered the 2nd Virginia forward in a localized attack.

Upon reaching the wood line, the Virginians received a hurricane of "terrific fire" that swept through the ranks. As a regimental commander Botts elected to accompany his regiment into battle mounted on his horse, making himself a conspicuous target above the black powder smoke. Hard campaigning in hot weather also affected Botts's health like his fellow brother colonel in the 33rd Virginia. Ignoring his "delicate frame and feeble health," Colonel Botts remained determined to follow his regiment into the evening attack. And just like Neff, the former lawyer was shot in the face by a musket ball, entering his check and exiting behind his ear. Miraculously, Botts somehow seemed to survive the wound that had killed John Neff, and some of his men soon found and evacuated their commander to a field hospital. Discharged from the army hospital, Lawson Botts was recovering in the home of a friend a few miles away in Middleburg when he died on September 16 from a "secondary hemorrhage."[23]

After losing their original commander, more officers and men went down with debilitating wounds. Nineteen-year-old John Weir left his job as a miner in 1861 to join the Nelson Blues in time to be wounded in the left arm in the fighting for Henry House Hill at the first battle of Manassas. After recovering from his wound Weir found himself promoted to sergeant. In the fight near the Brawner Woods, Sergeant Weir went down with yet another wound, giving him the unenviable distinction of being the only soldier in the 2nd Virginia to be wounded at both Manassas battles.[24]

Soon the 2nd Virginia's battle line began to show signs of stress. If the situation remained the same it was likely but a matter of time before the Virginians broke and fled to the rear or the regiment's men were all killed or captured. Before either event could take place, Lawton's Brigade of Ewell's Division arrived and formed onto the left of the regiment. Remaining in line until dark, the 2nd Virginia had become a spent force for the rest of the battle, losing 15 officers and men killed and an additional 43 wounded, for a casualty rate of 41 percent of all the men who went into the fight.[25]

23 *Biographical sketches of the graduates of the Virginia Military Institute*, 56.

24 Dennis Fry, *2nd Virginia Infantry* (Lynchburg, VA, 1984), 39.

25 *OR* 12, pt. 2, 661.

The introduction of the Stonewall Brigade turned the Brawner fight into an infantry fight, with foot soldiers engaging in most of the combat and taking most of the casualties. Shumaker's three batteries lent artillery support in their new position off to the left of the Stonewall Brigade. Totaling just ten guns, as a trained artillerist Jackson knew he needed additional guns to transform Shumaker's line into a truly decisive position. The wooded area between Sudley and Groveton continued to hinder reinforcing batteries in their deployment from the wing reserve position near the Sudley Church.

Fortunately for Baylor's beleaguered soldiers, and especially the 4th Virginia, additional artillery support was on the way. Nominally part of J. E. B. Stuart's command so long as the cavalry remained with Jackson's Wing, Maj. John Pelham's Horse Artillery was integrated into the overall artillery command structure. When Jackson's order to move twenty cannons from Sudley to Groveton reached the artillery reserve park, Pelham's guns became part of the redeployment.

One of six brothers serving in the Confederate army, 23-year-old John Pelham was fast becoming one of Stuart's favorite subordinates. From the first battle of Manassas through the fighting in 1862, Pelham demonstrated a rare mixture of energy and restraint, placing his artillery in positions producing maximum damage to the enemy without bringing unnecessary risk to his command. The youthful officer forged a strong personal and professional relationship with Stuart, one in which Pelham earned the opportunity to grow into a confident, aggressive artillerist.[26]

Reaching the Brawner farm battlefield proved almost as taxing as the actual fighting. Leaving Sudley, Pelham encountered the wooded terrain of Stony Ridge that had already encumbered other cannoneers traveling to the Brawner farm. After detaching one cannon earlier in the day, Pelham left the reserve artillery park with three guns. Appreciating the urgency of his orders, Pelham spurred his horse and ordered his men to follow him, at a gallop, "through a thick woods." Following a narrow, meandering trail through the forest, the setting sun cast long shadows among the trees, making it difficult to see more than a few yards. In the confusion one of Pelham's guns became separated from the main group. Losing a third of his combat strength Pelham faced a dilemma. The Alabamian could stop and allow his lost cannon to rejoin his command, which could take a few moments, or possibly never rejoin that evening, or he could continue on with the two remaining guns and hope that the wayward cannon eventually

26 Jerry Maxwell, *The Perfect Lion: The Life and Death of Confederate Artillerist John Pelham* (Tuscaloosa, AL, 2011), 122.

found him. The urgency of his orders forced Pelham's hand. Advancing with two cannons, a glorified section, without the possibility of infantry support seemed risky, but without additional artillery support the Confederate attack might falter and put Jackson's command at risk of capture or destruction. The loss of two guns would be a small price to pay to safeguard Jackson until the army could be reunited.[27]

Arriving on the battlefield with his two guns, Pelham reported directly to Jackson. Supervising the unfolding battle, Stonewall passed Pelham to Major Shumaker for instructions to deploy his battery on the Confederate right. Moving far beyond the right flank of the Confederate line, Pelham's experience now proved critical. Guided by the rolling sounds of musketry, Pelham used the sounds to locate the end of the Federal line fighting the Stonewall Brigade. Passing beyond the Brawner buildings, Pelham finally unlimbered about 50 to 60 yards on the left flank of the Federal infantry battling the 4th Virginia for possession of the Brawner buildings. Loading double rounds of canister, an anti-personnel round that converted his cannons into giant shotguns, Pelham unleashed withering blasts onto the exposed left of the enemy, helping relieve some of the pressure off the Virginians.[28]

Although Pelham's missing gun did not arrive in time for the battle, guns from other Confederate batteries eventually found their way through Stony Ridge to the new battlefield. Setting up well to the rear of the Stonewall Brigade, the 4th Maryland Light Artillery added weight to Maj. Shumaker's growing line. Unlike Pelham's gunners, the Marylanders focused their efforts on the Federal batteries in the distance.

Finding the range of the Federals, the Marylanders began a methodical fire to knock out the enemy's guns. In the midst of firing, one Marylander spied Jackson nearby watching the battery in action. Being under the personal observation of Stonewall Jackson sent an electric shock of pride through the battery. Temporarily abandoning the fight, the cannoneers ignored the Federals and instead gave "three hearty cheers" to the "grim old soldier." Displeased by the Marylanders' loss of focus, Jackson "instantly ordered the battery to renew its firing."[29]

Taking aim at six Federal cannons, the Marylanders renewed the contest after their mild rebuke. Under annoying fire from the Confederates, the Federal

27 *OR* 12, pt. 2, 754.

28 Ibid., 754.

29 Richter, *Three Cheers for the Chesapeake*, 41.

artillerists focused their efforts on silencing the source of their troubles. In the ensuing artillery duel, the Confederates disabled or drove from the field five of the six enemy cannon for the loss of three artillery horses and two walking wounded both of whom remained at their post for the duration of the fight.[30]

As the Marylanders dueled with the Federal cannon, Pelham remained fixated on the Federal infantry. Sending blasts of canister into the ranks of the Yankees, Pelham uncharacteristically lost situational awareness. With only two guns in line, Pelham played gunner instead of battery commander. Focusing solely on the operation of the right gun, the young major became oblivious to the role his other gun was playing in the battle. The setting sun was making it difficult to see what or who was operating on the battlefield. Exposed for over half an hour, Major Shumaker worried that Pelham's position was becoming untenable. An unidentified officer, probably Shumaker, rode up to Pelham's left gun and ordered the cannoneers to withdraw toward the main line near Stony Ridge.

Pelham's position was now fast becoming critical. The departure of his left gun now meant that Pelham had a single artillery piece to protect the flank. Initially relieving pressure on the 4th Virginia, Pelham's fire was so effective that Federal soldiers redirected some of their musketry fire towards the artillerists. While firing, the pole of Pelham's gun broke, making quickly moving the gun difficult. Alone, under fire, and now partially immobilized, if the Federals charged towards him Pelham faced the possibility of the unthinkable: losing his gun. Infantry support was needed, and it had to arrive soon.[31]

30 Ibid., 41–42.

31 *OR* 12, pt. 2, 754.

Chapter 24

"Shall I Run"

Brawner Farm: August 28, 1862

In the 6th Wisconsin, Pvt. Albert Young was struggling with a range of emotions. His first thought "was that the prospects for getting killed were growing bright" and perhaps he should run to safety. He felt very pale, and it seemed his blood had stopped with waves of intense heat flashing in quick succession through his entire being. He began to tremble to the point he might drop his musket. His legs could scarcely support his weight and he had trouble moving one foot ahead of the other. He was suffering a terrible thirst and with trembling fingers managed to get his canteen to his lips for a long drink. It did not quench his thirst and he again questioned, "Shall I run?"

But the answer was negative. He was too cowardly to endure being called a coward by his comrades if he survived. In the dusk light he could see "a black mass was moving out from the timber in front, directly towards him. His hair began to rise and something lifted his hat from his head and he had to grab it and pull it down tight so it would not come off. Then he heard his colonel's steady voice giving commands though he was sure he could not himself utter an audible sound.[1]

The Union line was now "a roaring hell of fire," in the words of one Wisconsin officer as he moved along just behind the shooting soldiers. All of General Gibbon's regiments were hotly engaged. Never retiring an inch, with "no confusion, now standing up, now flat upon the earth, now swaying backwards or forwards to get advantage of ground," the Black Hats fired hot muskets over and over again. Line after line of Rebels was swept away or broke in confusion. Fresh regiments would again appear and move forward to face them with a screeching yell that Gibbon's men would never forget because of a "peculiar

1 *Telegraph*, May 6, 1888.

corkscrew sensation that it sends down your backbone." But the Rebel yell was drowned out by a Black Hat cheer as well when the new attempt failed.[2] At one point the Rebels rallied and came on in a line overlapping the Union line both ways. It was met with volley after volley as the Wisconsin and Indiana boys fired with "the energy of madmen, and a recklessness of death truly wonderful." The "terrible wasting fire" opened "great gaps in the line, but isolated squads would rally together and rush up right into the face of Death."

On the left the men of Indiana's 19th "suffered terribly" with the "lines of battle close enough to do effective work." In the approaching dusk, Colonel Meredith's horse was hit in the neck by a ball and fell, pinning the colonel until he was pulled free by two officers. The horn on his saddle kept Meredith from serious injury. But he was stunned with broken ribs and escorted out of the fighting. Lieutenant Colonel Alois Bachman assumed command. Meredith's son, Samuel, serving as a lieutenant in one company, was also shot in the neck. The buckshot passed between the jugular vein and windpipe and to the soldiers helping him the wound appeared mortal. Major Isaac May was shot from his horse and crawled to a nearby clump of trees.

At one point two Rebel guns were pulled up on the 19th's left flank and two Indiana companies were ordered to wheel to the left. Their "deadly" musket fire forced the two artillery pieces to withdraw, but only to a position further back where they again opened firing. The move of the two companies left a gap in the Indiana line and the Confederates surged forward to push into it.

Out of the smoke and confusion Gibbon came up on foot to help reform the line near the back slope of a gentle ridge. Half of the regiment was down or dying. The regimental flag was "completely riddled—barely enough of it to hold together, and the staff shot through." The general left his small "sorrel horse" tied to a peach tree and the animal broke loose and ran away, leaving the general on foot and "in a dangerous and exposed position."[3] Gibbon watched a "most terrific musketry fire" rolling along the Union and Confederate lines which were engaged in a "regular stand up fight during which neither side yielded a foot."[4] His old Battery B was firing case shot and canister up and down along the enemy line, concentrating much of its fire to keep the Confederates from

2 Haskell, letter, Sep. 22, 1862; Byrne and Weaver, *Haskell of Gettysburg*, 44.

3 *Richmond* [IN] *Palladium*, Sept. 12, 1862; *Beaver Dam Home League*, Oct. 18, 1862; Dawes, journal, undated; Rufus R. Dawes, "Skirmishes of the Rappahannock and Battle of Gainesville," T. C. H. Smith Papers, Ohio Historical Society, Columbus; Bushnell, *Herald*, undated; Stine, *Army of the Potomac*, 131–132; Gaff, *Bloody Field*, 158

4 Gibbon, *Recollections*, 54.

advancing into the gap between the three regiments and the 6th Wisconsin. One officer noticed how the roar of artillery and musketry deadened "the cries and groans of the wounded as they fell and passed away."

The fighting was a blur of confusing sights and incidents. Private Philo Wright of the 2nd Wisconsin was shot about an hour into the battle. He was kneeling on his right knee with his left knee bent up with its side toward the rebels. The ball entered the left side of his calf, tearing ligaments and making a bad wound. In the ranks of the 6th Wisconsin, a private was shot through the arm. He tried to load his rifle-musket, but could not, and "then busied himself giving the remaining cartridges of his box to the comrades." Nearby, Pvt. W. H. Church of the same regiment was shot three times through the leg, grazed by a bullet on his left hand, and had another bullet cut the shoulder strap near the cartridge box. Dawes watched a mounted Confederate officer ride within 20 paces of his line and then be shot off his horse.[5]

The two lines were so close that the Wisconsin men by the flash of muskets could see the enemy as distinctly as the Confederates could see them. There was no time for orders except an occasional "Give them hell! Boys, give them hell!" The regimental line was all a jumble with each soldier firing as fast as he could load; artillery shells passing over made it seem as if "the heaven was a furnace." The Wisconsin men fired 40 or more times without stirring from their tracks and one observed his brigade could not advance and the Rebels could not drive it back despite the Johnnies having the advantage of numbers and cover of some woods while Gibbon's men were in an open field.

Into the gathering night, Western Brigade cheers "were promptly answered by the rebel yell." In the 7th Wisconsin Colonel Robinson's horse was killed by a bullet that passed through the animal and lodged on the inside of the officer's left leg just below the knee.[6] Lieutenant Colonel John Hamilton took command of the regiment and rode into the very face of the enemy where he was shot, the ball passing through his left thigh and lodging in the right groin. Hamilton refused to leave the fight even though the Confederates came again and then again. Major George Bill was shot in the head and was taken from the firing line. Captain George H. Brayton was shot dead along with Sgt. Philo C. Buckman.

5 W. H. Church, manuscript, WHS; Johnson, *Telegraph*, Nov. 30, 1884; Bushnell, *Herald*, undated; Brown to his father, Sept. 5, 1862; Edward Bragg to Earl Rogers, Apr. 3, 1900; Earl Rogers, *Telegraph*, Aug. 29, 1884; Dawes, journal, undated.

6 One soldier wrote: "Col. Robinson was sick and unfit for duty and has been very sick for several weeks but he led us nobly until wounded, all of the officers and men stood nobly to the work and were as cool as if shooting rabbits."

A 7th Wisconsin man was caught in a swirl of "bullets from front, at right flank,—the air full of them, whistling by our ears,—scratching our clothes,—burning our faces,—bullets seemingly everywhere." The Johnnies advanced, flags flying, and closed to within 30 yards of the Wisconsin men, who could hear the voice of the enemy commander calling, "Forward! Guide, center!" and the Badgers poured in their fire "through the dim and smokey light" and watched the Confederate ranks "grow thinner and beautifully less until the last man of them seemed to drop into the ground." And yet again, a line of Johnnies came, "their ranks outlined against the sky above the hill [and] went out into nothingness."

Chapter 25

"A Question of Endurance"

Brawner Farm: August 28, 1862

Unknown to Pelham and Shumaker, Confederate infantry was already marching toward their location. Nominally, Brig. Gen. William Taliaferro had four brigades in his division. One, the Stonewall Brigade, was already engaged with the enemy while another, Johnson's, was pulled back after the morning's skirmishing. Taliaferro still had half his division unemployed, waiting in reserve along Stony Ridge. Brigadier General William Starke's Louisiana brigade remained to the left rear of the Stonewall Brigade connecting Taliaferro and Ewell while Col. Alexander Taliaferro's brigade remained massed further to the rear as a general reserve.

William Taliaferro was fighting in his first battle as a divisional commander and his inexperience soon showed. Likely responding to an order from either Ewell or Jackson to support the artillery at the far end of the Confederate line, Taliaferro selected his old brigade. Perhaps owing to the pressure of command, wishing to see this important maneuver successfully carried out, or just wanting to be with his men for the fight, Taliaferro reverted back to being a brigade commander, leaving his division without tactical leadership.

Later in his after-action report, Taliaferro weakly defended his actions by rationalizing that since Starke's brigade was on the left on his line, it "was not in my (Taliaferro) power to be with this brigade after the action had progressed far," but the Virginian had confidence in Starke's ability as a "guarantee that it did all that the gallant Louisianans who composed it were required to perform." On August 28 Taliaferro had only about three weeks' worth of experience working with Starke. After the fighting around Cedar Mountain, Alexander Lawton's brigade of Georgians was removed from Taliaferro's Division and replaced by Starke's men who had previously served with A. P. Hill. Taliaferro, then, was basing his opinion of Starke mainly on the Louisianan's reputation

General William B. Taliaferro
Library of Congress

and recommendations from other officers, with a few weeks of practical experience added on.[1]

Taliaferro's decision to revert back to a brigade commander effectively removed a key link in the chain of command during a critical time. Accompanying his old brigade toward the far end of the Confederate line increased the distance and time it took for couriers from Jackson and Ewell to reach Taliaferro. With Baylor's brigade already engaged, his old command nearby, and Johnson far to the rear recuperating, Taliaferro effectively abandoned Starke's Brigade. The increased difficulty getting messages to Taliaferro also produced an unnecessary burden on forwarding commands to Starke's Brigade, now that the divisional commander was far on the flank. Unless Ewell or Jackson directly intervened and ordered the Louisianans into the fight, Starke was likely to sit out the battle, effectively reducing the division's combat weight by a quarter of its nominal strength.

Taliaferro's decision to accompany his old command may have derived from a combination of the terrain and its new commander. The division commander wanted his Third Brigade to advance from Stony Ridge in support of the Stonewall Brigade. Navigating the same terrain that was proving difficult to the Southern artillery, the mixed brigade of Virginians and Alabamians was likely to have trouble and delay in traversing the ground towards Pelham's guns. The undulating, woody terrain posed the risk of the brigade becoming mixed up, requiring a steady hand to ensure order.

After his elevation to division command, Taliaferro's old brigade received a new commander but retained its old name. On August 28, Col. Alexander Taliaferro led Taliaferro's Brigade. At 54 years old, Taliaferro was older than his distant relative. At the outbreak of war, Alexander converted his commission as

1 Ibid., 658.

major in the Virginia militia to become lieutenant colonel of the 23rd Virginia Infantry, the same regiment that William B. Taliaferro served as colonel. The two Taliaferros served together in the 23rd Virginia before William assumed command of a brigade. Serving together in the same regiment, and later in the same brigade, the two Taliaferros developed an established command relationship by August.

But things had changed since the two men served together in the Shenandoah Valley. As Jackson's command marched towards Richmond in July, William Taliaferro took a leave of absence from commanding his brigade. During the fighting around the capitol his replacement was killed. Colonel Taliaferro likewise missed the fighting around Richmond. Upon his return to the 23rd Virginia, Taliaferro found himself senior colonel and assumed command of the brigade.

Colonel Alexander Taliaferro's brigade was also undergoing changes. The core remained the three Virginia regiments that William Taliaferro commanded in the Valley, but the fighting in 1862 had wrecked its combat strength. Unable to take an extended period to recuperate its strength, after Richmond two freshly recruited regiments from Alabama were added to the brigade. Lacking the training and experience of their Virginia comrades, the Alabamians at least brought the brigade back up to its earlier numerical strength. Organized just three months earlier, the 47th and 48th Alabama both missed the fighting near Richmond. Experiencing combat for the first time at Cedar Mountain, questions lingered about the quality of the Alabamians. While the Virginians of the brigade marched towards Pelham, the two Alabama regiments remained behind.[2]

Brigadier General Taliaferro either did not believe the colonel had the requisite ability to maneuver his brigade into position by his own or felt comfort in commanding his old regiments. Regardless of the rationale behind his decision to accompany his old brigade, Taliaferro's actions were more suitable to those of a staff officer than a divisional commander. His actions unnecessarily undermined his ability to command the rest of his division in battle.

The two Taliaferros arranged the three Virginia regiments moving towards Pelham in two lines. In the front stood the 337 men of the 10th Virginia and the 206 soldiers of the Taliaferros' original regiment, the 23rd Virginia. Formed in their rear, the 37th Virginia (429 men) could either extend the flank of the line if necessary or move forward and plug any gaps. The 972 Virginians were veteran soldiers with numerous engagements emblazoned on their flags, but those battles had wrecked the junior officer corps in every regiment. Although

2 John Hennessy, *Second Manassas Battlefield Map Study* (Lynchburg, VA, 1985), 54.

in the service for a short time, the 759 soldiers in the twin Alabaman regiments had not experienced the same amount of turnover in company officers as their Virginia comrades and were likely just as combat effective. However, Taliaferro's decision to keep them in the rear effectively removed about 40 percent of his brigade even before becoming engaged.[3]

Approaching the fight, Taliaferro's front line deployed on the right of the 4th Virginia. Arranged in a 45-degree angle from the Stonewall Brigade's line, the right of Taliaferro's brigade projected forward, allowing the infantrymen to join Pelham in enfilading the left flank of the Federal regiment directly opposite the Brawner farm.

Emulating their comrades in the Stonewall Brigade, Taliaferro's men attempted to take advantage of nearby cover. While a portion of the brigade entered the farmhouse and its western outbuildings, the rest of the line deployed along an orchard, and possibly a vegetable garden. Not as effective as a fence line, Taliaferro's men likely also copied their fellow Virginians to their left and laid on the ground, shrinking their profile and the corresponding chance of being hit by Federal bullets.[4]

Settling into their position, the new arrivals fired into the flank of the Federal line. The enemy soon took advantage of terrain by hugging the small ridges, making it difficult work for the Virginians to drive the Yankees away from the Brawner house and its orchards back towards the turnpike. In line of battle, Taliaferro's men attempted to destroy their enemy with overwhelming musketry but found a hard time accomplishing that goal. In the process of this firefight, the two front regiments quickly lost many of their mounted field officers. The 23rd Virginia went into the fight with just two of its three field officers present. After its colonel was mortally wounded at Cedar Mountain, Lt. Col. Simeon Taylor and Maj. Andrew Van Buren Scott led the regiment recruited from Southside Virginia into the Brawner orchards. Like the leaders in the Stonewall Brigade, the two men went into the fight on horseback, making them more conspicuous targets. After getting their men in line, Major Scott went down with a war-ending wound, leaving Lieutenant Colonel Taylor the sole officer responsible for the entire regiment.[5]

3 John Owen Allen, "The Strength of the Union and Confederate Forces at Second Manassas" (MA thesis, George Mason University, 1993), 155.

4 *OR* 12, pt. 2, 657.

5 Compiled service record, Andrew Van Buren Scott, 23 Virginia Infantry, Record Group 94, National Archives, Washington D.C.

It was even worse in the 10th Virginia. Lieutenant Colonel Samuel Walker and Maj. Joshua Stover assisted Col. Edward Warren in leading the ten companies recruited in the Shenandoah Valley. Larger than its sister regiment, Colonel Warren needed both men to properly lead the 10th Virginia into battle. Continuing a story common to Confederate regiments this evening, both Walker and Stover soon went down with wounds, necessitating a quick shuffling of officers to fill the vacant command slots, as battle raged around them.[6]

Brigadier General William Taliaferro later remembered the main characteristic of his two brigades' fight as "no maneuvering, and very little tactics—it was a question of endurance, and both endured." From the first battle of Manassas in 1861 to bloody fields in the Shenandoah Valley and around Richmond a year later, Confederate units, especially those in Stonewall Jackson's command, developed a strong reputation for carrying offensive actions on the tip of the bayonet. However not every assault proved successful, with Confederates falling back after failed charges at first Manassas, first Kernstown, Gaines' Mill, Malvern Hill, and Cedar Mountain.[7]

Unlike previous battles in which Confederate assaults failed to immediately drive away the Federals, Baylor's and Taliaferro's brigades almost immediately stopped to engage the enemy in an extended firefight. After the war Brig. Gen. William Taliaferro curiously remembered that

> there was cover of woods not very far in rear of the lines on both sides, and brave men—with that instinct of self-preservation which is exhibited in the veteran soldier, who seizes every advantage of ground or obstacle—might have been justified in slowly seeking this shelter from the iron hail that smote them; but out in the sunlight, in the dying daylight, and under the stars, they stood, and although they could not advance, they would not retire.

Forgiving his Victorian embellishments, Taliaferro does advance an interesting observation. Baylor's and Taliaferro's men did not retreat when the charge stalled.[8]

Without Ewell's after-action report (which he never submitted), it is hard to piece together the Confederate battle plan for the 28th, but Taliaferro's observation corroborates Campbell Brown's account of Ewell planning a coordinated attack with both divisions. A year earlier at Henry House, the Virginians of the

6 *OR* 12, pt. 2, 567.

7 Taliaferro, "Jackson's Raid Around Pope," *Battles and Leaders*, 2:510.

8 Ibid., 510.

Stonewall Brigade first saw major combat in a bayonet charge against Federal artillery pieces. After momentarily capturing them, the survivors fell back from a Federal counterattack. Regrouping, the Stonewall Brigade launched another bayonet charge across the Henry House Hill, starting a series of charges and countercharges for possession of the hill and those Federal artillery pieces.

In the 13 months since its baptism of fire at Manassas, the Stonewall Brigade, along with comrades in Taliaferro's Brigade and much of the Army of Northern Virginia, engaged in other charges that initially failed. Instead of engaging in deadly firefights with the enemy during the Valley or Richmond campaigns once the opportunity arose to withdraw, regiments either fell back, regrouped, and attempted to engage in another charge, or retreated too exhausted and disorganized to continue to fight. Only in unusual circumstances did a failed attack dissolve into a stand-up firefight with no attempt to either advance or withdraw. The lack of aggressiveness in arguably the Confederacy's premier division in 1862 supports the theory that Ewell planned for Taliaferro's men to either drive the enemy away or at least hold their attention until Ewell's division came onto the battlefield to hit the enemy on the flank.

The heavy casualties among his officers, especially those serving in field and staff positions critical to lead regiments, contributed to Taliaferro's Division's assault stagnating into a prolonged firefight. The number of field and staff officers killed or wounded on August 28 was higher proportionally than most Civil War battles. The time of battle and the conditions of the fight likely contributed to these higher causality rates. Fighting near dusk, the silhouettes of most of the infantry soldiers became harder to distinguish from the forest to their rear. The Federals likely had a hard time differentiating Baylor's and Taliaferro's men from the dark tree line. The mounted field officers likely were better silhouetted against the dim skyline, especially if portions of the Federal line emulated the Stonewall Brigade and fought from a prone or kneeling position.

Three Federal soldiers were likely crouching towards the slight protection of the earth when they spied a mounted Confederate officer in the distance and fired. Shot three times, Brig. Gen. William Taliaferro refused to abandon the field and relinquish command to Starke. Bleeding from three wounds and coping with tremendous pain, and the survival of his command hanging in the balance, Taliaferro's ability to influence the battle on his part of the battlefield was quickly evaporating. Fortunately, on the left flank of the Stonewall Brigade, Ewell's Division began its assault. The culminating point of the battle was fast approaching.[9]

9 Gaff, *Brave Men's Tears*, 82.

Chapter 26

"Help in the Nick of Time"

Brawner Farm: August 28, 1862

In the quickening darkness, both lines alight with musket fire, the gap between the isolated 6th Wisconsin and the rest of the brigade was readily apparent. Major Dawes watched two fresh Union regiments from the turnpike double-quick into the gap in the "very nick of time" and fire a crashing volley. The Confederates responded with two separate bayonet attacks, only to be repulsed. Dawes galloped down the line of the regiment crying, "Cheer, boys cheer! As loud as you can holler 'Call out Bully for Sigel' and 'three and a tiger for the reinforcements.'" Of course, it was all just a ruse, and Sigel and the reinforcements were not at hand.[1]

But the fighting along the Union front was still not settled and a worried Dawes rode to Cutler, who asked, "Our men are giving ground on the left, Major?" No sooner had Dawes replied, "Yes, Sir," when he "heard that tchug so ominous in battle." Cutler "gave a convulsive start, and clapped his hand on his leg," but "not a muscle of the old man's face quivered as he quietly asked, 'Where is Col. Bragg? I am shot.'" At the same instant, the colonel's horse, "Old Prince," was hit, but carried Cutler safely from the field.

Dawes found Lt. Col. Edward Bragg still on foot behind the right of the regiment. To the left there was distant cheering and the two officers concluded that the Federal line "was again standing firmly." The arrival of the two regiments was helping to turn the battle in the favor of the Union line. Bragg pushed his regiment forward several rods only to have the enemy come on again. On the far left of the line, Dawes saw the men on the Union line "on the hill in the infernal light of the powder flashes, struggling as furiously as ever." Among the distant figures, he recognized Fairchild of the 2nd Wisconsin and Hamilton of

1 Dawes, "Skirmishes," Dawes, *Service*, 62.

the 7th Wisconsin as well as other officers "working among and cheering up their men." A steady stream of wounded men was also leaving the line for the woods and the turnpike.

The 2nd Wisconsin had been shot to pieces but was still holding. Colonel Edgar O'Connor was on his horse in a shower of bullets, encouraging his men, when he was shot in the arm. He kept his horse until he was gravely wounded in the groin and was carried to the rear and the shelter of the woods. Fairchild was now in command. Major Thomas Allen was hit in the neck and wrist. He wrapped the wounds and stayed on the line. Captain Randolph was shot in the head and killed. Wounded men in the 2nd told friends trying to help them, "Never mind me, fight! Hold your positions! I will get off if I can and if not, never mind, fight boys, don't give up the ground." The regiment's eight-man color party went into the fight carrying the same flag the 2nd Wisconsin used at Bull Run. It went up and down in the heavy musketry as one after another of the members of the color party were shot until only Color Corporal Joseph Minor was left. He held up the flag despite a leg wound, and then he was hit again in the other leg and fell to the ground still holding the banner. The ground was so littered with the dead and wounded the Badgers still firing had to watch where they stepped.[2]

In the front rank, kneeling, Pvt. Albert S. Cole was beside Cpl. E. B. Stickney when he heard his friend exclaim "There, my little finger is gone, but I can shoot yet." A few minutes later Stickney said aloud, "I am shot through the arm, but I can shoot yet." A few minutes later, Stickney fell on his shoulder—he was dead, shot through the head. Nearby, Cpl. Joshua Jones watched the man on his left get shot and then two men on his right. One ball passed through Jones's hat and one through the left side of his coat. Another private in the 2nd Wisconsin was biting the tail off his paper cartridge when he found himself sitting on the ground. He managed to stand up on his right leg, continuing the loading procedure, when he shifted to his left leg and went down. Feeling along his leg he found blood and a hole in his shin. Private P. B. Wright was kneeling and firing when a ball hit him in the calf, tearing out ligaments and making a bad wound.

In the gathering darkness, the 6th Wisconsin fell back by a backward step, keeping up its rate of fire and keeping in line with the brigade. Private Chester Wyman and the men of his company had fired at the flash of the enemy muskets as fast as they could load and fire. The man next to him was knocked out of line, "apparently dead," then Wyman himself was hit in the right thigh. He tried a step, but his leg gave way and he fell heavily to the ground. One of the companies

2 Wm. DeLoss Love, *Wisconsin, War of the Rebellion* (Chicago, 1866), 305.

of the right wing became broken marching backward into a ditch. Lieutenant Colonel Bragg halted to enable the regiment to reform the line, and it was upon that ground the regiment stood until the enemy ceased firing.

The soldiers on both sides were unable to see in the gathering darkness and the fighting finally sputtered to a halt after about 90 minutes. Dawes was surprised to discover that he "alone of all field officers in the battle remained mounted and unhurt." Across the dismal field could be heard "the groans of the wounded, their cries for help and calls for water" and to one Wisconsin soldier it was more difficult to endure those calls than going into battle. Private John Johnson of the 6th Wisconsin heard calls of "O, God, O mother" that made him shudder even though they were coming from the enemy lines.[3]

The first battle had not been like anything they expected. There was no brave charge, just a frantic scramble to load and shoot, load and shoot, again and again at the flashes from the enemy line. It had been all noise and confusion, dense powder smoke, and the lines merely surging crowds. Muskets became hot and so foul that the ramrods were hammered with rocks or against the ground to push down the lead bullet. It ended as suddenly as it began. The Black Hats stopped firing, facing an enemy they could no longer see. Officers pulled shaken soldiers to fill gaps and straighten the line. Details were organized to carry the wounded to the rear. Bragg, "after an interval of quiet," called for "three cheers" and the defiant "Hurrahs!" echoed into the blackness. No response of any kind was given by the enemy.[4]

Satisfied the fighting had ended and his line was secure, Gibbon rode to the Warrenton Turnpike. He was in "a very bad temper" and convinced that his brigade had been left unsupported. He came up to General King and his staff sitting in a fence corner alongside the road with two other brigade commanders, John Hatch and Abner Doubleday. Hot words were exchanged, but Gibbon calmed down somewhat after learning that Doubleday had sent two regiments to assist his brigade by filling the gap in the Union line. Hatch said he reversed his march but arrived too late. A short time later Gen. Marsena Patrick arrived.

The question was what to do now? Where was General Pope? Were other Federal units close enough to provide support? How strong was the Confederate force on the ridge and was it Jackson's men? King said his orders were to march to Centreville. "From whom were the orders received?" someone asked. "From General McDowell," said King. "Where was General McDowell?" another asked.

3 Dawes, *Service*, 62–63; Dawes, journal, undated; *Telegraph*, May 6, 1888; Fairfield, diary, Aug. 28, 1862; Johnson, *Telegraph*, Nov. 30, 1884.

4 Haskell to his brothers and sisters, Sept. 22, 1862; Dawes, *Service*, 63, 70.

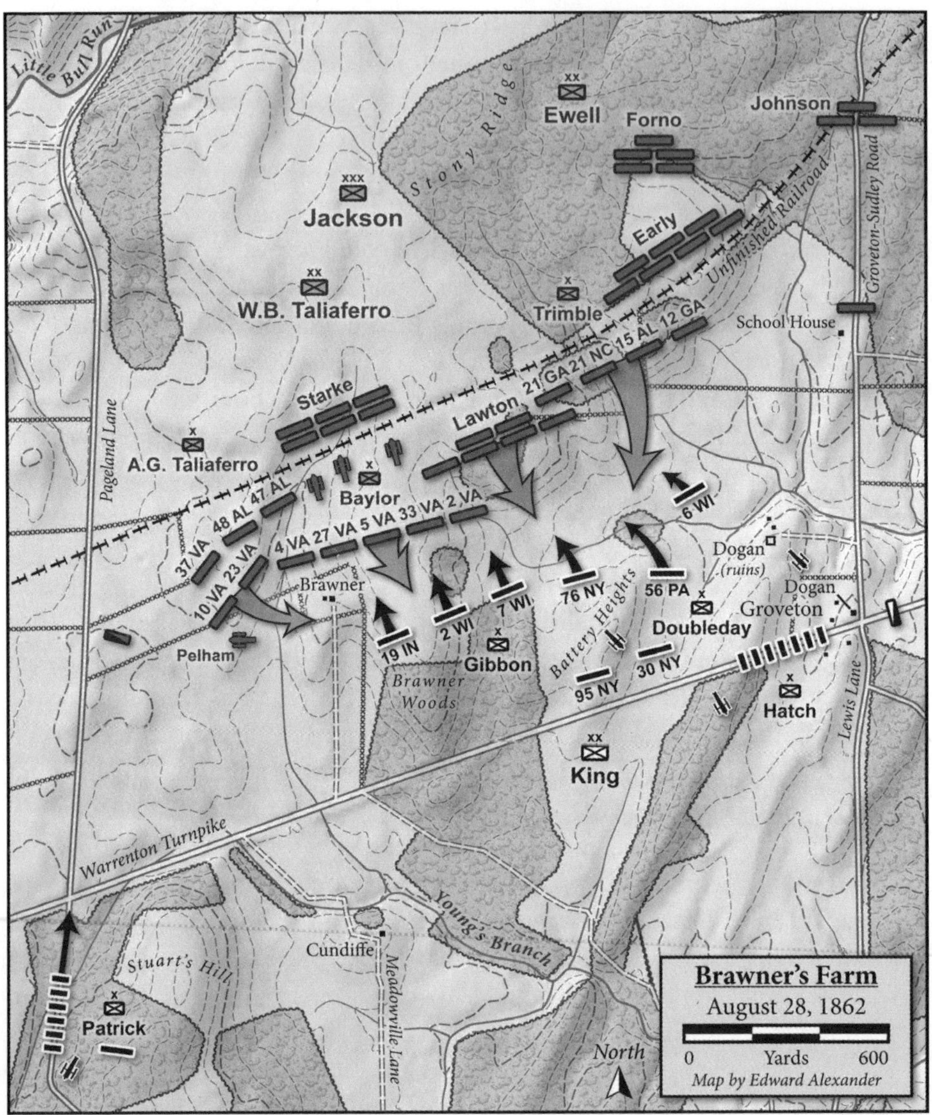

No one knew. Gibbon—still shaken by the fighting—said he felt that Jackson's "whole force might be in the woods just a few hundred yards away." He was the junior officer present, but none of the others expressed an opinion except King who wanted to obey his orders and march to Centreville.

Gibbon proposed the division take the road to Manassas Junction with the hope that they might meet troops coming from there. When no one expressed any opinion, he took a piece of paper and by the light of a candle wrote what he proposed and showed it to the other generals, finally handing it to General King.

They all agreed it was the best thing to do under the circumstances. Doubleday protested to the wording, saying the note omitted the role of his two regiments in the fighting. General King, after adding a sentence in his own handwriting, signed it as a dispatch to General McDowell:

> August 28, 1862—10:45 p.m.
>
> General McDowell.
>
> General: From prisoners taken tonight there is no doubt that Jackson's main force is in our immediate front. Our position is not tenable, and we shall fall back toward Manassas, with the expectation of meeting forces sent to our support. If [James] Ricketts should attempt to join us he might be cut off unless he falls back by way of Greenwich. Prisoners report Jackson has 60,000 to 70,000. Gibbon's brigade was pretty badly cut up—Colonels O'Connor, Cutler and Robinson being wounded, Major May killed.
>
> Doubleday's brigade also suffered severely.
>
> Colonel O'Connor has just died.
>
> Rufus King
>
> Brigadier-General, Commanding

The action decided on, the officers returned to their commands to make ready for the march to Manassas Junction.[5]

5 Gibbon, *Recollections*, 55–57.

Chapter 27

"Put Me Down and Give Them Hell"

Brawner Farm: August 28, 1862

In many ways the evening of Thursday, August 28, 1862, proved a life-changing event for the 45-year-old Dick Ewell. A few miles and many years ago, growing up on his family's farm, Stony Lonesome, young Ewell encountered a rabid dog while plowing his family's fields. Unarmed, Ewell unhitched his plow and mounted his plow horse, following the dog and raising the alarm to his family and neighbors. Eventually given a rifle from a trembling neighbor, Ewell killed the sick animal before it could hurt anyone or cause substantial damage. Young Dick's calm demeanor and level head foretold of his great potential to lead in challenging situations.[1]

Dick Ewell exhibited the same rational foresight on the evening of August 28 just north of Groveton as he had decades earlier at Stony Lonesome. This night arguably proved to be the high-water mark of Ewell's career since although he eventually rose to be a corps commander, Ewell rarely flashed the same tactical brilliance he routinely showcased as a divisional leader. At Groveton, Dick Ewell was not only a divisional commander but likely served as a multi-divisional commander.

Unfortunately, Ewell never submitted an after-action report. Jackson's final report included the entire campaign with just a few paragraphs on the fighting and maneuvering of August 28, so it is unlikely that historians will ever fully grasp the command organization for the fighting around Brawner farm. Campbell Brown's contemporary journal entry mentioning Ewell's temporary elevation as the ranking commander leading both his and Taliaferro's Divisions has yet to be substantiated by another source. But Brown's account is highly plausible for several reasons.

1 Donald Pfanz, *Richard S. Ewell: A Soldier's Life* (Chapel Hill, NC, 1998), 12–13.

General Richard S. Ewell. *Library of Congress*

Stonewall Jackson had risen fast in the thirteen months between his Civil War baptism of fire around the Henry House and his return to Manassas. From a brigade commander, Jackson now served as a semi-independent wing commander in the Confederacy's largest army. While he occasionally took an interest in the tactical deployment of some of his regiments and brigades during the Shenandoah campaign, by the summer of 1862 Jackson began trusting his commanders on the tactical level. Although when planning and conducting campaigns at the operational level Jackson continued to keep his divisional commanders routinely in the dark, when fighting occurred Jackson allowed his immediate subordinates to fight as they deemed best while Stonewall busied himself moving reinforcements to the front or shifting his line in response to the changing fortunes of battle.

Engaging the Federal column on the Warrenton Turnpike was but one of many responsibilities on Jackson's shoulders that afternoon and evening. Fighting the enemy on ground advantageous to the Confederates remained important but it did not override other pressing concerns for the wing commander. At a most basic level, Jackson needed to retain an over-all picture for his command. Stretched from Brawner farm to Sudley, the physical area of Jackson's command was about as large as a single commander could realistically be expected to lead with mid-nineteenth century communication techniques and technologies. Hill's Division and most of Jackson's artillery remained around Sudley holding the left end of Jackson's Wing. Remaining aware of the fighting occurring, but not directing the tactical details, allowed Jackson to funnel reinforcements into the fight, provided they could negotiate the terrain in time, a difficulty to which both Shoemaker and Pelham could attest.

The Confederate left flank remained important even if fighting had yet to occur there. The previous day's fight north of Manassas Junction revealed that at least some elements of McClellan's Army of the Potomac had arrived in northern Virginia. It remained to be seen if the Federals in Fairfax County were the advance guard of the Army of the Potomac or if McClellan's army was arriving piecemeal. Hill's roundabout march from Manassas Junction to Sudley via Centreville likely alerted the Federals north of Bull Run that Confederates were on the move north and west of Manassas. An enemy force approaching Centreville would more than likely find evidence of the Confederate column turning to cross Bull Run via the Stone Bridge. If the Federals remained on the Warrenton Turnpike from Centreville they would soon be approaching the vicinity of Sudley and Hill's hidden division.

As the fighting around the Brawner farm intensified, Jackson needed to remain vigilant on his left flank. How likely a Federal advance from Fairfax remained to be seen but if the enemy marched south on the turnpike, Hill's Division would likely become the most important part of Jackson's line. Hill's men held the only viable escape route for Jackson if disaster befell his wing. With Longstreet's concurrent fight, Jackson's original route across the Bull Run Mountains at Thoroughfare Gap remained closed. If Stonewall had to retreat from the Stony Ridge/Sudley position the most direct route his men could take back towards Thoroughfare Gap was along Catharpin Road to the northwest toward the mountains and a cross at the smaller, unguarded Hopewell Gap.

Another potential route towards the Bull Run Mountains remained Sudley Ford. Crossing Bull Run at the ford, Jackson's Wing could march north through neighboring Loudoun County towards the village of Aldie and recross the mountains. A significantly more round about escape route than Hopewell Gap, it still left the Confederates options. Both escape routes originated from Sudley. If Jackson lost Sudley his command would have no escape open to it without discipline falling apart.

As counterintuitive as it seemed to think about retreating just as part of his wing launched an assault, Jackson was too much of a competent, seasoned commander to recklessly put his command in a situation in which it could be attacked and destroyed in detail. Remaining aware of Hill's Division and his left flank precluded Jackson from reverting back to a brigadier general fighting a battle. These two routes to the west became increasingly important as open lines of communication to Lee and the rest of the Army of Northern Virginia. Thoroughfare Gap's temporary closure meant the severing of the Confederates' direct line of communication between the two wings. The rumble of artillery off towards Jackson's right signaled fighting for possession of the gap. In addition to his left, Stonewall also had to remain vigilant towards his right, for news of Lee's progress. Prior to the attack a courier reached Jackson from Lee with a message noting the main army's presence at Thoroughfare Gap and its expectation of moving across the mountain in the morning. While good news, until the junction with the rest of the Army of Northern Virginia, Jackson's detached left wing remained in elevated danger, that although not probable, still offered the possibility of being destroyed in detail if he made the wrong move.[2]

Tasked with the many responsibilities of high command, delegating the tactical fight to a key subordinate with a long-established relationship was a rational choice for Stonewall Jackson. Fortunately for Jackson, his relationship with Ewell was arguably the strongest Stonewall ever had with an immediate subordinate.

Ewell's four-brigade division, along with its battalion sized artillery, was unit-for-unit one of the best Confederate organizations in 1862. Blessed with experienced and competent commanders from division to regimental level, in many ways Ewell's division proved a stark contrast to Taliaferro's unstable command. While the past 48 hours showcased the tough fighting capabilities of Isaac Trimble's mixed brigade of Alabamians, Georgians, and North Carolinians,

2 Blackford, *War Years with Jeb Stuart*, 118.

and Henry Forno's Louisianans, Ewell's remaining two brigades proved equally reliable in combat.

Although a portion of his brigade fought at Bristoe Station the day before, the majority of Brig. Gen. Alexander Lawton's Georgians were fresh, if a bit tired from marching. A graduate of West Point, Lawton had served briefly in the prewar army as an artillerist before resigning his commission to study law at Harvard. Settling in Savannah, Georgia, Lawton's law career flourished. His subsequent forays into politics and managing new railroad concerns likewise proved successful. At the outbreak of war Lawton first won a colonelcy to an infantry regiment before being promoted and tasked with protecting Georgia's Atlantic coast. The 1862 campaigns in Virginia required more troops and soon Lawton and his brigade found themselves boarding trains to the main theater of war to the north.[3]

Lawton's brigade consisted of six Georgian regiments. They had served the first year of the war in the relatively quiet theater guarding the cities of Savannah and Charleston. Drilling, construction details, and light skirmishing comprised the lion's share of the Georgians' experiences in their first months of service. Later assigned to Jackson's army at the tail end of his Valley campaign, the Georgians endured a withering introduction to forced marches that helped prepare them for August's endeavors. Most of the brigade experienced major combat for the first time outside Richmond at Gaines' Mill, but after that substantial bloodletting the unit found itself held in reserve or in quiet parts of the line for most of July and August. Seasoned campaigners with combat experience, Lawton's brigade had yet to experience the intense turnover in personnel heavily engaged units such as the Stonewall Brigade were experiencing by August.

Ironically the largest brigade in Ewell's Division happened to be one of the most depleted by August. Brigadier General Jubal Early's command comprised seven regiments from the Old Dominion, veterans of extensive service in the Shenandoah Valley. That service came at a cost, with additional causalities in the regiments sustained a few weeks earlier at Cedar Mountain. Well below regulation strength, the Virginians still retained solid regimental commanders. The greatest asset to the brigade, however, was its commander. Like Lawton, after graduating from West Point Jubal Early resigned his commission to pursue a lucrative career as a lawyer and politician in Virginia. A reluctant secessionist, Early emerged as both a committed Confederate and a solid regimental commander. Promoted to brigadier, Early committed costly errors that both mauled his command and left him wounded at the battle of Williamsburg in

3 *New York Times*, July 3, 1896.

May 1862. Assigned his current brigade of Virginians during the Seven Days' campaign, Early apparently learned from his mistakes at Williamsburg and transformed himself into a competent commander, showcasing his skill both outside Richmond and at Cedar Mountain. A breakdown in communication prior to the flank march potentially put parts of his brigade in danger but was eventually fixed before the Federals could act. That scare by the Rappahannock River had so far been the only action Early and his men had yet experienced in this campaign.[4]

Geography complicated the Confederate advance. Positioned between Taliaferro and Hill and stretched out on Stony Ridge, Ewell's Division angled backwards away from the Brawner farmstead. Following Taliaferro's Division in its earlier march from Sudley, Early's Brigade stopped at the edge of the woods, with its left flank resting on an unfinished railroad bed and its right flank "a short distance in rear of Starke's brigade." Hay's Louisianans formed up close in the rear of Early's Virginians.[5]

Resting behind Starke's brigade, Ewell's initial position complicated any future offensive design. Attacking from their current position, Confederates would strike the enemy *en echelon*, Taliaferro on the right hitting the Federals first followed by Ewell. Attacking in this fashion posed the possibility of overwhelming Federal resistance, as enemy units fighting against Taliaferro would soon be outflanked by Ewell's men once they arrived on the battlefield. Ideally Ewell's men would be just a few moments behind Taliaferro's attack, but the friction of war (a slow courier delivering the orders for Ewell's men to attack, difficult terrain, etc.) could transform this attack into separate piecemeal attacks as first Taliaferro and later Ewell emerged onto the battlefield.

Desiring to support Taliaferro's men, geography transpired to hamper Ewell's efforts. There simply was not enough land to deploy his division. Staying in his current position, Ewell could not deploy his entire division, being squeezed between Taliaferro in his front and Stony Ridge in his rear. Massing his division in a tight column, with brigades stacked upon one another, might work while the troops waited for battle, but once committed to the fighting the formation would have enough room to deploy into a standard battle line. While attacking in dense columns was not unheard of (it was a favored tactic of the French armies during the Napoleonic Wars and eventually used by the Federals when piercing Confederate entrenchments in the last year of the Civil

4 Warner, *Generals in Gray*, 132; John Hennessy, *Return to Bull Run: The Campaign and Battle of Second Manassas* (New York, 1993), 71–72, 83–89.

5 *OR* 12, pt. 2, 710.

War) attacking in column contained far more risks than benefits. Likely wiping away anything in its path, without proper reconnaissance, its narrow frontage risked hitting either a light or non-exist enemy. If it did find the enemy, the column would be exposed to murderous volleys into its mass of humanity until the weight of numbers decided the charge. With daylight quickly fading away, Ewell decided to split his division in half. Ewell would take two brigades to find some open space to deploy and extend Taliaferro's line while Early commanded the remaining two brigades on Stoney Ridge.

As a commander, Ewell possessed a keen eye for competent subordinates. His decision to split his division into two halves appeared risky. Ewell gambled that Early's two brigades would receive their orders quickly, with little complication, and they would be inserted into the battle immediately, a series of events not always guaranteed to happen on a Civil War battlefield.[6]

Unlike the stacked column of Early and Forno, Ewell had enough room to position Lawton's Georgians in a standard battle line. Trimble's mixed brigade deployed next to Lawton, with its left resting near Starke's Louisianans of Taliaferro's command. Resting along an unfinished railroad cut, Lawton's tired men cheered the approach of Jackson riding by the line. Cheering Jackson had become so prevalent in the 31st Georgia that one solider remembered joking that when cheering broke out, soldiers hollered "There is Old Jack or a rabbit."[7]

Buoyed by what the soldiers thought was Jackson's presence, Ewell's two brigades were in position and ready for action. As an extension of Taliaferro's original line, Jackson and Ewell seem to have expected the two brigades to quickly advance in line with Taliaferro's main advance. One of Ewell's staff officers remembered the terrain in front of Lawton and Trimble as "gently undulating—quite open, except on our left, where a ravine ran down towards the pike, full of small trees & old-field pines." The difference between their new position and Stoney Ridge could not have been starker.[8]

Electing to hold Trimble's brigade in reserve, Ewell ordered Lawton's men to enter the firefight, advancing until they came in line with the Stonewall Brigade to their right. Unable to negotiate the ground as easily as their comrades, a gap soon emerged between the Virginians and Georgians. Recognizing the trouble that Lawton's men had, many soldiers thought Jackson had decided to ride forward, advancing behind the Georgians, cheering the men on. An officer in

6 *OR* 12, pt. 2, 710.

7 White, *This Most Bloody and Cruel Drama*, 43.

8 *OR* 12, pt. 2, 645; Jones, *Campbell Brown's Civil War*, 155.

the 26th Georgia remembered advancing "just after dark" so although the man has never been satisfactorily identified, rumors in the army (later picked up in the Southern press) quickly turned the officer into Stonewall Jackson.[9]

Advancing on Lawton's right and linking the brigade to the Stonewall Brigade were the officers and men of the 26th Georgia. Like the rest of Lee's army, heavy campaigning around Richmond left the 26th Georgian understrength, especially in officers. Riding in command of the regiment was 32-year-old Maj. Eli S. Griffin. A wealthy farmer from central Georgia, at the outbreak of the war Griffin left his young family to join the "Faulk Invincibles" as its company commander. During the unit's reorganization that spring, the regiment decided that Griffin possessed enough leadership skills and experience to be elected major. As the only serving field officer, Griffin had a few orderlies and Adjutant Andrew Lyles to help lead and maneuver the regiment in battle.[10]

The sun setting fast, daylight became premium. Advancing from Stony Ridge, Griffin saw an unoccupied portion of the fence line adjacent to the 2nd Virginia in the distance. Marching towards the limited protection of the fence, stray artillery rounds and Federal musket balls that had missed the Virginians landed in the ranks of the Georgians. Twenty-four-year-old Capt. James Blain remembered the effects of those rounds as "occasionally a man would drop from the ranks, yet not one faltered." Within minutes the Georgians gained the fence and "were ordered to lie down and commence firing."[11]

Darkness coupled with the close proximities of the opposing battle lines and the normal terror of a battlefield produced an unusual sense of confusion characteristic of most Civil War firefights. After the fight, rumors of friendly fire, especially between the Stonewall Brigade and Lawton's Georgians, percolated so widely that they eventually became part of the historiography of the battle. The foundation of the friendly fire claim stems from a postwar account of the campaign by James Hendricks. A wartime member of the 2nd Virginia, Hendricks wrote an article in the *Confederate Veteran* about the campaign offering a vivid account of the fight that warrants being reproduced in full:

> The brigade lost heavily in this encounter, and afterwards was weak in numbers. A very unfortunate occurrence caused much of this loss. The Federals had been

9 *Weekly Columbus Enquirer*, Sept. 23, 1862; Styple, ed., *Writing & Fighting from the Army of Northern Virginia*, 139.

10 Compiled service record, Eli Griffin, 26 Georgia Infantry, Record Group 94, National Archives, Washington D.C.

11 Styple, ed., *Writing & Fighting from the Army of Northern Virginia*, 139.

> driven from their position, but the firing was still heavy. It was now getting dusk, and with the smoke of battle the exact situation was not known to our commander. The 28th Georgia was sent to our support. They mistook us for the enemy and opened a low and rapid fire; and not meeting any resistance, they doubled their efforts. We were ordered to lie down, and some even attempted to run to their lines, but were shot down before they had gone far. The firing ceased finally, but many were killed and wounded.[12]

Written decades after the war, the author probably meant the 26th Georgia since the 28th Georgia was serving in D. H. Hill's Division then on its way to the main army from Richmond. Besides misremembering the unit's identity, Hendricks's account is at odds with Captain Blain's contemporary account of the 26th Georgia's advance. Worse yet for this persistent story, Hendricks's account is likely the result of years of rumors and conversations by his fellow hometown comrades. A native of Shepherdstown, Virginia, Hendricks originally enlisted with a hometown unit that soon joined the 2nd Virginia Infantry. By spring 1862, Hendricks had left his comrades and joined the 12th Virginia Cavalry as a trooper, a unit in which he served through the rest of the war. Not actually present at the battle, Hendricks's sole account of Confederate friendly fire is likely fictitious.[13]

Among Lawton's brigade reaching the fence line were the 18 officers and 173 men of the 26th Georgia. Although roughly the same size as the 4th Virginia fighting near the Brawner outbuildings, the 26th Georgia had yet to experience the campaigning of the Virginians. Losing men to disease earlier in their service and adding more names to the causality list after fighting in the Seven Days' campaign, the hard marching from the Rappahannock to the old Manassas battlefield, and the resulting straggling, contributed to the dwindling numbers in the ranks. The south Georgians in the 26th Georgia were "brought up in a thinly settle[d] country" with few schools but ample opportunity to hunt "fleet-footed deer, panther, wolf, bear, wild-cat and fox running at break-neck speed." Hunting skills learned at home translated well to the army as one soldier remembered, "When the Twenty-Sixth had to fight the enemy it always punished them severely."[14]

Using their civilian hunting skills against an enemy about 100 yards away, the men of the 26th Georgia and the rest of Lawton's Brigade traded volleys with

12 James Hendricks, "Jackson's March to Rear of Pope's Army," *Confederate Veteran* 17 (1909): 549.

13 Fry, *2nd Virginia Infantry*, 104.

14 Gaff, *Brave Men's Tears*, 83; Nichols, *A Soldier's Story of His Regiment*, 16.

the enemy, although not without loss. A soldier in the 31st Georgia remembered "our men were simply mowed down in the dark by the Yankee guns." Seeing his men holding to the protection of the fence line, Lawton rode through his brigade ordering the regiments to continue their advance. To Capt. James Blain in the 26th Georgia, rushing from the fence line, the Georgians were met by a Yankee volley that "did fearful execution; men fell from the ranks by the dozen." The combination of the growing darkness, wooded terrain through which the brigade charged, and fierce enemy fire resulted in added confusion in the Georgian ranks, with some men advancing while others remained at the fence line, as well as a stream of soldiers moving between the two lines.[15]

Confusion reigned in the Georgian ranks. To the left of Major Griffin's regiment, Sgt. J. F. Kelly and some of his comrades in the 31st Georgia refused to budge from the protection of the fence. Soon elements of the brigade that did advance drifted in front of Kelly's regiment, forcing the men to hold their fire for fear of hitting their friends. Ordered to cease firing, Kelly and his friends tried to make out as best they could the progress of the assault.[16]

Corporal Joseph Truett summarized Lawton's charge in his own style: "we went rite to work on them and give them one of the worst whipens you ever saw yankees get." An officer in the 26th Georgia remembered "one volley sent the enemy flying over the hill to the woods." Following the enemy into the woods, mounting casualties slowed and then stopped Lawton from closing towards the turnpike. In the 31st Georgia the ranking captain commanded the regiment. After he was killed his successor was shot almost immediately. Lacking leadership and receiving renewed enemy fire, the 31st Georgia "was in great confusion, and scattered in the woods, where they had been beaten back."[17]

Waiting close towards the rear as Lawton's Georgians advanced was Isaac Trimble and his mixed brigade of Alabamians, North Carolinians, and Georgians. Their commander felt vindicated after leading a portion of his men capturing Manassas Junction, and likely thought a well-deserved promotion to brigadier general was in his future. The cheerful Trimble led the only brigade in Ewell's Division comprised of regiments from different states. Waiting in reserve, one civilian later remembered the effects of the combination of war weariness and exhaustion from the campaign. Lying down trying to get some rest, "you can only see their faces, and they are not the faces of the soldiers of

15 White, *This Most Bloody and Cruel Drama*, 43; *Augusta Weekly Chronicle*, Sept. 23, 1862.

16 White, *This Most Bloody and Cruel Drama*, 43.

17 Ibid., 43–44; *Augusta Weekly Chronicle*, Sept. 23, 1862; I. G. Gradwell, "Cedar Mountain to Sharpsburg," *Confederate Veteran* 29 (1921): 297.

novels. They are sunburned and dirty, and pinched, their eyes do not blaze with the lust of battle. . . . On the whole, they are rather calm eyes, but there is a tensity in this calm that rather chills you, and you feel uncomfortable."[18]

Rest for Trimble's men was broken sometime between 7:00 p.m. and 7:30 p.m. Destined to fight at Little Round Top nearly a year later, in 1862 27-year-old William Oates had yet to rise to command of the 15th Alabama. Serving as a company commander of the "Henry Pioneers," Captain Oates was close enough to Trimble to see one of Ewell's staff officers ride up with orders to advance his brigade.[19] Orders raced through the regiments to make ready for battle. A soldier in the 21st Georgia remembered his comrades preparing "for desperate work" when they received orders to drop everything and take only their cartridge boxes. The men ready for action, the advance began. To Captain Oates and his comrades in the 15th Alabama, Trimble roared "Forward, guide center, march!" in the "loudest command I ever heard." To the soldiers in the 21st Georgia, Trimble simply said, "Forward." As Trimble remembered, after giving the command "my brigade moved forward in beautiful line of battle."[20]

Unlike the other brigades that charged towards the Warrenton Turnpike that evening, Trimble's is the only one that was preceded by a skirmish line. At the time of its enlistment in 1861, the 21st North Carolina contained an unauthorized 12 companies, two more than official Confederate War Department regulations. During an army wide reorganization in 1862, the two extra companies of the 21st North Carolina were carved off to create a new unit, the 1st North Carolina Battalion Sharpshooters. Too small to add additional firepower to most stand-up fights, the 80 men of the of the 1st North Carolina Battalion settled into a role as default skirmishers for Trimble's Brigade, a role they again took up this evening as they screened the advance of the brigade. Forming on the right flank of the brigade line were the 242 officers and men of the 21st Georgia. Next to the Georgians was their sister regiment, the 21st North Carolina fielding another approximately 250 soldiers. To the left of the Carolinians were the 300 Alabamians serving in the 15th Alabama while

18 John Ware, "Second Manassas: Fifty-Eight Years Afterwards," *Confederate Veteran* 30 (1922): 61.

19 In his account Oates identifies the staff officer as Captain McKim. However, McKim served as a staff officer to General Steuart. Oates likely mistook Campbell Brown for McKim as Brown records being ordered by Ewell to "order up the second line." Jones, *Campbell Brown's Civil War*, 155.

20 Oates, *The War Between the Union and Confederacy*, 138; Thomas, *History of the Doles-Cook Brigade*, 353–354; "Report of General I. R. Trimble of Operations from 14th to 29th August, 1862," *Southern Historical Society Papers* 8 (1880): 307.

Trimble's largest regiment, the 12th Georgia, held the left. Altogether Trimble's brigade advanced with nearly 1,800 men.[21]

Advancing over open fields, men began falling from enemy musketry. A Georgina remembered the landscape becoming so dark that the enemy "could not be seen or located only by the flash of their guns." Trimble's goal was to reach the same fence line behind which Baylor and Lawton took cover. While advancing to the main Confederate line, Captain Oates recalled that the Alabamians immediately fell to the ground when confronted with the first Federal volley and opened fire towards an increasingly hidden foe. When the men of the 1st North Carolina Battalion gained a fence line parallel to Lawton's line, the enemy fire slackened, and the brigade rushed towards the anticipated cover of the fence.[22]

Twenty-one-year-old Lewis Powers, serving as a lieutenant in the 21st North Carolina between the Alabamians and Georgians, supervised his men as they tore down the fence, piling the rails for better protection. Like their comrades in the Stonewall Brigade a few hundred yards up the line, Trimble's men laid on the ground under the protection of their *ad hoc* defensive line as they began to empty their cartridge boxes into a Federal battle line positioned in a woodlot about 100 yards away, firing in the direction of the flashes of musketry from the enemy. A soldier serving in the 21st Georgia remembered that once at the fence, "the work of death commenced at short range."[23]

Echoing the experiences of most Confederates, once in possession of the fence line, Trimble's men stopped. The psychological effects of fighting behind cover, limited though it may be, proved too tempting to abandon. Officers, especially the brigade commanders and their staffs, had a particularly hard time locating and moving their men on this dark, smoky battlefield. A lieutenant in the 15th Alabama worried that his men were firing into fellow Confederates. An enlisted soldier swore they were Yankees after seeing the gleam of brass buttons by the flash of their guns and joked that if they were indeed Confederates, he killed "some of our best men."[24]

All humor quickly left Trimble's ranks. Attempting to take maximum protection from the fence, a soldier remembered himself and a comrade

21 Sherrill Jr., *21st North Carolina*, 154.

22 McClendon, *Recollections of War Times*, 107; Oates, *The War Between the Union and Confederacy*, 138.

23 Clark, ed., *Histories of the Several Regiments and Battalions from North Carolina*, 2:155; Thomas, *History of the Doles-Cook Brigade*, 354.

24 McClendon, *Recollections of War Times*, 119.

crouching, fighting on their knees, with one soldier firing between a crack in the fence and another firing over the top rail. The Federal fire against the Confederates became so intense that the musketry "literally tore the old rotten fence into fragments." Resting an elbow on his friend, Alonzo Watson, to steady his aim, William McClendon was horrified to hear a "thud" and feel a jolt. Writing decades later, the death of Watson remained frozen in McClendon's mind. "Lonzo began to relax and sink, exclaiming in a low tone, 'Oh Lordy, I am a dead man.' These were his last words, life soon became extinct, but I didn't move but kept loading and firing until the fight was over."[25]

Lawton and Trimble's assault soon stalled, and Ewell attempted to get the Confederate lines moving. Officers from Jackson down to the lowliest staff officer attempted to fashion order out of the growing chaos and get the assault back on track. After being dispatched by Ewell, Campbell Brown came across Jackson trying to rally some stragglers, "more excited & indignant than I ever saw him—riding rapidly about among them & threatening with his arm raised." Brown admitted that seeing Jackson attempting to dragoon the stragglers in that way left him and a comrade squeamish, "to see conduct on his part—such evidence of uneasiness."[26]

Riding back towards the fighting line Brown felt "plainly the blank feeling of astonishment with which I looked up & down the line for a mounted officer & saw not one. It was about sunset—but I could see fully half a mile of the line." Ewell's aide later learned that because the men were fighting prone behind fences and mounted officers became silhouetted against the evening sky, most of the surviving officers dismounted and sent their horses to the rear. Better protected from enemy fire, dismounting slowed the officers from traversing the battle lines, making it more difficult to get the brigades advancing again. Among the dismounted men was Dick Ewell. Unlike other officers, Ewell decided to dismount not from fear of enemy fire but from the fear of his horse. The noise of battle startled his new mare and, exhausted from the fatigue of marching and lack of adequate sleep, Ewell was afraid that he did not have enough strength to properly handle his mount. Instead of risking being thrown, Ewell decided to dismount.[27]

Slowly officers began to reassert limited order among their troops, some resulting in localized attacks. Lawton appeared to the men of the 26th Georgia

25 Ibid., 119–120.

26 Jones, *Campbell Brown's Civil War*, 155.

27 Ibid., 155.

on foot, encouraging them to fire into the enemy. After a few rounds Lawton ordered the Georgians to fix bayonets and charge. Rising from the protection of the fence line the 26th Georgia, "with a true Georgia yell, rushed upon them." Advancing over open ground, the regiment quickly wilted under intense enemy small arms fire. Within moments the color bearer fell along with most of the color guard. Eight out of the ten company commanders fell killed or wounded. A Georgian later remembered his comrades "fell from the ranks by the dozen," slowing and eventually stopping the charge. Before reaching the Federals the disintegrating regimental line turned around and the Georgians fell back to the fence.[28]

Lawton's superior also tried to get the Confederate line moving again. Towards the left of Trimble's Brigade a ravine ran perpendicular to the stalled Southern firing line. Some astute Federal soldiers grasped the importance of the ravine and took up position in its protection, enfilading Trimble's men. Realizing what a small number of soldiers could do in that position, Ewell decided to clear the ravine with an unknown regiment.

In the summer of 1989, the venerable historian Robert Krick attempted to reconstruct the events surrounding Ewell's wounding. In the ground-breaking article that ensued, Krick surmised that the regiment Ewell led was the 31st Georgia of Lawton's Brigade. Krick's evidence centered on a post-war veteran's remembrance and the notion that the 31st Georgia did not participate in Lawton's charge because of its relatively light casualties. During the fighting on August 28, the 31st Georgia lost seven killed and twenty-six wounded for a total of 33 casualties. While certainly low for Lawton's Brigade, the 61st Georgia in the main battle line sustained similar casualties (16 killed, 32 wounded) so the 31st Georgia likely fought with the brigade.[29]

Moreover, the postwar account by I. G. Bradwell implies that the 31st Georgia participated in Lawton's attack. Sustaining casualties from an unseen enemy, including its acting regiment commander, the Georgians broke and retreated. Among the retreating soldiers was Dick Ewell, now remounted. Dismounting, Ewell supposedly grasped the regimental flag, rallied the 31st Georgia, and led them back in another attack. During the charge, Ewell went down with a wound to the leg. Since Campbell Brown's contemporary account has Ewell dismounting well before entering the battle, Bradwell's account of

28 Alton Murray, *South Georgia Rebels: The True Wartime Experiences of the 26th Regiment, Georgia Volunteer Infantry* (St. Mary's, GA, 1976), 78–80.

29 "Ewell's Division," *Confederate Causality Reports*, Record Group 109, Roll 0007, 15, National Archives, Washington D.C.

Ewell and the 31st Georgia is likely one of many apocryphal postwar stories created by veterans.[30]

After dismounting from his horse, Ewell likely studied the progress of the battle via sound. The experienced division commander heard firing towards the left of his line and recognized the importance of neutralizing that Federal threat before it endangered the entire line. Walking towards the end of the line to take personal charge of the nearest regiment, Ewell walked parallel to Trimble's Brigade. As he passed the 15th Alabama a soldier yelled out "Here is General Ewell, boys" followed by a thunderous volley.[31]

Ewell may have been addressing the threat to this left flank with Trimble's left end of his line, the 15th Alabama and the 12th Georgia, potentially explaining the two regiments' absence in the subsequent charge. Leading the 12th Georgia and an unknown regiment (a soldier in the 21st Georgia wrote on September 9 that in their charge they were assisted by the 26th Georgia and 61st Georgia of Lawton's Brigade, but no other contemporary accounts corroborate this sole account), Ewell cleared most of the ravine of the troublesome Yankees. While most retreated towards the main Federal line, some withdrew eastward, still on the flank of Trimble's Brigade. A scattering fire drew Ewell's attention. Kneeling to get a better view of this annoying fire, a Federal minie ball struck Ewell's knee and traveled down the leg "for some inches." Seeing their division commander fall, a few Alabamans offered to carry Ewell to the rear to which the feisty Virginian replied "Put me down, and give them hell!"[32]

Ewell's wound was a disaster to Lee's army. In an immediate sense the overall directing hand of the battle was incapacitated. Until news percolated up through the Confederate chain of command, any chance of a concerted Confederate attack evaporated. The lateness of the hour almost guaranteed that by time word reached Early of his superior's wounding the battle would be over. Except for the intuition and leadership of regimental and brigade commanders, the Confederate line remained at the fence line for the remainder of the battle, a direct result of Ewell's wound.

His protests notwithstanding, eventually Ewell was evacuated from the battlefield. It remained to be seen the severity of his wound and thus the likelihood of him either dying, recovering and returning to the army, or

30 I. G. Bradwell, "Cedar Mountain to Antietam," *Confederate Veteran* 29 (1921): 297.

31 Oates, *The War Between the Union and Confederacy*, 141.

32 Jones, *Campbell Brown's Civil War*, 157; Thomas, *History of the Doles-Cook Brigade*, 219; Robert E. L. Krick, "The Wounding of Richard Stoddert Ewell," MNBP; Styple, ed., *Writing & Fighting from the Army of Northern Virginia*, 141; Pfanz, *Richard S. Ewell*, 257.

discharged a crippled general. Ewell was wounded at the height of his career with a reputation as Lee's best division commander. The effects of Ewell's absence continued to be felt within the Confederate army from Antietam to Fredericksburg.

Ewell's wounding did not end the fight. Around 8:00 p.m. Trimble assembled the last major Confederate charge of the battle. Stemming from the confusion of navigating a smoky, loud, dark battlefield, only half of Trimble's brigade heard the order to prepare for a charge. As the two 21s began their advance, word failed to reach the 15th Alabama or the 12th Georgia and they remained prone behind their sections of fencing. By the time the regiments advanced the sun had set and moonlight began illumining the battlefield.[33]

Leading the Tar Heels was 27-year-old Lt. Col. Saunders Fulton, who was said to be "a man who was absolutely without fear, and who evidently believed that he was not to be killed in battle." After ordering his men to fix bayonets in preparation to "charge the pillaging wretches of the infamous Pope," the Carolinians nervously awaited word to advance. Within moments it arrived and the twin 21s "went over the fence with one of [their] most blood-curdling rebel yells."

Advancing alone on the moonlit field, the Georgians and Carolinians quickly received hellacious fire from the front and both flanks. Within moments after leaving the fence line the Tar Heel color bearer fell; Fulton quickly seized the colors. Waving the flag and bellowing "Forward boys!" the former physician soon went down with a musket ball to his thigh but within a few moments was back on his feet again encouraging his men forward. After advancing no more than fifteen steps the young lieutenant colonel was shot in the other thigh. Unfortunately, a third bullet hit him in the stomach, mortally wounding the intrepid officer.[34]

Within 30 yards of the Federal line, the Yankees redoubled their efforts, firing as fast as humanly possible, stopping the twin 21s. The Georgians and Tar Heels attempted to take cover nearby and settled into trading volleys with the unseen enemy. Realizing that the attack had failed, Trimble sent messengers to bring both regiments back to the main line. During the firefight along the fence line and subsequent charge, the 21st North Carolina sustained nearly 20 percent casualties in the fight, but its sister regiment took the more severe beating. Going into the fight with 242 officers and men, the next morning only

33 "Report of General I. R. Trimble of Operations from 14th to 29th August, 1862," *Southern Historical Society Papers*, 307–308.

34 Sherrill Jr., *21st North Carolina*, 157, 447.

69 answered the roll call, amounting to an initial 71 percent casualty rate for the Brawner fight. Soldiers separated from the regiment during the night fighting trickled in the following hours revising the Georgians casualty rate to a still shocking 58 percent.[35]

After the repulse of the two 21s, musketry continued to ring out along the battlefield but slowly began to ebb as darkness engulfed the Brawner fields, woods, and fence lines. For the Confederates, the battle was over.

35 "Report of General I. R. Trimble of Operations from 14th to 29th August, 1862," *Southern Historical Society Papers*, 308; Sherrill Jr., *21st North Carolina*, 158.

Chapter 28

"A Grim and Weary Night"

Brawner Farm: August 29, 1862

The soldiers never forgot the grim night, the air damp and thick and greasy with the smoke of the fighting and marked by the troubling calls of the wounded. Private Alvin Eager of the 2nd Wisconsin, shot through the mouth and in pain, searched for his brother Amos, who was with the 7th Wisconsin. Amos had been shot in the hand and leg and was unable to walk. He was to be left behind with the wounded in make-shift field hospitals near the turnpike. Alvin assisted his brother to a tree, said a hurried good-bye, and then joined his regiment as it was readying to march off. Amos, desperate not to be left behind, dragged himself to catch the rear of a passing ambulance. He pulled himself aboard, falling on the wounded already in the wagon.[1]

Not far away, Pvt. Chester Wyman of the 6th Wisconsin, wounded in the right leg, was back in the small woods by the turnpike where a field hospital was set up. Many of the wounded were piled around at different points in the woods and there were only a few men to help them. The walking wounded got water and food for the others, but there was little to go around. The small field station would be surrounded by the fighting of second Bull Run over the next three days and more wounded would be brought in until there were about 500 there. Wyman soon realized that with no help it was every man for himself. One man near him died and had a blanket. Wyman took it and spread it over himself to keep warm.[2]

1 Eager family records compiled by Jennifer Eager Ehle. Amos was transferred to the Veteran Reserve Corps on Nov. 15, 1863. *Wisconsin Roster*, vol. 1, 552

2 Wyman, letter, May 28, 1918. He added: "Our men came with a flag of Truce and carried us to Washington some 50 miles from there. The city of Washington contributed carriages to bring in the wounded, but the suffering we endured that night over the rough roads can be imagined but not told. When we arrived there a number of dead were removed from the carriages and at least

Across the fields could be seen flickering torches and lanterns as soldiers from both sides searched for fallen friends and messmates. A Wisconsin man and his friends found all the dead and wounded men of his regiment along a line, a rod or two in width. In the darkness, they encountered enemy pickets who fired on them but missed. Fairchild formed the 2nd Wisconsin's survivors on the roadway and was shaken to find so few. He called, "Where is the regiment—have they scattered?" Out of the darkness, someone replied, "Colonel, this is all that is left of the Second, the rest lay on the field." Through tears Fairchild replied, "Thank God, they are worthy of their name."

Several lost Confederates came out of the darkness into the Wisconsin line where they were disarmed. They said they were Jackson's men of Ewell's Division, and the Johnnies asked with friendly curiosity about the soldiers in the "big hats" they had been fighting.[3] Told they were Wisconsin and Indiana men, one Confederate private nodded and said that one of his officers had remarked, "It was no use to fight them damn fools; they did not know enough to know when they were whipped." Captain Brown was told by one that it was the first time the soldiers in his brigade "ever turned their backs to the foe."[4]

Toward midnight, the line moved back to the edge of the timber where the weary soldiers rested for an hour or two. While there, one of the regiments which had advanced to plug the gap in the line came out of the darkness marching toward the turnpike. Captain John Marsh saw it was the 76th New York and heard an officer call "Halt!" The column, however, kept on moving. Marsh heard the colonel say, "Seventy-sixth New York, won't you halt? Seventy-sixth New York, you have behaved so well tonight, won't you halt?" But the plea went for naught, and Marsh watched the regiment move away "with steady tread."[5]

It was a night to stampede any brigade, especially one staggered and battered in its first fight, but the Wisconsin and Indiana men stood steady in the darkness. It was about a half hour after midnight when the regiments marched through the woods to the turnpike. The moving soldiers found many of the dead and wounded scattered in the dark shadows, suffering and groaning and some were dying. They sometimes stumbled over the dead and wounded. On the turnpike, the soldiers found hasty preparations for retreat and at about

---

one third of the wounded died within 2 weeks after we were in the hospital." Wyman was soon discharged and sent home.

3 Harries, in Otis, *2nd Wisconsin*, 253; *Beaver Dam Home League*, Oct. 18, 1862; Dawes, *Service*, 63–64; Bragg to his wife, Sept. 13, 1862.

4 Sullivan, *Telegraph*, Oct. 21, 1883; Brown to his father, Sept. 5, 1862.

5 Marsh, *Telegraph*, Jan. 16, 1881.

1:00 a.m. they silently filed away into the darkness, muffling the rattling tin cups, and turning toward Manassas Junction.

A soldier in the 23rd New York of Patrick's brigade, which had halted and took cover in a wood following the artillery bursts, watched the fighting from 1,000 yards away and wrote about it in a letter home. "It was a grand yet terrible sight to behold," he ventured with appropriate drama. "The thunder of the cannon and sound of musketry was incessant, while amid the shades of evening, their flashes of smoke and fire filled the air with a lurid glow. Cheer after cheer went up with the groans of the dying and wounded, and to one not filled with the excitement of battle, or inured with the dangers of a soldier, it would have been a scene too fearful to behold."[6]

In the darkness, the 6th Wisconsin was ordered east. The remaining regiments of the brigade followed along with all the division ambulances filled with wounded. Captain Brown of the 6th Wisconsin was troubled to leave behind in the care of the doctors and nurses his friend, Lt. Jerome Johnson, who suffered a severe wound to the groin, and 12 others from his company. Gibbon rode at the head of the column and Adjutant Edward Brooks of the 6th Wisconsin rode ahead now and then to scout the fields. A 7th Wisconsin man was among the last to leave the field and he found one of Gibbon's men on the ground, shot through the lungs. He gave the man the last drops of water in his canteen, then, just before sunrise, marched after his regiment. Now and then as he left, a bullet whizzed over his head.[7]

Not far away accompanying the wounded was Pvt. Philo Wright of the 2nd Wisconsin. He was leaning against a hollow tree in the woods. He shoved his musket into the tree and waited through the long hours with many of those around "uttering death groans." By daybreak, he and the others were prisoners. He was troubled when a few of the wounded around him cried and told the Rebels they had been forced to enlist or were drafted. After a time, he could hear battle sounds in the distance and realized his only hope was to crawl for safety. He crawled about twenty rods when some Pennsylvania men gathered him up, telling him "You will make better time with us." He was taken to a small field hospital. The hospital was soon in danger from the fighting and Wright and the other wounded were hauled to ambulances. Wright's ambulance already was carrying two men. He had to sit beside the driver, but when the ambulance crossed a ditch after moving some 80 rods, a wheel broke, and he was thrown to

6 Seymour Dexter to Charles Tubbs, Sept. 9, 1862, National Archives, Washington D.C.

7 Cheek and Pointon, *Sauk County*, 40–41; Longhenry diary, Aug. 27–29, 1862.

the ground. A surgeon riding a horse near the ambulance told the two soldiers in the ambulance to crawl to the woods and wait. The doctor loaded Wright on his horse and took him to a field hospital.[8]

A brigade staff officer witnessed the somber men and officers as the column left behind the wounded, as the ambulances would hold up the line of march for Manassas Junction. One private observed in the darkness the men around him were "bleeding, angry, hungry, tired, sleepy, foot-sore and cut to pieces." Drained of all energy by the hot emotions and numbing fear, the bone-weary young men were just able to put one foot ahead of the other. Little was heard from the column above the scuffling feet, the dull clink of accouterments, and the creak of the wagons and ambulances. If there was a halt, half of the soldiers fell instantly to sleep, each man sitting or lying down on the spot where he stopped. Now and then, the quiet night was broken by a soft sigh or the jarring cry of a wounded man. But to be left behind was more feared than enduring the weariness or the agony of the march; so, they walked through a seemingly endless night.[9]

Captain John Marsh of the 6th Wisconsin found his wounded knee too painful to walk. He was about to drop out of the column when Major Dawes came along, dismounted, and helped Marsh onto his horse. Presently there sifted out of the marching columns wounded men who had been struggling to keep up with their companies and to avoid falling into the hands of the enemy. As Dawes walked beside his horse, soon each stirrup strap and even the animal's tail became a crutch to help along the weak and weary. The darkness was sometimes broken by calls for water, but the canteens were empty.[10]

The next few hours were very hard. One Badger fell asleep as he walked, his gun dropping out of his hand, jerking him awake with a start. It was morning when the column reached Manassas Junction and with the halt the weary soldiers dropped where they stood and fell asleep. Gibbon endeavored to secure food and ammunition, but the junction was a "scene of desolation and ruin." The Confederates had just days before seized the depot and destroyed everything they could not eat or carry off. Long trains of cars which had been filled with

8 P. B. Wright, *Rhymes at Odd Times*, no date, n.p. 163–173. Wright served in "Grant County Grays," Co. C, 2nd Wisconsin Volunteer Infantry. After the war he practiced medicine and surgery in and about Grand Rapids, MI. His collection of poems and war memoirs was privately printed.

9 Haskell to brothers and sisters, Sept. 22, 1862; Sullivan, *Telegraph*, Oct. 21, 1883; Fairfield, diary, Aug. 28, 1862.

10 Marsh, *Telegraph*, Jan. 16, 1881; Dawes, *Service*, 64.

supplies for the army were now "a smoldering mass of ashes, the rebel troops, first supplying themselves, having set the balance on fire two nights before."

With dawn a Wisconsin soldier found his brigade, but the men were so dirty and powder-stained he could barely recognize his own tentmates. It also seemed to him that their dispositions changed with their appearance. As the men stood around small coffee fires, there was praise for Gibbon's bravery and leadership in the fighting and hard words for King's failure to send reinforcements. One soldier said it seemed in Pope's army it was "every one for himself and the devil take the hindmost."

One Wisconsin officer tried to find the words in a letter he was writing home. "None of us could look upon our thinned ranks, so full the night before, now so shattered, without tears," he wrote. "And the faces of these brave boys, as the morning sun disclosed them, no pen can describe. The men were cheerful, quiet and orderly," he went on, in a poetic vein. "The dust and blackness of battle were upon their clothes, and in their hair, and on their skin, but you saw none of these,—you saw only their eyes, and the shadows of the 'light of battle,' and the furrows plowed upon cheeks that were smooth a day before, and now not half filled up. I could not look upon them without tears, and could have hugged the necks of them all."[11]

Around the officer as he wrote home the Wisconsin and Indiana men cooked the remains of the fresh beef ration issued the previous day and boiled coffee. The brigade's ammunition wagons came up and each man drew 60 rounds. About mid-morning they began to hear the "heavy sound of cannon and an occasional ripple of musketry," seemingly very near the place where they had fought the previous night. Dawes, sleeping alongside the roadway, awoke to the "heavy tramp of hurrying feet" and found a thick blue column moving back along the very road his 6th Wisconsin had covered the previous night. The soldiers, they were told, were just up from McClellan's Army of the Potomac and they were marching to the sound of the fighting. The arrivals were the veterans of the battles outside Richmond and were in good spirits and full of contempt for Pope's soldiers, especially those dirty fellows in black hats and frock coats alongside the roadway.

One of the passing soldiers called in a sneering voice. "We are going up to show you 'straw feet' how to fight." That set up a chorus of cat calls by both sides. One of the arriving veterans belonged to a colorful Zouave organization still outfitted in baggy red trousers. As it passed, a frustrated Badger went out to the edge of the road with narrowed eyes and raised fist to yell, "Wait 'till you get

11 Haskell to brothers and sisters, Sept. 22, 1862.

where we have been, you'll get the slack taken out of your pantaloons and the swell out of your heads."[12]

The Western Brigade was engaged on and off over the next two days in fighting at Bull Run and found itself part of the rear guard. It was obvious to all that John Pope's Army of Virginia had suffered a disaster and the broken units made their way toward the safety of the defensive lines around Washington. As the head of the Western Brigade finally approached Upton's Hill, regimental commanders had their color bearers wave their flags to prevent being fired upon by the Union guns in the front upon the height.

At Upton Hill, dismay gave way to grim acceptance. "You see we are back near our first starting point," a Wisconsin officer wrote home. "It is a sorrowful conclusion of a mismanaged campaign Pope has played out with the army." Otherwise, there was little change and routine again prevailed. Peddlers reappeared, but soldiers' pockets were empty. "Sutlers are asking outrageous prices," one Black Hat reported. "Molasses 50 cents a bottle. . . . As a result the soldiers are obliged to steal."[13]

12 Sullivan, *Telegraph*, May 16, 1884; Longhenry, diary, Aug. 29–30, 1862; Dawes, *Service*, 68–69. "Fitz-John Porter's corps from the army of the Potomac passed as we lay along the road. We felt good thinking we would be reinforced by the Army of the Potomac." Cheek and Pointon in *Sauk County*, 42.

13 Cheek and Pointon, *Sauk County*, 46; Thomas Allen, letter, Sept. 4, 1862; Longhenry, diary, Sept. 3, 1862.

Chapter 29

"Oh How We Suffered"

Manassas Battlefield: August 29, 1862

The battle of Groveton was over by 9:00 p.m. In the course of that evening's fighting, Jackson's Wing was bloodied. Besides losing two divisional commanders in Taliaferro and Ewell, four brigades were decimated. Historian John Hennessy has calculated that approximately a third of the soldiers that entered the fight became a casualty.[1]

In a letter to his hometown newspaper a soldier-correspondent lamented "The old Stonewall Brigade suffered on Thursday. . . . Oh how we suffered in the loss of noble, valuable men and officers." The brigade did indeed suffer with the five regiments taking a combined 340 killed, wounded, and missing, or 40 percent of the soldiers that entered the battle. Just as devastating to the future effectiveness of the brigade were who the casualties were. The brigade lost an unusually large number of officers. In terms of regimental commanders, the brigade took a 60 percent casualty rate with two regimental commanders, Colonel Botts of the 2nd and Colonel Neff of the 33rd, either dead or dying and Colonel Grigsby of the 27th wounded. In the 2nd Virginia, the only officers remaining by the dawn of August 29 were a single captain and one lieutenant.[2]

The heavy losses in the Stonewall Brigade overshadowed the damage that other brigades of Taliaferro's Division took. The three Virginia regiments of Taliaferro that fought alongside the Stonewall Brigade sustained about 100 casualties. Taliaferro's regiments lost just over 10 percent of the men that entered the fight. Not as severe as Baylor's brigade, Taliaferro's Virginians were still literally decimated that evening. Like the Stonewall Brigade, an unusually

1 Hennessy, *Return to Bull Run*, 188.

2 *Lexington Gazette*, Sept. 11, 1862; Jeffry Wert, *A Brotherhood of Valor: The Common Soldiers of the Stonewall Brigade, C.S.A, and the Iron Brigade, U.S.A.* (New York, 1999), 154.

high proportion of officers also went down in the fight. That evening Lieutenant Colonel Taylor was the only field officer serving in the 23rd Virginia and a similar situation faced Colonel Warren in the 10th Virginia. Added to the officers lost at Cedar Mountain, Taliaferro's Virginians found themselves increasingly led by junior officers.[3] All told, Taliaferro's Division lost about 500 officers and men at Brawner farm.

The loss in officers was capped with the wounding of Taliaferro in his debut battle after assuming command of Jackson's old division. The severe loss of officers from the company to the division portended a reduction in the effectiveness in Jackson's old division. In both the short and long term, the division remained in flux. After Taliaferro's wounding, William Starke left his Louisiana brigade and assumed command of the division and led it through the rest of the Manassas fighting, only to be killed less than a month later leading the division at Antietam.

As unfortunate as the rapid turnover in divisional commanders was, the turnover in company and regimental officers threatened long term damage to the effectiveness of one of Lee's best divisions. Lost leaders were usually replaced by the elevation of junior officers. Some, like Elisha "Bull" Paxton, developed into excellent commanders provided they survived. Bull Paxton was killed leading the Stonewall Brigade at Chancellorsville. Not all battlefield promotions turned out so favorably, with some officers promoted beyond their command ability. At the company level the high turnover in officers disrupted not only the battlefield performance but all units suffered administratively as newly promoted officers learned the bureaucratic nature of Civil War army paperwork. Some superb combat commanders never mastered administrative duties, slowly but surely diminishing the efficiency of their command.

The losses in Taliaferro's Division threatened disaster. Ewell's Division was in danger of devolving in one campaign from one of the Confederacy's best divisions to a shell of its former self. Ewell's first brigade took the heaviest number of casualties suffered during the battle. Lawton's Brigade of Georgians lost 113 killed, 296 wounded, and 5 missing for a total of 414 casualties. The one killed and five wounded in the 13th Georgia suggests that regiment served in a detached, reserve role during the battle. If that is the case, Lawton's Brigade likely took a higher casualty rate than the Stonewall Brigade. One of Lawton's regiments received one of the highest casualty rates of the war during its time fighting on the Brawner farm. The 26th Georgia lost 42 men killed, 87 wounded, and 5 missing (likely men killed but never accounted for in the confusion of

3 Gaff, *Brave Men's Tears*, 159.

the fight). The 26th Georgia lost 134 men, nearly 72 percent of the soldiers that entered the fight.[4]

Similar to the Stonewall Brigade, the officer corps in Lawton's Brigade was wrecked. Between the four regiments actively engaged in the fight, eight officers were killed, including two captains and six lieutenants, while another 23 officers went down with wounds. The loss of 31 officers on August 28 endangered the long-term combat effectiveness of Lawton's Brigade. The fight at Brawner was but one battle in a larger campaign that lasted over a week from August 27 to September 1. Fortunately, after the 28th, Lawton's Brigade remained in reserve but still managed to lose an additional five officers killed and wounded. During a single week of fighting Lawton's Georgians lost a stunning thirty-six officers.[5]

Trimble's Brigade barely emerged from the August 28 fighting in better shape than their Georgian comrades. The last major Confederate unit committed to the fight, Trimble's mixed brigade, still lost 90 officers and men killed, 214 wounded, and 6 missing. The total loss of 310 men was not evenly distributed in the brigade. The 15th Alabama, 21st North Carolina, and the 12th Georgia each sustained roughly 50 casualties in the fight, with the 1st North Carolina Battalion losing an additional 15 officers and men. Over 50 percent of the brigade's casualties were concentrated in a single regiment. The 21st Georgia lost 36 killed, 109 wounded, and a single soldier missing. The Georgian's 146 casualties amounted to a loss of 71 percent of all officers and men that the 21st Georgia brought into the fight. Factoring in random shell bursts in the brigades held in reserve, Ewell's Division lost 759 men killed, wounded, and captured.[6]

The single greatest loss in the division was the wounding of its leader. By the evening of August 28 Ewell had not only developed into a rock-solid division commander but was one of the few men to successfully establish a close, working relationship with Jackson. As A. P. Hill learned earlier in August, being a subordinate to Stonewall Jackson was not an easy assignment. The partnership that Ewell and Jackson established in the first half of 1862 formed the foundation for Jackson's subsequent victories and renown. It remained to be seen how the loss of Ewell would impact Jackson and the success of his wing.

Over 1,200 soldiers of Jackson's Wing fell fighting near the old Manassas battlefield on August 28, 1862. Compared to the recent fighting on the Virginia peninsula, Confederate losses were light. An engagement with only portions

4 *OR* 12, pt. 2, 813.

5 Ibid., 810–813.

6 Ibid., 812.

of both armies engaged, Brawner farm had more in common with the fighting at Williamsburg in May or Beaver Dam Creek in June. In those battles the Confederates lost more men than at Brawner, with nearly 1,500 men falling at Beaver Dam Creek and nearly 1,700 at Williamsburg. Like Brawner both battles were at the beginning of their respective campaigns, Williamsburg preceding the Confederate retreat towards Richmond and Beaver Dam Creek kicking off the Seven Days' battles.

Compared to similar battles, Brawner was not extraordinarily bloody. It was noteworthy as Jackson's second major semi-independent fight since the Valley campaign. The fighting in August starting at Cedar Mountain and extending to Brawner farm highlighted Jackson's continued ability to perform admirably on the operational level by marching his troops literally around the enemy. Both fights also highlighted Jackson's continual uninspiring execution at the tactical level. Historian John Hennessy has categorized the Confederate performance at Brawner as "ill-managed and indecisive" and a "mediocre battlefield performance" by Jackson. Joe Harsh likewise viewed Jackson's decision to attack a "curious one." Taking Jackson to task for viewing the destruction of a single Federal division as worthwhile to committing the Army of Northern Virginia to battle, Harsh rebukes Jackson's decision to attack on August 28 as a victory "through bloody combat and from tactical blunders by the enemy. There would be no heavy victory from easy fighting."[7]

Jackson, Taliaferro, and Ewell all deserve some criticism for their performance. After conducting one of the most successful operational movements in American military history, everyone in Jackson's Wing from commander to private was reaching the limits of physical endurance. Marching over 50 miles to reach his objective of severing the Orange and Alexandria Railroad at Bristoe Station, Jackson risked his command for the secondary objective of Manassas Junction. The small Federal garrison at Manassas and the uncoordinated attempts by the Federals on August 27 proved fortunate for Jackson who reaped the benefits more from luck than from skill. His decision to move his wing away from the railroad after August 27 was correct, but in typical Jacksonian style his desire for operational secrecy led to unnecessary marching for his already tired wing.

Jackson's biggest mistake of August 27–28 was the abandonment of Thoroughfare Gap. Detaching a portion of his wing to guard the important gap may have been risky, seeing how Stonewall was operating between two Federal forces of Pope along the Rappahannock River and McClellan arriving in

7 Hennessy, *Return to Bull Run*, 189; Harsh, *Confederate Tide Rising*, 154.

Alexandria. Faced with a potential fight sooner rather than later, Jackson decided to keep his wing concentrated. However, Stonewall completely misused J. E. B. Stuart and his cavalry. After recognizing his error by not providing enough mounted men at the start of Jackson's flank march, Lee overcompensated by detaching the majority of his army's cavalry to serve with Jackson's column. Earlier in the Valley campaign Jackson routinely took a dim light on cavalry operated under Turner Ashby.

Acting as a semi-independent commander, Jackson never fully appreciated how to use cavalry. The mounted arm's superb performance on August 26 at Bristoe Station, and August 27 at Manassas Junction and Bull Run Bridge, derived more from Stuart's ability than Jackson's. After that initial success Jackson allowed most of the cavalry to literally gallop out of the campaign. The raid into Fairfax County netted almost no new information about Federal movements. Instead Jackson would have been better served by directing Stuart and his troopers to actively patrol the area between his Wing and Thoroughfare Gap. Outnumbered by the Federals that marched to the gap from Warrenton, Confederate cavalry would still have reported Federals in the gap more quickly and efficiently, likely making any subsequent fight for the gap easier for the Confederates.

After arriving at the old Manassas battlefield Jackson's aggressiveness almost got the better of him. Rather than remaining under cover until word of Lee's whereabouts was known, the sight of a Federal column marching on the Warrenton Turnpike that morning offered too tempting a target for Stonewall. By the time Jackson's Wing got in motion to attack the enemy, the enemy had shifted to a road that allowed him to march away from Jackson's position and towards Manassas.

Frustrated by the lack of success in the morning, when Jackson saw another Federal column marching on the turnpike that afternoon he allowed his wing to attack. The destruction of a Federal division would likely have buoyed Confederate chances of a successful northern Virginia campaign. To fulfill that objective Jackson needed to attack in time with enough force. Unfortunately for Confederate arms, the attack was launched late in the day. Most of the subsequent confusion and piecemeal attacks owed more to the decision to start a fight at dusk rather than from any particular command failure by any specific general. The subsequent movements of Jackson, Ewell, and Taliaferro were hindered by the lateness of the attack.

Jackson would likely have been better served postponing the attack. Naturally aggressive and frustrated by the fizzling of the morning attack, Jackson characteristically decided to press his offensive. The lateness of the hour likely doomed Confederate success before the first shot was fired. Jackson's attack, however, alerted the Federals to his new location and presaged another tough 24 hours of fighting before the Army of Northern Virginia was reunited. The Confederate victory at second Manassas is arguably Lee's most complete battlefield victory of the war. While skill certainly played a role, an undue portion of the victory—especially on August 28—derived more from luck and a lackluster Federal command than brilliant Confederate generalship. The battle of Brawner farm devolved into a brutal standup fight, one in which the Confederate army was not well placed to quickly replace losses. Unknown to all, the battle of Brawner farm was but one of many battles from northern Virginia to Maryland that summer and fall.

Chapter 30

"We Found Your Beloved Son"

Virginia: December 1862

In early December 1862, a light wagon left Centreville, Virginia. It displayed a white flag of truce as a battle was apparently brewing at nearby Fredericksburg and the countryside was being patrolled by soldiers of both sides. The expedition was headed to the old battlefield near Gainesville where it was hoped could be recovered the body of Col. Edgar O'Connor of the 2nd Wisconsin Infantry, who was buried in a shallow grave following the fighting there August 28.

William Selleck of the Wisconsin Soldiers Aid Society had been promised a soldier escort, but the pending battle precluded the assistance of a detail of Union cavalrymen. His party included a light wagon and driver, himself, and a former member of O'Connor's regiment. Selleck carried diagrams of the graves of Wisconsin soldiers at the site, but upon arrival it was soon discovered they were useless. He located a local resident who was acquainted with the battlefield and who joined the party.

In a December 14 letter to the colonel's father at Beloit, Wisconsin, Selleck wrote: "There was one, having a board, with your son's name and Regt. on it, but on examination was found not to be the one; whereupon I picked out one which, from its appearance, I thought must be an officer. We opened it and got to the shoulder, pulled aside the blanket, and could see the eagle on the strap which satisfied me that it was the body of your son."

The body was removed from the grave. The blanket was pulled aside, and a rubber blanket lifted off the face. The face "was found to be undecayed and as white as the day it was buried." Selleck said he recognized "it as that of your beloved son, as would any who was at all acquainted with him and familiar with his appearance when in life." The colonel's body was placed in the black walnut coffin brought along for the purpose. The little party then made its way for Washington arriving well after dark after a 46-mile trip along what Selleck called "a very bad road."

In Washington, Selleck consulted with Gen. Rufus King and others and a funeral was organized in the parlor of the boarding house where Selleck lived. The ceremony was attended by a large delegation of Wisconsin officials, including Governor Alexander Randall, other dignitaries, and a number of citizens. The service was performed by an Episcopal clergyman. The coffin was placed in the hearse and covered with a U.S. flag. The escort included the 26th regiment of Maine volunteers and its band and the procession moved along Pennsylvania Avenue to the Congressional burial site. "The remains now repose, encased in a black walnut coffin which is placed in a stout outside case made of thick pine," Selleck wrote.[1]

Almost a year after O'Connor's remains were recovered, on November 1, 1863, now Brig. Gen. Lysander Cutler of the First Division of the I Corps sat down to write a letter to the editor of the *Wisconsin State Journal* back home. He wanted to address rumors that the remains of the men who fell "in the bloody fight of August 28th 1862 were carelessly buried."

On the way to Thoroughfare Gap, he explained, the old battlefield was visited, and the rumors proved true. Lying about in every direction were the bleaching bones and ghastly skulls of the men who fell. The rebels had only slightly covered the dead with earth, which was quickly washed off by the heavy rains, leaving the bodies fully exposed to view. The opposing lines could still be traced by the litter of cartridge papers and half-buried bodies. The shallow graves were also easy to discover—the grass grew a little greener and taller.

Cutler wrote: "I have today had details from all the regiments who fought there sent to the ground under the charge of Captain [Hollon] Richardson, of the Seventh Wisconsin. We have carefully interred the remains. Many of them could be recognized by the positions where they fell, or by articles found about them. As the friends of those who fell will doubtless hear of the loose manner of the first burial, I write to assure them that all has been done that could be given them decent burial."

1 W. Y. Selleck to B. O'Connor, Dec. 14, 1862. Selleck would soon sit on a platform at Gettysburg, PA, with President Lincoln. He was a member of the committee which organized the establishment of a National Cemetery for Federal soldiers killed in the battle there in 1863.

Chapter 31

"More of True Valor"

Present Day

In the immediate hours after Gainesville, regimental officers and the soldiers of Gibbon's Western Brigade quietly took stock. It seemed as if suddenly everything had changed. Gone finally was the lingering doubt how they would perform in combat—they had stood fire in a murderous exchange of musketry for an hour and more. The long days on a drill field, they discovered, gave them the ability to maneuver and deliver a sustained fire that broke apart approaching enemy units. Also recognized was that the other regiments in the brigade could be counted on in a tight place. Deep concerns remained, however. Left behind in the make-shift hospitals along the Warrenton Turnpike were friends and kinsmen, some wounded, others dead. How would faraway mothers in Indiana and Wisconsin take the terrible news?[1]

The losses were numbing. Colonel Edgar O'Connor of the 2nd Wisconsin was killed and the three other colonels—Meredith of the 19th, Robinson of the 7th,

1 The nation's population shift west began at the end of the Revolutionary War when unsettled land beckoned west of the Appalachian Mountains. It soon led to the formation of the new states of Indiana, Illinois, Michigan, and Wisconsin, and that brought more settlers—men and women of ambition and vigor interested in making a future. It mattered not where they came from, it was life on what was sometimes a harsh frontier that changed and shaped them. "They were young men and women in their very prime; a sturdy, stalwart, self-reliant element such as pushed out to develop a new country . . . their superiority was noticeable," one man observed. In many ways, these settlers and arriving immigrants filling the Upper Middle West were a new kind of American with only faint memory of earlier colonial days. They had a certain kinship with those who first pushed into the Ohio River Valley and Kentucky, but they were better educated and riding the growing wave of industrial revolution. They had a sharp sense of place and distance and an understanding of the times heightened by the growth of newspapers, railroads, highways, canals, and the telegraph. They counted among their friends others who were White, Black, and Red; immigrant or native born; as well as sons and daughters of local tribes and early French trappers. As soldiers, these "Western boys" had a certain dash and sense of themselves never before seen in the United States. When a Western regiment appeared—one volunteer said—the "fine physique, the self-reliant carriage of its men at once challenged attention."

This drawing is found in the 1900 edition of *The Iron Brigade* by Charles King, who followed his father, Rufus King, as an aide in the early days of the war before heading to West Point. *Lance J. Herdegen*

and Cutler of the 6th—wounded or injured. Major Isaac May of the 19th was shot and would soon be dead after lying without shelter in a rainstorm. His grave was never found. Special praise was voiced for wounded Lt. Col. Charles Hamilton of the 7th who did not leave until the fighting ended and his horse fell dead. He was soon out of the war, writing a friend: "I was this day discharged [from] the service. I could have probably retained my position to the prejudice of junior officers in the regt, but as my idea was that those who fight should have the honors."

In the stunning confusion of their first battle, most of the company commanders demonstrated their worth. And it was also noted with silent nods that the soldiers of the 2nd Wisconsin, who boasted so long of their service at first Bull Run, again showed their true mettle, and they in turn finally accepted the men in the other regiments as full comrades.

It was the hated and distant John Gibbon who won their hearts. His appearance during the heaviest of the fighting proved his individual courage and the fighting demonstrated his heavy schedule of drills and camps of instruction had somehow turned them into a real fighting brigade. The defining moment came when Gibbon was listening to verbal reports of the "frightful loss" to his regiments. He waved his hand to stop, and one soldier watched as the general "dropped his head and wept most bitterly. His sorrow was that of the father who had been bereft of his children."

The 90 minutes of fighting was a true "stand up and knock down" fight in a mostly open field with the desperate lines sometimes 100 yards apart, or 70 yards, or even 30 yards, both sides firing with the fury of madmen. There was little maneuvering, just steady shooting with the muskets so hot and fouled they were hard to load. The Black Hats were issued 40 rounds for their boxes and another 20 rounds to carry in haversacks, but soon the cartridges were expended. Even the extra cartridges passed forward by wounded men and the first boxes of ammunition arriving from supply wagons back on the roadway did little to ease the short supply.

The steady and accurate shooting of the Indiana and Wisconsin men stalled attempts by the enemy to drive them and the stubborn resistance surprised the Confederates. The long hours drilling "load in nine counts" was now recognized as an important part of being a soldier: "Could you have seen the men of this brigade stand up in line on the night of Aug. 28, not a man skulking or wavering, breasting the terrible fire of nearly a whole division of the enemy, until their ranks were fearfully thinned, and until the enemy had ceased firing, you would have been as proud of them as we were," a Wisconsin man said of Gainesville.[2]

Of course, the 2nd Wisconsin, the first to be engaged, suffered the most—a staggering 276 out of the 430 carried off the field. For almost 20 minutes the outnumbered regiment stood alone in a violent exchange of musketry at close range. "I went into the fight of Thursday, the 28th, with fifty-one men, and came

2 Quiner, *Correspondence*; Bushnell, *Iron Brigade*; *Indianapolis Daily State Sentinel*, Sept. 12, 1862.

out with only eight," said one lieutenant. The 7th Wisconsin lost 164 of 580 engaged, and the 19th Indiana 210 of 423. In the 6th Wisconsin, less exposed on low ground, eight were killed, 61 wounded, and three missing out of 504 engaged. Initial reports showed more than one-third of the brigade—725—were casualties. The two regiments of Doubleday's Division sent to assist the Western Brigade also suffered heavy losses—the 56th Pennsylvania lost 136 out of 300, and the 76th New York 100 out of 250 officers and men. Eight of Gibbon's 12 field officers were injured, wounded, or killed. With no field officers available in the 7th, Gibbon consolidated the 2nd and 7th under Fairchild, the senior officer of the two regiments still on his feet.[3]

The fierce combat forever marked the farmers, shopkeepers, mechanics, and piney camp boys from far away Wisconsin and Indiana. A one-time hired man the next morning could hardly recognize his tentmates. An officer looked at the lines on the faces so unmarked the day before and wanted to hug their necks. A general listened to the grim roll calls and wept. "I never liked anything better than to stand right up among the bullets and shells and give it to the rebels," one soldier said. Another survivor would write to a friend that it "has got so that it does not excite me any more to be in action than to be in a corn field hoeing or digging potatoes." Gainesville taught his brigade how to fight, a third soldier wrote home.[4]

The Westerners recognized the road had taken a dark turn and a certain Confederate general involved in the change of fortunes caught their attention and they singled him out as a dangerous and worthy foe. His men were described as "half-soled, full-souled" fellows by one who saw them. "Jacksons men fight like devils," a Wisconsin officer wrote home. The Johnnies "will march to the cannons mouth without flinching. They march barefoot endure any and every privation. They shout for Jackson." Efforts to counter the Confederate army's move into Maryland—even with Little Mac back in command—were in doubt, he reported. The Rebels "think and are certain Jackson can and will whip the north and they have been taught their homes and lives and everything thing [they] hold near and dear depends on this march of Jackson to the north."[5]

3 Gaff, *Brave Men's Tears*, 156–158; Stine, *Army of the Potomac*, 132; Dawes, journal, undated; Allen, letter, Sept. 4, 1862; Wheeler, journal, Aug. 30, 1862; *Telegraph*, Dec. 7, 1879; *Milwaukee Sentinel*, Sept. 6, 1862; *Wisconsin State Journal*, Sept. 17, 1862. The actual number of casualties is always problematic. Some officers overstated numbers on their returns while others understated them and some officers just got them wrong.

4 Hutchins, letter cited in *Brandon* [VT] *Monitor*, Oct.10, 1862.

5 Young to wife, Sept. 3, 1862, *Dear Delia*, 90.

After the fighting on the Brawner farm fields, Gibbon's Brigade was engaged over the next two days in what became second Bull Run but escaped the heavy fighting. That was immediately followed by a troubling and gloomy retreat from the battlefield with the brigade part of the rear guard. No sooner were the men of the Western Brigade safe in the Washington defenses when they learned that Jackson and the victorious Confederate Army of Northern Virginia was apparently moving into Maryland. The overall success of Union arms was now uncertain.

Surprisingly, to cheers and calls of encouragement from the ranks, George Brinton McClellan, who failed outside Richmond, was given command of Pope's men and the arriving reinforcements from the Army of the Potomac. He faced the daunting task of untangling the defeat of the past few days and readying the newly combined force for active campaigning against the invading Confederates. There was much to do. Command structures were in disarray. The men in ranks were shaken by the changing fortunes of the recent days. Everything was in a hurry. Animals had to be gathered and made ready. Wagons had to be repaired and the food and ammunition found to fill them. Soldiers needed refitting. Orders had to be drafted. But the man who had built the Army of the Potomac into a force so strong it was able to stand almost any blow, or any defeat, was equal to the task. It was McClellan at his very best. No other general, Confederate or Union, could have pulled it off, but Little Mac accomplished the impossible and advance elements of his cobbled together army were on the road and giving chase just one day after the Confederates crossed into Maryland.

In less than two weeks, the Union forces reached South Mountain in Maryland and found Confederates holding the three main crossings. On September 14, Gibbon's men fought their way up the National Road to Turner's Gap, and three days later—on September 17—found themselves in a hellish swirl of fighting in a cornfield near Sharpsburg, Maryland. It was their fourth pitched battle in less than a month.

The long climb up South Mountain astride the National Road under McClellan's eye became a transforming moment. Other soldiers were now not talking about a "Gibbon's Brigade," a "Western Brigade" or a "Black Hat Brigade," but an "Iron Brigade of the West." It became a mighty epithet and McClellan claimed to have a role in creating it; perhaps he was a factor. The story he told a former Wisconsin officer during a reception at the Continental Hotel in Philadelphia after the war included this exchange between himself and Gen. Joseph Hooker:

McClellan: "What troops are those fighting on the pike?

Hooker: "General Gibbon's Brigade of Western men."

McClellan: "They must be made of iron."

Hooker: "By the Eternal, they are iron! If you had seen them at Bull Run as I did, you would know them to be iron."

McClellan: "Why, General Hooker, they fight equal to the best troops in the world."

The general said it was sometime after the fighting that Hooker rode up to headquarters and called out, "General McClellan, what do you think now of my Iron Brigade?" It was an exchange that could have happened. John Gibbon said that during the battle of Gainesville "the men we took prisoner asked who 'those black hatted fellows' were they had been fighting and after that the men were accustomed to refer to themselves as 'The Black Hat Brigade.' How or when the name of the 'Iron Brigade' was first given I do not know but soon after the battle of Antietam the name was started and ever after was applied to the brigade." Rufus Dawes, in his brilliant history of his 6th Wisconsin, never identified the origin of the name.[6]

Other evidence provides a more acceptable explanation. The slope of South Mountain was less cluttered in September 1862 than now, with clumps of woods, some large clusters of boulders, and stone fences marking the open fields. From the viewing platform built by his engineers on a rise of ground near his headquarters well back from South Mountain, Little Mac had a clear view of the advance. In his report of the battle, McClellan wrote a glowing description: "[Gibbon's] brigade advanced steadily, driving the enemy from positions in the woods and behind stone walls, until they reached a point well up towards the top of the pass, when the enemy, having been reinforced by three regiments, opened heavy fire on the front and on both flanks. . . . Gen. Gibbon, in this delicate movement, handled his brigade with as much precision and coolness as if upon parade, and the bravery of his troops could not be excelled."[7]

It was a display of brave fighting that was remembered because it occurred in full view. At Gainesville, in the fighting the day before second Bull Run, the four regiments fought almost alone in the gathering darkness against elements of the Stonewall Brigade, another fighting organization with a storied battle name. But it was still then an unknown brigade of soldiers in big hats against a

6 Gibbon, *Recollections*, 93

7 George B. McClellan, *McClellan's Own Story*, 582.

"Stonewall Brigade." The Westerners also covered the retreat at second Bull Run but won little fame. At South Mountain, however, the general commanding the Army of the Potomac and others watched as Gibbon's brigade fought its way up to Turner's Gap, and perhaps, just perhaps, Little Mac did ask what brigade was moving up the hill, and when told, perhaps, just perhaps, did make a clever remark about "iron men."

A newspaper reporter standing nearby overheard something along those lines from McClellan and his officers and noted it in his own notebook long before McClellan's memory was romanced a bit. The correspondent worked for the *Cincinnati Daily Commercial*. He wrote a report that was printed September 22, 1862, just eight days after South Mountain and five days after Antietam. In it he said of Gibbon's men: "The last terrible battle has reduced this brigade to a mere skeleton; there being scarcely enough members to form half a regiment, the 2nd Wisconsin, which but a few weeks since, numbered over nine hundred men, can now muster but fifty nine. This brigade has done some of the hardest and best fighting in the service. It has been justly termed the Iron Brigade of the West."[8]

The name was linked to McClellan in letters home. Captain Aleck Gordon Jr. of the 7th Wisconsin wrote in late September that "Gen. McClellan has given us the name of the Iron Brigade." Private Hugh Perkins of the same regiment also wrote to a friend September 26th that "Gen. McClellan has given us the name of the Iron Brigade." Even Dawes as early as September 18 used the word "iron" to describe the men of his regiment: "I have come safely through two more terrible engagements with the enemy, that at South Mountain and the great battle of yesterday [Antietam]," he wrote his mother. "The men have stood like iron."[9]

The missed opportunity at Gainesville became a subject of controversy. General John Pope wrote that the decision to march King's division from Jackson's front to Manassas Junction was a tragic error. He also said that he had directed orders to King to "hold his ground at all costs"—a claim refuted in

8 *Cincinnati Daily Commercial*, Sept. 22, 1862. Wisconsin and Indiana men always believed there was no confusion and that it was McClellan who singled them out as an "Iron Brigade of the West." From the first they were careful to include the reference to their Western roots and said it was a name won by hard fighting. Jerome Watrous of the 6th Wisconsin, one of the newspaper "prints" himself, first told the correct version of how the name was used by a newspaper man who was at McClellan's headquarters during South Mountain. Then the editor of his own newspaper, Watrous had been asked about the famous name in an interview with the *Chicago Chronicle* before the 1898 Iron Brigade Association reunion at Baraboo, WI. When it was published by the Chicago newspaper, Watrous ran the story in the columns of his own *Milwaukee Sunday Telegraph*, Sept. 12, 1898.

9 Wisconsin Newspapers, Vol. 4; "Letters of a Civil War Soldier," ed. Marilyn Gardner, prepared for syndication for April 9, 1983, *Christian Science Monitor*.

print by King's son, Charles King. In fact, by August 28, Pope's Army of Virginia was scattered and there was confusion about the movement of the Confederate columns. One Federal division had been ordered to the Thoroughfare Gap to contest the arrival of the rest of the Rebel army, but the commander, realizing he was outnumbered, retreated on the approach of Confederate James Longstreet's brigades. Hearing King was taking his division to Manassas Junction, Union Gen. James Ricketts took his soldiers and marched to Bristoe. Pope insisted later that it was the worst move King or Ricketts could have made—if they had maintained their positions, the two might have kept Longstreet's soldiers from reaching Jackson.

Upon hearing of King's engagement, Pope became convinced that Jackson was in full retreat to Thoroughfare Gap and Union forces could be hurled at the rebels while King and Ricketts blocked their retreat. In truth, the situation was much different. Jackson was not retreating—he was digging in along a strong defensive position. His lines of communication to Longstreet were open and the head of Longstreet's column was already through the gap and bivouacked within supporting distance. Not expecting Longstreet before Saturday night, or even Sunday, Pope issued orders for an attack on Jackson. Even as his aides went to the division commanders, Federal skirmishers were already exchanging fire with Jackson's men along the turnpike east of Groveton. Other Union forces joined and soon an engagement was in progress.

There were three critical moments in the confusion and uncertainty. Gibbon's move to advance a regiment on the Rebel battery shelling his column was questioned. Was it simply a pesky enemy horse battery or was it something more? Gibbon did not know, of course, and the advance of infantry probably stirred up Jackson and could have led to the defeat of a portion of the Union army. General Massena Patrick of King's division said he declined to put his brigade in on Gibbon's left because he disapproved of Gibbon's making the attack without more consideration and knowledge of the strength of the enemy.[10]

The gathering darkness and the flicker of musket fire also lifted the fog of war for both sides when it revealed the large gap between the 6th Wisconsin and the rest of the brigade. It clearly showed the danger that was finally addressed by the arrival of two regiments from Doubleday's brigade.

The decision to leave the battlefield to the enemy was also questioned with some anger and much blame laid on Rufus King, who was recovering from an epileptic seizure just days before. A Wisconsin officer, unaware the general was ill and not drunk, wrote in his journal:

10 Stine, *Army of the Potomac*, 132.

> It would not do for Gen. McDowell's troops to have had a battle when he was not there, or to have found any Confederate force of the enemy where according to his theory of the situation there was only a reconnoiter party. It might look as though he didn't know where the enemy was. Neither would it do for a division General (King) to have his troops fight a battle at the beginning of which he was almost dead drunk, and which he did not show his precious head. Nor is he anxious to any thing particularly said about the matter of his withdrawing his division without orders, ill-natured folks would say hurriedly, to Manassas.

The same sentiments were being echoed in ranks by a 2nd Wisconsin soldier: "Then our division commander, Brigadier General Rufus King, orders a retreat, the first and only command he is known to have given since the opening of the battle, and we march by the Bethlehem Road to Manassas Junction."[11]

Long after the war, however, in a written defense of his father, Charles King, a soldier in his own right and a popular author, said that "no order or message of any kind, sort, or description reached General King that night from General Pope or another superior officer; no staff-officer of General King saw or heard from General Pope that night." He also quoted from a letter of May 7, 1863, from Gibbon to King: "I deem it not out of place to say that the retreat was suggested and urged by myself as a necessary military measure." Gibbon added, "I do not hesitate to say, and it is susceptible of proof, that of the two courses which I considered open to you, of obeying your orders to march to Centreville or treat on Manassas on your own responsibility, the one you adopted was the proper one."

In the end, of course, the decision to march King's division away from Jackson's front was a mistake and played a large role in the defeat of Pope's Army of Virginia in the next two days.[12]

From the first, the 90 minutes of fighting had trouble finding a name. As clearly part of the opening of the larger engagement, it often was lumped into second Bull Run even though the engagement in the late afternoon of August 28, 1862, was in some way a separate and distinct encounter. Of some significance and despite the fighting over the next two days, both sides singled out the clash of infantry with their own names.

11 Rufus Dawes, journal, undated; Wheeler, journal, Aug. 28, 1862. For a full discussion see John J. Hennessy, *Return to Bull Run: The Campaign and Battle of Second Manassas* (New York, 1993), 193.

12 General King, "In Vindication of General Rufus King," *Battles and Leaders*, 2:495. See also Gaff, *Brave Men's Tears*, 164–169. As an example of how the battle cast a long shadow over the King family, Charles King, in endorsing a copy of his novel, *The Iron Brigade*, to his daughter on Aug. 28, 1902, added a brief note: "The Anniversary of 'Gainesville.'"

The Wisconsin and Indiana men always called the fighting "Gainesville"—for the small nearby crossroads community—and that was the name painted on their flags and listed in their reports. The Confederates called it "Groveton," for another nearby community. The Manassas National Park Service did not acquire the site until 1985 and after a time settled on "Brawner's Farm," a name first given the engagement by Alan Nolan in his 1961 book *The Iron Brigade: A Military History*. The NPS improved the site with signage and walking paths starting near the rebuilt Brawner farmhouse to the area where the 19th Indiana fought, and farther on to where the 2nd Wisconsin opened the fighting, and all the way to the right flank of the Union line.[13]

Those who fought on the Brawner farm fields struggled to find the words to describe the fighting. One Wisconsin man called it "a rude baptism of blood," but it was Confederate W. B. Taliaferro who was the most eloquent. He described the fighting as

> a stand-up combat, dogged and unflinching. . . . There were no wounds from spent balls, the confronting lines looked into each other's faces at deadly ranges, less than one hundred yards apart, and they stood as immovable as the painted heroes in a battle-piece. . . . [But] out in the sunlight, in the dying daylight, and under the stars, they stood, and although they could not advance, they would not retire. There was some discipline in this, but there was much more of true valor.

A long time afterward, following an examination of the records, Rufus Dawes sat down to write a history of his 6th Wisconsin and in it was his bitter summary of Gainesville. "On the afternoon of this day, August 28th, 1862 . . . the best blood of Wisconsin and Indiana was poured out like water, and it was spilled for naught. . . . Our one night's experience at Gainesville had eradicated our yearning for a fight. In our future history we will also be found ready but never again anxious."[14]

The Western men traveling along the long road started in 1861 would come to several crossroads much like Gainesville. One of those places was located not far ahead in the Herbst woodlot just northwest of a small community called Gettysburg, in Pennsylvania.

13 Nolan. *Iron Brigade*, 315–316.

14 W. B. Taliaferro, "Jackson's Raid Around Pope," *Battles and Leaders of the Civil War*, 2:510; Dawes, *Service*, 69–70.

Bibliography

Primary Sources

Archival Sources

Duke University, Durham, NC.
Munford-Ellis Family. Papers.
Emory University, Atlanta, GA.
George Wren. Diary.
Manassas National Battlefield Park, Manassas, VA.
Robert E. L. Krick. "The Wounding of Richard Stoddert Ewell."
John Neff. "Family History."
David Walton. Letter. 33rd Virginia file.
Maryland Historical Society, Baltimore, MD.
Trimble Papers.
National Archives.
Record Group 94.
Record Group 109.
Tulane University, New Orleans, LA.
George P. Ring. Diary.
Virginia Historical Society, Richmond, VA.
Robert Lee Traylor Papers.
Wisconsin Veterans Museum, Madison, WI.
William H. Washburn. "Jerome A. Watrous: The Civil War Years."

Government Documents

Biographical Directory of the American Congress, 1774–1960. Washington, D.C.: United States Government Printing Office, 1961.

Coggins, Jack. *Arms and Equipment of the Civil War*. Garden City, NY: Doubleday & Co., 1962.

Confederate States Ordnance Bureau, Field Manual. Richmond: Ritchie & Dunnavant, 1862.

Coppee, Henry. *Field Manual of Evolutions of the Line*. Philadelphia: J. B. Lippincott & Co., 1862.

Fuller, Claud E. *Springfield Muzzle-Loading Shoulder Arms*. New York: Francis Bannerman Sons, 1930.

Hardee, W. J. *Rifle and Light Infantry Tactics*. 2 vols. Philadelphia: J. B. Lippincott & Co., 1861.

McClellan, George B. *Manual of Bayonet Exercise*. Philadelphia: J. B. Lippincott & Co., 1862.

Reilly, Robert M. *United States Military Small Arms, 1816–1865*. Eagle Press, 1970.

Revised United States Army Regulations of 1861. Washington, D.C.: United States Government Printing Office, 1863.

Thomas, Dean S. *Ready . . . Aim . . . Fire*. Bilgerville, PA: Osborn Printing Co., 1981.

U.S. Infantry Tactics. Philadelphia: J. B. Lippincott & Co., 1863.

War of the Rebellion, Official Records of the Union and Confederate Armies. Washington, D.C.: United States Government Printing Office, 1889–1900.

Newspapers

Augusta Weekly Chronicle
Baraboo [WI] *News-Republic*
Baraboo [WI] *Republic*
Beloit [WI] *Free Press*
Beloit [WI] *Journal*
The Blackhat, Occasional Newsletter of the 6th Wisconsin Vols.
Charleston Daily Courier
Chicago Chronicle
Chippewa Herald
Christian Science Monitor
Civil War Times Illustrated
Confederate Veteran
Evening Wisconsin
Fond du Lac [WI] *Reporter*
Gettysburg Compiler
Gettysburg Magazine
Grant County [WI] *Herald*
La Crosse Morning Chronicle
La Crosse Republican and Leader
Lexington Gazette
Lexington Post
Mauston Star
Milwaukee Daily News
Milwaukee Free Press
Milwaukee History, Milwaukee County Historical Society
Milwaukee Journal
Milwaukee Sentinel
Milwaukee Sunday Telegraph/Milwaukee Telegraph
Mineral Point Tribune
Missouri Republican
The National Tribune
New York Times
Prescott Journal
Richmond Daily Dispatch
Richmond Dispatch
Richmond Enquirer
Rochester Union and Advertiser
Staunton Spectator
Vernon County Censor
Weekly Columbus Enquirer
Wisconsin Magazine of History
Wisconsin Necrology
Wisconsin Newspaper Volumes

Secondary Sources

Adams, James G. *History of Education in Sawyer County, Wisconsin.* McIntire, IA: M. E. Granger, 1902.

Aderman, Ralph M., ed. *Trading Post to Metropolis.* Milwaukee: Milwaukee County Historical Society, 1987.

Allardice, Bruce. *More Generals in Gray.* Baton Rouge: University of Louisiana Press, 2006.

Allen, John Owen. "The Strength of the Union and Confederate Forces at Second Manassas." Master's thesis, George Mason University, 1993.

Aubery, Doc. *Recollections of a Newsboy in the Army of the Potomac.* Milwaukee, 1900.

Beaudot, William J. K., and Lance J. Herdegen, eds, *An Irishman in the Iron Brigade: The Civil War Memoirs of James P. Sullivan, Sergt., Company K, 6th Wisconsin Volunteers.* New York: Fordham University Press, 1993.

Bean, W. G. *The Liberty Hall Rifles: Stonewall's College Boys.* Charlottesville, VA: University Press of Virginia, 2004.

Bohannon, Keith. *The Giles, Alleghany, and Jackson Artillery.* Lynchburg, VA: H. E. Howard, 1990.

Blackford, W. W. *War Years with Jeb Stuart.* Baton Rouge: Louisiana State University Press, 1993.

Bradwell, I. G. "Cedar Mountain to Sharpsburg," *Confederate Veteran* 29 (1921): 296–298.

Brown, Philip. *Reminiscences of the War of 1861–1865.* Richmond: Whittet & Shepperson, 1917.

Bruce, William G. *History of Milwaukee, City and County.* Chicago: S. J. Clare Publishing Co., 1922.

Buck, Samuel. *With the Old Confeds: Actual Experiences of a Captain in the Line.* Gaithersburg, MD: Butternut Press, 1983.

Buel, Clarence and Robert Johnson, eds. *Battles and Leaders of the Civil War.* 4 vols. New York: Thomas Yoseloff, 1956.

Buell, Augustus, *The Cannoneer: Recollections of Service in the Army of the Potomac.* Washington, D.C.: The National Tribune, 1897.

Carmichael, Peter. *The Purcell, Crenshaw, and Letcher Artillery.* Lynchburg, VA: H. E. Howard, 1990.

Casler, John. *Four Years in the Stonewall Brigade.* Columbia, SC: University of South Carolina Press, 2005.

Chamberlayne, C. G., ed. *Ham Chamberlayne—Virginian: Letters and Papers of An Artillery Officer in the War for Southern Independence 1861–1865.* Wilmington, NC: Broadfoot Publishing Company, 1992.

Cheek, Philip, and Mair Pointon. *History of the Sauk County Riflemen, Known as Company "A" Sixth Wisconsin Veteran Volunteer Infantry, 1861–1865.* N.P., 1909.

Clark, Walter, ed. *Histories of the Several Regiments and Battalions from North Carolina in the Great War 1861–65.* 5 vols. Goldsboro, NC: Nash Brothers, 1901.

Cockrell, Monroe, ed. *Gunner with Stonewall: Reminiscences of William Thomas Poague.* Lincoln: University of Nebraska Press, 1998.

Conard, Howard L. *History of Milwaukee: From its First Settlement to the year 1895.* Chicago: American Biographical Publishing Co., 1895.

Cozen, Kathleen Neils. *Immigrant Milwaukee, 1836–1860.* Cambridge, MA: Harvard University Press, 1976.

Cozzens, Peter. *Shenandoah 1862: Stonewall Jackson's Valley Campaign.* Chapel Hill: University Press of North Carolina, 2008.

Crabtree, Beth and James Patton, eds. *"Journal of a Secesh Lady": The Diary of Catherine Ann Devereux Edmondston, 1860–1866.* Raleigh: North Carolina Division of Archives and History, 1999.

Crist, Lynda, ed. *The Papers of Jefferson Davis:1862.* Baton Rouge: Louisiana State University, 1995.

Current, Richard N. *The History of Wisconsin: The Civil War Era 1848–1873.* Madison: Wisconsin Historical Society, 1976.

Daniel, Larry and Lynn Bock. *Island No. 10: Struggle for the Mississippi Valley.* Tuscaloosa: University of Alabama Press, 1996.

Dawes, Rufus R. *Service with the Sixth Wisconsin Volunteers.* Dayton, OH: Morningside Books, 1984.

Dictionary of American Biography. 10 vols. New York: Charles Scribner's Sons, 1946.

Dictionary of Wisconsin Biography. Madison: Wisconsin Historical Society, 1960.

Donald, David, ed. *Gone for the Soldier: The Civil War Memoirs of Private Alfred Bellard.* New York: Little, Brown and Company, 1975.

Douglas, Henry Kyd. *I Rode with Stonewall.* Chapel Hill: University of North Carolina Press, 1940.

Dowdey, Clifford, and Louis Manarin, eds. *The Wartime Papers of R. E. Lee.* New York: Bramhall House, 1961.

Driver, Robert, Jr. *1st Virginia Cavalry.* Lynchburg, VA: H. E. Howard, 1991.

______. *5th Virginia Cavalry.* Lynchburg, VA: H. E. Howard, 1997.

Dudley, William W. *The Iron Brigade at Gettysburg, Official Report of the Part Borne by the 1st Brigade, 1st Division, 1st Army Corps.* Cincinnati: privately printed, 1879.

Dunn, Craig L. *Iron Men, Iron Will: The Nineteenth Indiana Regiment of the Iron Brigade.* Indianapolis: Guild Press of Indiana, 1995.

Durkin, Joseph, ed. *Confederate Chaplain: A War Journal of Rev. James B. Sheeran, c.ss.r 14th Louisiana, C.S.A.* Milwaukee: Bruce Publishing Company, 1960.

Dyer, F. H. *A Compendium of the War of the Rebellion.* Dayton, OH: Morningside Bookshop, 1987.

Earley Judith and Kay Fanning. *Manassas National Battlefield, Brawner Farm Cultural Landscapes Report.* Washington D.C.: U.S. Department of the Interior, National Park Service, 2005.

Edgar, Alfred. *My Reminiscences of the Civil War with the Stonewall Brigade and the Immortal 600.* Charleston, WV: 35th Star Publishing, 2011.

Engle, Stephe. *Yankee Dutchman: The Life of Franz Sigel.* Fayetteville: The University of Arkansas Press, 1993.

Everett, Donald, ed. *Chaplain Davis and Hood's Texas Brigade.* Baton Rouge: Louisiana State University Press, 1999.

Fitch, Michael H. *Echoes of the Civil War As I Hear Them.* New York: 1905.

Flower, Frank A. *History of Milwaukee, Wisconsin.* Chicago: Western Historical Co., 1881.

Ford, Benjamin and Stephen Thompson. *Archaeological Investigations Associated with the Fauquier and Alexandria Turnpike.* Charlottesville, VA: Rivanna Archaeological Services, LLC, 2013.

Freeman, Douglas A. *Lee's Lieutenants.* New York: Charles Scribner's Sons, 1942–1944.

Fry, Dennis. *2nd Virginia Infantry.* Lynchburg, VA: H. E. Howard, 1984.

Fry, Zachery. *A Republic in the Ranks: Loyalty and Dissent in the Army of the Potomac.* Chapel Hill: University of North Carolina Press, 2020.

Fulton, William. *War Reminiscences of William Frierson Fulton II.* Gaithersburg, MD: Butternut Press, 1986.

Gaff, Alan. *Brave Men's Tears: The Iron Brigade at Brawner Farm.* Dayton, OH: Morningside House, 1988.

______. *On Many a Bloody Field: Four Years in the Iron Brigade.* Bloomington: Indiana University Press, 1997.

_____. ed. *The Second Wisconsin Infantry, with letters and recollections by other members of the regiment.* Dayton, OH: Morningside Press, 1984.

Gannon, James. *Irish Rebels, Confederate Tigers: A History of the 6th Louisiana Volunteers, 1861–1865.* Campbell, CA: Savas Publishing, 1998.

"General I. R. Trimble's Report of Operations of his Brigade from 14th to 29th August, 1862," *Southern Historical Society Papers* 8 (1880): 306–309.

Gibbon, John. *Personal Recollections of the Civil War.* New York: G. P. Putnam's Sons, 1928.

Glatthaar, Joseph. *General Lee's Army: From Victory to Collapse.* New York: Free Press, 2008.

Gold, Thomas. *History of Clarke County, Virginia and its connection to the War Between the States.* Berryville, VA: C. R. Hughes, 1914.

Goss, Thomas. *The War within the Union High Command.* Lawrence: University Press of Kansas, 2003.

Gregory, John B. *History of Milwaukee, Wisconsin.* 4 vols. Chicago: S. J. Clarke, Publishing Co., 1931.

Hardy, Michael. *General Lee's Immortals: The Battles and Campaigns of the Branch-Lane Brigade in the Army of Northern Virginia, 1861–1865.* El Dorado Hills, CA: Savas Beatie, 2018.

Harsh, Joseph. *Confederate Tide Rising: Robert E. Lee and the Making of Southern Strategy.* Kent, OH: The Kent State University Press, 1998.

Hendricks, James. "Jackson's March to Rear of Pope's Army." *Confederate Veteran* 17 (1909): 549–550.

Hennessy, John. *Return to Bull Run: The Campaign and Battle of Second Manassas.* New York: Simon & Schuster, 1993.

Hennessy, John. *Second Manassas Battlefield Map Study.* Lynchburg, VA: H. E. Howard, 1985.

Herdegen, Lance J. *The Men Stood Like Iron: How the Iron Brigade Won its Name.* Bloomington: Indiana University Press, 1997.

Herdegen, Lance J. and William J. K. Beaudot. *In the Bloody Railroad Cut at Gettysburg.* Dayton, OH: Morningside House, 1990.

Herdegen, Lance J. and Sharon Murphy, eds. *Four Years With the Iron Brigade: The Civil War Journal of William Ray, Seventh Wisconsin.* New York: DaCapo Press, 2001.

Hill, Alonzo. *Our Boys. Personal Experiences of a Soldier in the Army of the Potomac.* Philadelphia: John Potter and Company, 1866.

History of Crawford and Richland Counties, Wisconsin. Springfield, IL: Union Publishing Company, 1884.

History of Vernon County, Wisconsin. Springfield, IL: Union Publishing Co., 1883.

Johnson, John. *The University Memorial: Biographical Sketches of Alumni of the University of Virginia.* Baltimore, MD: Turnbull Brothers, 1871.

Johnston, David. *Four Years a Soldier.* Princeton, WV, 1887.

Jones, Terry, ed. *Campbell Brown's Civil War with Ewell and the Army of Northern Virginia.* Baton Rouge: Louisiana State University Press, 2001.

_____. *Lee's Tigers Revisited: The Louisiana Infantry in the Army of Northern Virginia.* Baton Rouge: Louisiana State University Press, 2017.

Kelly, Tom, ed. *The Personal Memoirs of Jonathan Thomas Scharf of the First Maryland Artillery.* Baltimore, MD: Butternut and Blue, 1993.

Kessinger, Lawrance. *History of Buffalo County, Wisconsin.* Alma, WI: 1888.

Koss, Rudolf. "Milwaukee. Milwaukee, Wis." *The Milwaukee Herald*, 1871.

Krick, Robert. *Civil War Weather in Virginia.* Tuscaloosa: University of Alabama Press, 2007.

Lawrence, Lee, ed. *Society of Rebels: Diary of Amanda Edmonds.* Warrenton, VA: Piedmont Press, 2016.

Longstreet, James. *From Manassas to Appomattox: Memoirs of the Civil War in America.* Philadelphia: J. B. Lippincott Company, 1896.

Love, William D. *Wisconsin in the War of the Rebellion*. Chicago: Church & Goodman, 1866.

Lowe, Jeffrey and Sam Hodges, eds. *Letters to Amanda: The Civil War Letters of Marion Hill Fitzpatrick, Army of Northern Virginia*. Macon, GA: Mercer University Press, 1999.

Madaus, Howard Michael and Richard H. Zeitlin, eds. *The Flags of the Iron Brigade*. Madison: Wisconsin Veterans Museum, 1998.

Manassas National Battlefield, Environmental Assessment Rehabilitation of Brawner Farm House. Washington D.C.: U.S. Department of the Interior, National Park Service, 2005.

Marshall, Michael. *Gallant Creoles: A History of the Donaldsonville Cannoniers*. Lafayette: University of Louisiana at Lafayette Press, 2013.

Marszalek, John. *Commander of All of Lincoln's Armies: A Life of General Henry W. Halleck*. Cambridge, MA: The Belknap Press of Harvard University Press, 2004.

Marvel, William. *Lincoln's Autocrat: The Life of Edwin Stanton*. Chapel Hill: University of North Carolina Press, 2015.

Matsui, John. *The First Republican Army: The Army of Virginia and the Radicalization of the Civil War*. Charlottesville: University of Virginia Press, 2016.

Maxwell, Jerry. *The Perfect Lion: The Life and Death of Confederate Artillerist John Pelham*. Tuscaloosa: University of Alabama Press, 2011.

McCaslin, Richard, ed. *A Soldiers Letters to Charming Nellie*. Knoxville: University of Tennessee Press, 2008.

McClendon, William. *Recollections of War Times: By an Old Veteran while under Stonewall Jackson and Lieutenant General James Longstreet*. Tuscaloosa: University of Alabama Press, 2010.

McDonald, Archie, ed. *Make Me a Map of the Valley: The Civil War Journal of Stonewall Jackson's Topographer*. Dallas: Southern Methodist University Press, 1989.

McGuire, Hunter. *An Address by Hunter McGuire, M.D., Medical Director of Jackson's Corps at the Dedication of Jackson Memorial Hall, Virginia Military Institute*. Richmond: R. E. Lee Camp, No. 1, C.V., 1897.

_____. "General Thomas J. Jackson." *Southern Historical Society Papers* 19 (1891): 298–318.

McMullen, Glenn, ed. *The Civil War Letters of Dr. Harvey Black*. Baltimore: Butternut & Blue Press, 1995.

McMurry, Richard, ed. *Footprints of a Regiment: A Recollection of the 1st Georgia Regulars 1861–1865*. Atlanta: Longstreet Press, 1992.

Military Order of the Loyal Legion of the United States, *Commandery of the State of Wisconsin, War Papers*. Vol. I. Milwaukee: Armitage & Allen, 1891.

_____. *Commandery of the State of Wisconsin, War Papers*. Vol. II. Milwaukee: Armitage & Allen, 1896.

_____. *Commandery of the State of Wisconsin*. Vol. III. Milwaukee: Armitage & Allen, 1903.

Moore, Edward. *The Story of a Cannoneer under Stonewall Jackson*. Lynchburg, VA: J. P. Bell Company, 1910.

Muir, Rory. *Tactics and the Experience of Battle in the Age of Napoleon*. New Haven, CT: Yale University Press, 1998.

Murray, Alton. *South Georgia Rebels: The True Wartime Experiences of the 26th Regiment, Georgia Volunteer Infantry*. St. Marys, GA: Alton Murray, 1976.

Nolan, Alan T. *The Iron Brigade*. New York: Macmillan, 1961.

Nolan, Alan T. and Sharon Vipond, eds. *Giants in Their Tall Black Hats: Essays on the Iron Brigade*. Bloomington: Indiana University Press, 1998.

Nevins, Allen, ed. *A Diary of Battle: The Personal Journals of Colonel Charles S. Wainwright, 1861–1865*. New York: Harcourt, Brace &World, 1962.

Nichols, George. *A Soldier's Story of his Regiment (61st Georgia)*. Tuscaloosa: University of Alabama Press, 2011.

Nisbet, James. *Four Years on the Firing Line*. Chattanooga, TN: Imperial Press, 1914.

Oates, William. *The War Between the Union and the Confederacy and Its Lost Opportunities with a History of the 15th Alabama Regiment*. New York: Neale Publishing Company, 1905.

Pearson, Johnnie, ed. *Lee and Jackson's Bloody Twelfth: The Letters of Irby Goodwin Scott, First Lieutenant, Company G, Putnam Light Infantry, Twelfth Georgia Volunteer Infantry*. Knoxville: University of Tennessee Press, 2010.

Peskin, Allan. *Winfield Scott and the Profession of Arms*. Kent, OH: Kent State University Press, 2003.

Pfanz, Donald. *Richard S. Ewell: A Soldier's Life*. Chapel Hill: University of North Carolina Press, 1998.

Phillips, Ulrich, ed. *The Correspondence of Robert Toombs, Alexander H. Stephens, and Howell Cobb*. Washington, D.C.: U.S. Government Printing Office, 1913.

Quiner, Edwin B. *The Military History of Wisconsin*. Chicago: Clarke & Co., 1866.

Rafuse, Ethan. *McClellan's War: The Failure of Moderation in the Struggle for the Union*. Bloomington: Indiana University Press, 2005.

Reidenbaugh, Lowell. *33rd Virginia Infantry*. Lynchburg, VA: H. E. Howard, 1987.

Richter, Rick. *Three Cheers for the Chesapeake! History of the 4th Maryland Light Artillery Battery in the Civil War*. Atglen, PA: Schiffer Publishing, 2017.

Robertson, James, Jr. *General A. P. Hill: The Story of a Confederate Warrior*. New York: Random House, 1987.

______. *Stonewall Jackson: The Man, The Soldier, The Legend*. New York: Macmillan, 1997.

Ross, Sam, *The Empty Sleeve: A Biography of Lucius Fairchild*. Madison: The State Historical Society of Wisconsin for the Wisconsin Civil War Centennial Commission, 1964.

Rothenberg, Gunter. *The Art of Warfare in the Age of Napoleon*. Bloomington: Indiana University Press, 1980.

Scarborough, William, ed. *The Diary of Edmund Ruffin: A Dream Shattered, June 1863–June 1865*. Baton Rouge: Louisiana State University Press, 1989.

Sherrill, Lee, Jr. *The 21st North Carolina Infantry*. Jefferson, NC: McFarland & Company, 2015.

Skoch, George and Mark Perkins, eds. *Lone Star Confederate: A Gallant and Good Soldier of the Fifth Texas Infantry*. College Station: Texas A&M University Press, 2003.

Soldiers' and Citizens' Album of Biographical Record. Chicago: Grand Army Publishing Company, 1888.

Steensma, Robert C., ed. *The Civil War Letters of James E. Northup and Samuel W. Northup*. Sioux Falls, SD: Augustana College, 2000.

Stevens, Michael E., ed. *As If It Were Glory: Robert Beecham's Civil War from the Iron Brigade to the Black Regiments*. Madison, WI: Madison House, 1998.

Stine, J. H. *History of the Army of the Potomac*. Philadelphia: J. B. Rogers Printing Co., 1892.

Stocker, Jeffrey, ed. *From Huntsville to Appomattox: R. T. Cole's History of 4th Regiment, Alabama Volunteer Infantry, C.S.A., Army of Northern Virginia*. Knoxville: University of Tennessee Press, 1996.

Styple, William, ed. *Writing and Fighting from the Army of Northern Virginia: A Collection of Confederate Correspondence*. Kearny, NJ: Bell Grove Publishing, 2003.

Sutherland, Daniel. *Seasons of War: The Ordeal of a Confederate Community 1861–1865*. New York: The Free Press, 1995.

Taaffe, Stephen. *Commanding the Army of the Potomac*. Lawrence: University Press of Kansas, 2006.

Tap, Bruce. *Over Lincoln's Shoulder: The Committee on the Conduct of the War*. Lawrence: University Press of Kansas, 1998.

Thomas, Emory. "'The Greatest Service I Rendered the State': J. E. B. Stuart's Account of the Capture of John Brown." *The Virginia Magazine of History and Biography* 94, no. 3 (1986): 345–357.

Thomas, Henry. *History of the Doles-Cook Brigade Army of Northern Virginia 1861–1865.* Atlanta: Franklin Printing and Publishing Company, 1903.

Trefousse, Hans. *Carl Schurz: A Biography.* Knoxville: University of Tennessee Press, 1982.

Tyler, Lyon. *The Letters and Times of the Tylers.* 2 Vols. Richmond, VA: Whittet & Shepperson, 1884–1896.

Walker, Charles. *Biographical sketches of the Graduates and Elévès of the Virginia Military Institute who fell during the war between the States.* Philadelphia: J. B. Lippincott Company, 1875.

Walterman, Thomas. *There Stands "Old Rock": Rock County, Wisconsin, and the War to Preserve the Union.* Friendship, WI: Rock County Historical Society, 2001.

Ware, John. "Second Manassas: Fifty-Eight Years Afterwards." *Confederate Veteran* 30 (1922): 60–62.

Warner, Ezra. *Generals in Gray: Lives of the Confederate Generals.* Baton Rouge: Louisiana State University Press, 2006.

_____. *Generals in Blue: Lives of Union Commanders.* Baton Rouge: Louisiana State University Press, 1964.

Welsh, Jack. *Medical Histories of Confederate Generals.* Kent, OH: Kent State University Press, 1999.

Welton, J. Michael, ed. *"My Heart is So Rebellious": The Caldwell Letters, 1861–1865.* Warrenton, VA: Fauquier National Bank, 1991.

Wert, Jeffery. *A Brotherhood of Valor: The Common Soldiers of the Stonewall Brigade, C.S.A, and the Iron Brigade, U.S.A.* New York: Simon & Schuster, 1999.

White, Gregory. *This Most Bloody and Cruel Drama: A History of the 31st Georgia Volunteer Infantry.* Baltimore: Butternut & Blue, 1997.

Whitehouse, Hugh L., ed. *Letters from the Iron Brigade: George W. Partridge, Jr., 1839–1863.* Indianapolis: Guild Press of Indiana, 1994.

Worsham, John. *One of Jackson's Foot Cavalry: His experience and what he saw during the war 1861–1865.* New York: Neale Publishing Company, 1912.

The War of the Rebellion: A Compilation of the Official Records of the Union and Confederate Armies. 128 vols. Washington, D.C.: 1880-1901.

Zen, E-An and Alta Walker. *Rocks and War: Geology and the Civil War Campaign of Second Manassas.* Shippensburg, PA: White Mane Books, 2000.

Zettler, B. M. *War Stories and School-day Incidents for the Children.* New York: Neale Publishing Company, 1912.

Websites

Griffin, Neal. "Thoroughfare Gap, and the Second Battle of Manasses." Accessed Nov. 14, 2020, http://www.sumtercountyhistory.com/wbts/2MANASS.htm.

Index

About the Authors

Lance J. Herdegen (left) is the author of several books. *Those Damned Black Hats: The Iron Brigade in the Gettysburg Campaign* (Savas Beatie, 2008) won the Army Historical Foundation's Distinguished Writing Award for Battle/Operational History and *The Iron Brigade in Civil War and Memory: The Black Hats from Bull Run to Appomattox and Thereafter* (Savas Beatie, 2012) received the Iron Brigade Association Award. Lance enjoyed a long career as a journalist with the United Press International (UPI) news wire service and was recently inducted into the Milwaukee Press Club Hall of Fame. He lives in Spring Prairie, Wisconsin.

A native of Connecticut, Bill Backus (right) graduated from the University of Mary Washington with a degree in Historic Preservation. Prior to his service with Prince William County, he worked with the National Park Service at Vicksburg National Military Park and Petersburg National Battlefield. Bill currently serves as the Curator for the Prince William County Office of Historic Preservation in Northern Virginia. He is co-author of *A Want of Vigilance: The Bristoe Station Campaign, October 9–19, 1863* (Savas Beatie, 2015).